A BRIGHT SPARK

A BRIGHT SPARK

WILLIE WILSON

THE INSPIRING STORY OF WILLIE WILSON'S
RISE FROM HUMBLE BEGINNINGS TO
EXTRAORDINARY BUSINESS SUCCESS

BLACK & WHITE PUBLISHING

First published 2006
by Black & White Publishing Ltd
99 Giles Street, Edinburgh EH6 6BZ

ISBN 13: 978 1 84502 135 1
ISBN 10: 1 84502 135 5

Typeset by RefineCatch Limited, Bungay, Suffolk
Printed and bound by Creative Print and Design Group Ltd

Acknowledgement

Grateful thanks to Graham Lironi for all his help with the writing of this book.

Dedication

This book is dedicated to my beloved wife, Mary, my sons, Scott and Richard, my grandchildren, Michael and Connor, and to the memory of my parents, Alec and Annie, and my granny, Maggie Nugent.

Contents

1

Challenging Prejudice at Birth

Family legend has it that my Spanish great-granny's family name of Mahon became Mallon when her family moved to Ireland. What is more certain is the fact that her daughter, Maggie Mallon, and Maggie's husband, Paddy Nugent, from the towns of Dun Laoghaire and Dundalk respectively, emigrated to Scotland in search of work in around 1910. They settled in Garnkirk, a housing scheme not far from Crow Wood golf course, near Muirhead, Lanarkshire, where many immigrants from Ireland were housed on their arrival in Scotland.

Whilst lots of immigrants found work on farms as labourers, my granddad landed a job at Gartcosh steelworks where he stoked the coke oven. His job proved to be the primary cause of his death as he developed a disease particular to steel workers called black spot, so called because it afflicted those stokers who had breathed in metal dust particles which stuck to their lungs, eventually rusting and producing deadly black spots.

Though the first three of my granny's five children were born in Ireland, my mum, Annie Nugent, and her younger brother, John, were born in Scotland. My mum met my dad, Alexander Wilson, a coach driver from Milngavie, when they both worked at the Stepps depot of Alexander's Coaches – he was a driver and she was a bus conductress. I was born a few years later at 2 Knowe Road, Muirhead, my granny's house, on 12 July 1943 – the very day that the Battle of the Boyne of 1690, which saw Protestant William III defeat Roman Catholic James II, is recalled each year in the celebrations of the Orange Order. Family legend has it that, at my birth, my granny, an Irish Catholic, turned to my dad and said, 'Get that wain below the bed and bring him out tomorrow!' But my dad, a Protestant, jumped at the opportunity presented by my date of birth to suggest that I should be called Billy – and so it was that I was named William Alexander Wilson.

I was never to discuss my religion with my dad until I reached my teens. It was only when I went to upper grade school that the matter of religion began to be discussed openly amongst my friends and I discovered that most of the guys I knew whose parents were in a mixed marriage had assumed their dad's religion. This discovery prompted me to ask my dad about why I had been raised a Catholic, my mother's faith. He told me it was because my mum had the stronger faith.

But though, throughout my childhood, religion was never a big issue at home, it was an issue in my granny's house. Indeed, whenever any of my cousins had occasion to bring someone back to my granny's house, invariably the first question she asked her houseguest was, 'And what school do you go to?' My wife Mary was a Protestant and she must have been one of the first to be fully accepted into my granny's house. My granny's was typical of the Irish attitude that prevailed at that time. I'm sorry about that but it's a fact. Later, prior to our wedding, Mary decided – without any interference from me – to convert to Catholicism. She felt that would make it easier on the children and remove any cause for dispute about religion so she took religious instruction under Father Walsh at St Joseph's in Helensburgh.

I was brought up at my granny's house in Knowe Road, a street known locally as the Duke. Locals would arrange to meet 'at the top of the Duke', the junction where Knowe Road met the main road in Muirhead. That was where all the young folk gathered of an evening, underneath the gas lamps.

Because my dad was still in the army when I was born – he was a driver in the infantry and remained in the army until 1945 – I was sent to live with my granny until such time as my parents were able to get themselves settled and my dad found a proper job.

My mum's brothers were miners and, twice a year, they would get a free ton of coal delivered to the house by a horse and cart, the coal bing was tipped out on to the pavement outside our house. I remember my granddad pushing a big square wooden box barrow out into the street and filling it with coal. I used to sit on top of the coal in the barrow as he wheeled it indoors to store in the scullery, next to the larder.

My mum's youngest brother, my uncle John, lived with

my granny and he kept greyhounds – in Lanarkshire you either kept greyhounds or pigeons – in one of his two sheds in the back garden. In the other shed, which he had fitted out with a couple of seats and a telephone, he operated as a bookmaker – an activity that was not strictly legal. One day my uncle John asked me to go and fetch my granny and I remember finding her bending over in the middle of a field picking potatoes with one of my aunt's babies wrapped around her back in a shawl. I might have been only about three or four years old at the time but I knew even then that there was something not quite right about that.

Much later I would go on to meet friends who had also been descended from Irish immigrants and they would tell me of how their grandparents had worked on farms and lived in bothies without running water, electricity – or even a proper floor. Given such living conditions, it's small wonder that many immigrants wound up suffering from pleurisy and pneumonia.

I hate exploitation. We like to kid ourselves that such exploitation doesn't happen so much nowadays but I recognise it all around me. I even recognise it in some people who are oblivious to the fact that they are exploiting someone. For example, our company recently brought some electricians over from Poland to work for us. We helped them find suitable accommodation and we paid them the then going rate of £11.54 an hour. They told me that they had been paid £5 an hour in England. That's exploitation. I don't believe that a Polish electrician working in Scotland should be paid any less than a Scottish electrician – and I'm a great believer in the saying 'What goes around comes around'.

Throughout my whole childhood, up until my mid teens, my gran would insist that every July all her relations would gather together in Dun Laoghaire for a fortnight's summer holiday – and if my gran insisted on it, then you best believe that that's what happened!

I remember as a wee lad standing in the queue for the boat at the Broomielaw. The Burns & Laird boat that took us over was also used to transport cattle between Ireland and Scotland. The boat would dock and the herd of cattle would be unloaded into big sheds at the side of the Broomielaw; then its decks would be hosed down quickly before all the holidaymakers would troop on and it would head back down the Clyde. The boat always set sail at nine o'clock at night and would arrive in Belfast at eight o'clock the following morning. We would then catch the train down to Dublin, passing through a border crossing en route.

At some point during the holiday, all my relatives – my gran, mum and dad, aunts and uncles and cousins – would set off to walk from Dun Laoghaire up to Blackrock and into the south side of Dublin. This was in the 1940s and, the first time I did this walk, I must have been only about five years old. In those days there were lots of what were called 'jaunting carts' – horses and traps – and I can clearly remember my gran flagging them down to give us children and herself a ride into Dublin while the adults walked. My gran always wore a spotless dark blue coat and she always wore her silver and black hair pulled tight in a bun under a hat held in place by a big silver hatpin. Those were fantastic times. Simple times. We walked everywhere on those holidays. The only place we didn't walk to in those days was when we took the train up to Dundalk to see my grandpa's relations.

It was not long after I'd enrolled at my first school, St Barbara's at Muirhead, that my father found work as a driver for Garelochhead Coaches. The job came with a tied house, at Bromley Place in Garelochhead, and so I left my granny's house to move in with my parents. I was enrolled in St Joseph's school in Helensburgh and travelled there from Garelochhead every day. I completed my primary education in St Joseph's and moved from there into St Pat's in Dumbarton.

But my gran had always ruled the roost. She was a bit of a control freak. So much so that, even when I left her house to go and live in Garelochhead with my mum and dad, I would still regularly go back to live with my granny at 2 Knowe Road. I had to go back – my mother didn't have any option. If my gran instructed her family to gather at her house at the weekend, then that was what happened.

I remember that, when I was very young, we all used to sit around the fireside at my gran's house on a Saturday night. I used to sit and listen to all her stories about what went on during her time in Ireland and find it all fascinating.

All the relatives would gather for Sunday dinner at my granny's. She had a big table that sat beneath the living room window and, every Sunday, she'd pull out its leaves and extend it to its full size. This was where all the adults would sit for their Sunday dinner while we children would be called in from playing outside to sit at a table in the scullery – a simple pine table that had been scrubbed so hard and so often with a scouring brush that it had always looked bleached. My granny would sit in the living room with the other adults but the door to the kitchen was left ajar so that she could keep a close eye on us. I remember sitting at the table in the scullery from where I could see my granny sitting through in the living room. Having finished my dinner and desperate to get back outside to play, I would not dare to make a move until she gave me the nod. She would see us sitting there waiting for her and, eventually, she would give a slight nod which was a signal that it was OK for us kids to leave the table and go back out to play in the Duke. And it was safe to play in the street in those days because there weren't any cars.

My lifelong interest in Celtic Football Club came from my gran's side of the family. My uncle John, my mother's sister's husband, Peter O'Hare, and my cousins were all great Celtic fans. At that time, it was simple – though people try and shy away from saying it – but, if you were a Catholic, you were usually a Celtic supporter and, if you were a Protestant, you were usually a Rangers supporter. But I'm not interested in sectarianism. I believe in the Burns' saying that 'a man's a man for a' that'.

Unfortunately, it was not long after I joined my parents in Bromley Place that my dad had a disagreement with his employer and we were evicted from the house. It seems that my dad had had a difference of opinion with his supervisor, a row had broken out, hands were lifted and the old man wound up losing his job over it. He then joined Cameron's Coaches in Helensburgh and Jimmy Cameron converted an old tyre store in the attic space above the garage into somewhere for us to live. I remember we had a Belfast sink outside our door, no hot water and the toilet was shared with a family living on the ground floor. Given the less than satisfactory accommodation, my parents applied to be put on the council list for a home, only to be informed that there was a lengthy waiting list.

Our next move was to 52 East Clyde Street, Helensburgh, an address known locally as 'Seagull Pen', so called because, at the end of the pen behind the house was a break wall for the tide upon which a flock of seagulls would perch. Seagull Pen comprised two rooms, a stairheid lavvy and an attic. It was in the attic that my brother John was born. I remember well the nurse who brought him into the world – Nurse McDonald was famous in Helensburgh. I was eleven at the time and had just started at St Pat's secondary school in Dumbarton.

Although I'd been quite content at primary school, I never really settled at St Pat's, to the extent that I bunked off school regularly. Indeed, throughout the summer months, more often than not I would step on to the school bus with a pair of swimming trunks wrapped in a towel tucked tightly under my arm and step off at Ardmore to go down to Ardmore Point for a swim rather than attend school. I used to swim at the weekends too. Saturday usually meant a visit to the public baths at the gas works very close to our house. I remember that, when we entered the baths, we were handed a big coarse towel, almost like a coal sack, and a large lump of bright red carbolic soap. I'll never forget the smell of that soap. I bunked school to go for a swim at Ardmore Point so often that everyone knew where I was and I suppose that ended up being a bit of a problem for my parents. My dad was certainly unhappy at my lack of application at school. My mother was always more inclined to let things take their course but my old man was more prone to push me, certainly where my education was concerned.

It was during this time that my parents finally received notice that there was a council house available for us and so we moved house once more to 30 Ben Bouie Drive, Kirkmichael. We had a lot of happy times there, despite the fact that, at that time, Kirkmichael had a reputation as one of the worst council estates in the area.

But, when we eventually moved from Seagull Pen to Kirkmichael, it was totally different from the reputation it had outside because there were some fabulous families there – probably more nice families there than you would find elsewhere – and there were no 'bad' families. I'm still at a loss to this day to explain why Kirkmichael had earned such a bad name for itself. I think maybe it was looked down upon because many of the families had large numbers of children which, at that time, seemed to be frowned upon - an absolute nonsense. My best man, Jim Shields, lived in Kirkmichael. There were families like the Malleys, the Murrays, the Youngs, the Currans, the McQueens, the Brabenders, the Friels and the McGinleys, whom we became very close to and ended up living next door to in Rhu. It was a tight-knit neighbourhood with a real community spirit and no gang violence or troubles that I can recall. There have been a lot of successful people that have come out of Kirkmichael – and I'm proud to count myself amongst them.

We ended up living in Kirkmichael for eight years before moving back into Helensburgh. My uncle John came to live with us when we were staying at Kirkmichael. Latterly, he'd lost his eyesight through diabetes and I remember the morning my father came to tell me that he'd died, having drowned from a build-up of fluid in his lungs.

It was a year or so after my brother was born that I started to notice a distinct change in my mother. I didn't know what it was to begin with, because it was alien to me. I'd never encountered this in my family before. And I began to wonder why my granny had started to visit us more often than usual. Finally, one day I asked her outright.

'Look Billy, there's a problem with your mum just now,' she said. 'Your mum's taken to drinking an awful lot lately.'

The fact was that my mother was struggling to manage and, with my father working all the hours of the day as a coach driver, he wasn't able to provide her with as much support as he would have liked. My mother was forty-three when John was born and she found it hard to cope. The way she tried to muddle through was by turning to drink – and she ended up an alcoholic. She didn't stop drinking for thirteen years – and then she stopped as suddenly as she'd started. It was her faith that made her stop. Before she started drinking, my mother had gone to church every day but, during the time she was an alcoholic, her church attendance became less regular. She would rarely go to church on a weekday any more but, if she happened to be sober on a Sunday, she'd make the effort to attend. In hindsight, I can see that the reason for the decline in the regularity of her churchgoing was embarrassment. When she was sober, she knew that she'd done wrong and she wouldn't want to go to church in case she caught sight of some members of her congregation gossiping about her behind her back.

I remember that, when I was about sixteen, I'd started to become more aware of gossip too. By that time Mary and I had started going out together and I remember asking her to visit me at home, rather than going to meet her in Helensburgh, because I didn't want to leave the house and run the risk of being embarrassed by catching sight of passers-by pointing me out as the son of the woman who'd taken to drink. I suffered from that sense of shame and wasn't able to cope with it for a while. But I always felt that I shouldn't be held responsible for my mother's drinking and that, although her drinking was affecting the family, it wasn't affecting any other people. Maybe it was because I'd skipped school and lacked the necessary education but I didn't really know how to express the sense of shame I felt whenever I was confronted with it.

One day I remember overhearing some neighbours openly discussing my mother's alcoholism and, ashamed, I told my dad about it.

'We're family and we'll support your mum,' he said. 'What we think about her is one thing – but we won't have anybody outside the family talking about her.'

My dad was lending me his support. He'd started to see the effect that my mum's alcoholism was having on me as I'd grown older and more aware of what was going on. And there's no doubt that it did affect me. I played amateur football throughout my teens – my position was left back – stopping before I started my own business at the age of twenty. After that, I followed football and was very much involved with Rhu Amateur Football Club but as a non-player. Every Thursday, after training, the team would go to the Rhu Inn for a few lagers and lime – but I'd never touch a drink. I was too scared to, having seen what alcohol had done to my mother. It was to be much later before I allowed myself my first taste of beer.

I was a member of Rhu Amateur Football Club, run by Donnie Thomson, as were many of my pals from primary and secondary school. Some of these guys were at my wedding but, for whatever reason, many of them were to die young. My best pal, Neil 'Pony' Welsh, John 'Jake' Orr, Billy Goodall, Billy Mooney, Spud Thomson, Alistair Glendie and Barry Irvine – seven guys all the same age as me – and all of them died in their forties from cancer, except Billy Mooney, who was killed in an accident in London.

We first played together as young boys and, as we grew older, we went on to play in the amateur league. Although I wasn't playing by then, Rhu Amateurs beat Pennilee in the final to win the Scottish Cup at Hampden in 1967 – the same year that Celtic won the European Cup. That was an unbelievable experience for me – many of my best pals had played that day and I was very proud of them. I remember coming back into Helensburgh that night and disembarking the bus at Clyde Street to find the whole town choc-a-bloc with people celebrating. We used to train with the football club at Rhu on Tuesday and Thursday nights. In between the football training, we ran from Rhu out to Kidston Park and back and a crowd of girls used to congregate at the corner of Manse Road in Rhu to watch us run past. That was how I met Mary, when I was sixteen, having left school at fifteen as soon as I had the chance.

I'd always wanted to be an electrician and the school careers officer arranged for me to have an interview with Small & McDonald, a Glasgow-based company with a branch in Helensburgh. I got the job and started as an apprentice electrician right after the Glasgow Fair.

2

An Immersion in Entrepreneurship and Marriage

At that time there was no day release so, two evenings a week, I would catch the bus to Lennox College in Dumbarton. But before I completed my five-year apprenticeship, I left Small & McDonald. My journeyman, Jim Thomson, had emigrated to Canada and so I decided to complete my apprenticeship working for GEC at St Helier, Jersey, where some of my pals were working on a house-building project. Not many people would have chosen to leave their job before completing their apprenticeship but I did though, in the event, it didn't work out quite the way I'd intended. Unfortunately, I didn't enjoy my time in Jersey as much as I'd hoped and so I only stayed long enough to qualify as an electrician before returning home to work for James Scott.

It was while I was working on a housing project in Dumbarton that, one day, I was asked by the foreman to report to the admin hut to speak to Ian McKinnon, the personnel manager. Ian McKinnon was a tall man, with black, sleeked-back hair and a bristling moustache. He looked me up and down.

'I thought you told me you were a journeyman?' he said, sarcastically.

'That's right,' I said. 'I *am* a journeyman.'

'You're not a journeyman, son,' he said. 'I've just checked your papers and you're only twenty years old.'

'That's right,' I said. 'I started my time when I was fifteen.'

'You don't start your time at fifteen at James Scott,' he said. 'At James Scott you do a pre-apprenticeship year – you might come in at fifteen but you don't start your apprenticeship at fifteen – and you've not done your time till you're twenty-one.'

'Well, what does that mean?' I said.

'It means that you're a fifth-year apprentice,' he said.

'Is that right?' I said. 'Well, you can stick your job up your arse!'

It was to be many years later, after I'd started my own business, before I bumped into Ian McKinnon again. It was at the annual association dinner dance in the Thistle Hotel in Glasgow that I saw him standing at the bar, an older man now, wearing a kilt. He was with a couple of his cronies, Ewan Mackenzie, the electrical contractor, and Frank Dunnet (who subsequently bought Ferguson Shipyard and was awarded an MBE) and he caught my eye as I was passing by.

'Hey, Wilson!' he shouted, beckoning me over. 'Come here a minute.' Then, after introducing me to his group, he told them, 'Wilson here's the only man who's ever told me to stick my job up my arse!'

We went on to become good friends.

Having resigned from James Scott, I went straight to Faslane where I landed a job with W. D. Aldridge, though, once again, I didn't hang about for any length of time. All the way through my apprenticeship I'd been thinking to myself, 'I'm not going to be working like this for long. I'm going to be working for myself as soon as I get the opportunity.'

My mum had an entrepreneurial nature and my dad had started his own coach business when I was in primary school. Although my dad had been keen for me to join him in his business, this didn't really appeal to me because I could see that he was working day and night – doing school runs during the day and theatre runs during the long winter nights – and often not returning home till midnight. What's more, any coach repairs needing doing had to be attended to first thing in the morning or last thing at night to ensure that the coaches were in full working order for the school run. I watched the long hours that my dad was putting in day after day and thought to myself, 'This isn't for me.' I don't mind hard work but my dad was working all the hours of the day and night.

The opportunity to start my own business presented itself when, one day, I stumbled across an advert in the *Helensburgh Advertiser*, our local paper. SSEB (South of Scotland Electricity Board) was offering to install electric immersers in homes for £15. Local authority houses were not constructed with electric immersers as standard in those days so they were much in demand. It occurred to me that I could install electric immersers in people's homes and make myself some money so, while I was still working at W. D. Aldridge, I took out an ad in the local paper,

15

offering to install electric immersers for £13. The response to the advert was immediate. The paper had come out on a Friday and over the course of that weekend I was inundated with work.

After working at W. D. Aldridge, I cycled around Helensburgh on my pushbike installing electric immersers in people's homes and because many of the customers knew me, they would often insist on paying me cash in hand as soon as I'd completed the job.

'You'll be needing your money, Billy Wilson,' they'd say. 'You've done a good job, there you go,' and more often than not they'd hand me £13 plus another couple of quid as a tip!

That was my very first business venture. Then Jim Shields and Alec Stewart, of Stewart and Shields Builders, who had always regarded me as something of a grafter, approached me with an offer to take my business venture a stage further. We soon struck a deal whereby they gave me the finance I needed to get my business up and running, including an office located within their own premises, in return for a fifty per cent share of the profits. Needless to say, fifty per cent of the profits would not have amounted to very much in the first few years but, because we were working out of the same premises, our overheads were minimal and much of the work I was undertaking was profitable.

After handing in my week's notice at W. D. Aldridge, I started my own business – W. A. Wilson Electrical – on 3 March 1964 at the age of twenty. Jim Shields and Alec Stewart were a fantastic help to me. In fact, Jim Shields' son – also Jim – now managing director of Stewart and Shields, was one of my schoolmates and became my best man and godfather to Scott, my elder son. Jim and Alec helped me diversify from immerser installations into other business areas, such as the electrics required for loft conversions. In those days people were beginning to buy more and more electrical equipment for their homes, such as fridges and televisions, and there was a rising demand for extra sockets to be installed. That kept me busy in the early days.

One of the first things I did after establishing my own business was to write a letter offering my services to all the builders in the Dumbarton area. One of the builders I wrote to, enquiring if there were any opportunities to tender for electrical work, was R. D. Robertson, which was at that time about to start building a new housing scheme in Colquhoun Street, Helensburgh. Although I received a reply explaining that an electrical contractor had already been appointed for that project, within weeks of the project starting, I received a phone call from Hugh Orr, R. D. Robertson's chief estimator, who told me that the original contractor had gone bankrupt and asked me if I'd be interested in taking on the job at the rate agreed with the original contractor. I confirmed that I'd be more than happy to take on the project at that rate, even if, at that time, I wouldn't have known a good rate from a bad rate. But what I did know was that I was doing the work, and, as long as I had enough funds to cover the cost of the materials I required – and a little bit extra – then that was all I needed to get me up and running.

I quickly took on my first apprentice, Ian Mundie, to help with the workload (tragically, Ian was to die from cancer at the age of twenty-two) and we soon started to pick up work on a number of other housing projects undertaken by R. D. Robertson. I was then approached by Frank Lawrie, an engineer from Dumbarton, who invited me to tender for the electrical contracting work required for a substantial school building project with which he was involved for Dumbarton County Council. When I told Frank that I'd have to pass up the opportunity as my company did not yet have the financial resources required to undertake such a sizeable project, he offered to enquire if the council would be prepared to pay me on a fortnightly basis. Although I thought that would be the last I'd hear of it, Frank duly came back to report that the council was happy to pay me fortnightly – and that was my introduction into sizeable commercial electrical contract work.

I was sixteen years old when I first met Mary and twenty-three when we were married on 24 June 1967 at St Joseph's in Helensburgh. Our reception was at the Ardencaple Hotel in Rhu, after which we planned to drive down to Blackpool for our honeymoon. But, before we left for Blackpool, the first person we went to visit after our wedding reception was Mary's father, who was by then a patient at Erskine Hospital.

Mary's father, Danny Bowen, was a Welshman who had been a gunner in the Royal Air Force during the Second World War. His plane had been shot down over the English Channel and he had been left fighting for survival for three or four hours in the freezing water before being rescued. But the traumatic experience had left a mark on his health. After the war, he flew to Rhu, which had an RAF presence with hangars for seaplanes, and the family settled there. Mary has an elder sister, Sylvia, and a younger sister, Christine, but, when her mother left the family home, Mary and Christine were raised by their father in Rhu.

Her father had worked for British Rail as a linesman but, after the war, his health had started to deteriorate. Mary looked after him for as long as she could in the family home, even though she was only in her early teens herself. Eventually, though, her dad's doctor insisted that he would have to go into Erskine Hospital to receive the constant care he needed. He was to remain a patient there for about sixteen years. Having suffered some damage to his nervous system, he had previously been admitted to Killearn Hospital where he had undergone brain surgery. I remember that we went to visit him a couple of days after the operation to discover that he'd lost his power of speech. Although his speech was to return, he was never really the same again.

My own father had been a driver in the infantry during the war, where he'd been based in Holland, and, unlike Mary's dad, he had a war pension. Although my dad's war pension was because of a damaged spine, it was due to his pension that his more serious illness came to light. A condition of his war pension was that he had to travel to Edinburgh every year to undergo a medical. This was a procedure designed to check that he was still eligible for the pension since, if his medical examination had shown any improvement in his health, then his pension would have been cut. A couple of days after one of these annual examinations he received a letter from his doctor asking him to pay a visit, at which point he was told that he had lung cancer. The disease had been discovered by an X-ray taken during the examination for his war pension.

By this time, my dad was working with me in Helensburgh and so I bought him a house next to the yard so that he could be close to me and I could see him. A very heavy smoker – going through at least sixty cigarettes a day – he was diagnosed with lung cancer at the age of sixty-four and died at the age of seventy. Mary's father died in March 1980. My father died the following March, in 1981, and my mother died a year later, in March 1982. So all three of our parents died in the March of three consecutive years.

But, on our wedding day, we paid a visit to Mary's father in Erskine Hospital prior to heading off on our honeymoon in Blackpool and as we were leaving the reception and saying our farewells to our family and friends before catching the ferry over to Erskine – at that time there was no bridge – Jim Thomson's wife Agnes shoved some confetti and petals down my trousers. Having visited Mary's father, we soon realised that we'd left it too late to drive all the way down to Blackpool that night, so we decided to stop off at Carlisle. I remember the two of us, nervous newly-weds, sitting in the car outside the big, imposing Station Hotel in Carlisle, arguing over which one of us should go and book us into the hotel for the night. Eventually I realised that Mary would never relent and that I'd have to do it. I remember enquiring at the reception desk if there was a room available for us, without wishing to reveal the fact that we were newly-weds. Having found us a room, I went to park the car before returning with Mary to the hotel reception to book us in. But as we walked, self-consciously, across the grand foyer towards the broad staircase with its curving balustrades, we were distracted by the sound of some people laughing behind us. When we turned around to find out the source of all the hilarity, I discovered to my horror that the confetti and petals that Agnes had stuffed down my trousers had now worked their way down my trouser legs to leave a trail behind me running right across the centre of the foyer for all to see! Mary and I turned and ran up the staircase to our room where we locked ourselves in for the rest of the evening.

3

Keeping My Name Above the Door

When the time had come for Mary's dad to be admitted to hospital, he transferred the family home to Mary's name so our first marital home was a council house at 24 Laggary Road, Rhu. Scott, my elder son, was born the year after Mary and I married and a couple of years later we moved to Westerton Villa in Helensburgh – a property which had been left derelict after being damaged by a fire following the mysterious disappearance of its previous owner, a naval officer at Faslane. He had suddenly vanished, leaving only his uniform abandoned on a remote jetty further along the west coast, prompting speculation that he'd been a spy who had been picked up by a Russian submarine and taken home.

I decided to buy the derelict property and apply for a grant from Dumbarton District Council to help fund the extensive restoration project required. I paid £8,300 for the house, only to then be refused a grant on the grounds that I'd known that it had been damaged by a fire prior to purchasing it. This infuriated me so I arranged to see Billy Petrie, a friend and my local councillor, and informed him that I wished to appeal the refusal of my grant application on the grounds that I considered the councillors to be inconsistent, given that there were clear precedents for giving grants to properties that owners had purchased knowing that they required restoration and conversion. The council had recently given my friend Jim Shields a generous grant to convert stables on Rhu back road into a home and had also awarded a grant to the Polombo family at Alexandria to convert the old blacksmith's at Balloch into housing. I threatened to pursue the matter in the courts unless Billy agreed to argue my case. Somewhat reluctantly, Billy agreed to raise the matter again with a few of the councillors.

Then, late one night, a couple of weeks later, there was a knock at our door and a proud Billy Petrie strode into our living room.

'I've managed to get you your grant!' he announced.

'You've managed to what?' I asked.

'I've managed to get you your grant!' he repeated, awaiting my gratitude. But gratitude's not what he got. Instead, I shot him down.

'You didn't get me anything,' I told him angrily. 'I got it for myself. You'd already accepted the council's decision to reject my application before I demanded that you do something about it.'

Billy never spoke to me for a few years after that, though the grant for £8,600 enabled me to undertake a considerable amount of work on the property. But one of the conditions of the grant was that the original stone walls had to remain. Since I didn't want the original walls, it took me a few weeks to come up with a solution to this problem. But then I had a brainwave. I spoke to Alan Berry, my architect.

'According to the condition of the grant, the original stone walls have to *remain*,' I said. 'But there's nothing in the condition that says that the stone walls have to be *seen*.'

'What's your point?' he asked.

'Well, I thought I would just leave them and build around them.'

'But you'd end up with walls that are four feet thick!'

'Maybe so,' I said, 'but that's not necessarily a bad thing.'

So that's what I did. I built a house within a house – and it looked fantastic.

I received a tremendous amount of help with the restoration project from R. D. Robertson and, when the house was finally finished, I got a phone call to report to their offices for a meeting with the firm's owners – Willie Gilchrist, Jimmy Bauchop and Buster Mackenzie. I'd been dreading that phone call for some time because I knew that I was about to be presented with a massive invoice for all the work they had done on the property. I arrived at the meeting with a sense of trepidation to find the three directors sitting waiting for me.

'We've come to a decision about the work we've undertaken on your property . . .' said Willie Gilchrist, the managing director.

'Here we go,' I thought.

'. . . and we've decided not to give you a bill. As a sign of appreciation for what you've done for us over the years – not just for us as a company but for each of us personally – this is our way of saying thanks.'

So I didn't get invoiced at all for all the work that went into restoring my house! That meant that, having paid £8,300 for the property and getting a grant for £8,600 and having it completely restored, the total cost of moving into the house, including all the furniture, came to a grand total of just £16,900. A decade later, when the housing market was booming, I sold it for £128,000.

From the start, my business grew very quickly, so much so that by the late 1960s we were already a large local contractor employing around thirty people, including my brother John, who had joined the company straight from school in 1969 to serve his time as an apprentice. In those first few years, the company was mostly involved in new housing and in commercial work and although local authorities had just started to invite tenders for the upgrading and rewiring of council homes, this was an area of business that I'd so far resisted becoming directly involved in.

Returning from a holiday in Jersey one year, I received a phone call from Willie Brock at Dumbarton District Council asking me to report to his office as a matter of urgency. I set off to meet him straight away but, as the business was only in its early days and I was still involved in the physical aspect of the work myself, it was only once I'd arrived at the council offices that I realised that I was still wearing my dirty work overalls. I remember being guided by Willie along a corridor of the architects' department and asking him where he was leading me.

'We're going into the council chamber,' he informed me.

I was only a young man at the time and I remember

feeling self-conscious about still wearing my overalls on entering the grand council chamber to report to all the councillors. All I knew about was getting on with my work and trying to build my business. I'd never been involved at this level before. Then Bob Miller – a big guy with silver hair and a bushy moustache who was chief architect at Dumbarton District Council – entered the chamber, sat down beside me, turned to face me and said, 'Willie, the council is very disappointed that the tenders are not being returned for this rewiring programme . . .' and proceeded to give me a real going-over before the whole chamber. I remember being taken aback by the ferocity of this unanticipated verbal assault.

On leaving the meeting, Willie Brock saw that I was shocked and took me back to his office for a cup of coffee. As we walked along the corridor, Bob Miller appeared and wrapped an arm around my shoulders.

'I had to be seen to be giving you a bit of a hard time in the chamber just now,' he confided. 'You see, these councillors in there are my bosses.'

That was my introduction to local council politics. I'd seen at first hand how the system worked – and I learned quickly. Bob Miller also gave me a useful piece of advice that day that I've never forgotten. He told me, 'If you don't really want to win a contract – price it high.'

The first tender I submitted was for the rewiring of 387 council houses in Renton, at Tontine and Burnbrae, opposite Vale of Leven Academy – and I won the contract! The margins for the rewiring and upgrading of local authority properties turned out to be very profitable and, at our peak, we were upgrading around 3000–4000 houses a year. For many years, that line of work came to account for around eighty per cent of our turnover.

A couple of years later I discovered that, although we were offering some of the most competitive prices for electrical contracting work, we were still not winning as much work as we might have, so I decided to go it alone and tender for projects as a main contractor instead of just an electrical contractor. That meant that I could retain all the electrical work, as well as any other trades that I wanted to undertake, then subcontract the other work required. The trades that I chose to retain were electrical, plumbing, heating and joinery and I subcontracted all the building, roof tiling, floor tiling and painting work.

We then started working on various projects for Glasgow District Council and one of the largest projects we won during that period involved the rewiring of 1400 houses at Pollock. The contract was valued at £572,000 and, by this time, I'd diversified the business considerably, though, by the early 1970s – the era of the three-day week and of power cuts – the electrical contracting side of the company alone was turning over about £7 million.

Then one day Jim Shields came to me and offered to make me a director if I agreed to fully integrate W. A. Wilson Electrical into Stewart and Shields Builders. I'll never forget the look on his face when I told him I wasn't interested. He was taken aback and he was furious.

'You don't want to become a director?' he asked, incredulous. Though I was just a young man, I said, 'No, I'm not interested in anything like that. I want to keep my own name. And anyway, I'll make more money than you.'

That riled him.

'You'll never have as big a turnover as us,' he said.

'I'm not interested in turnover,' I said. 'At the end of the day it's profit that matters.'

One of the best pieces of business advice my father gave me was 'keep your own name above the door'. My old man had always instilled that thinking in me – and that was very important to me at that time. It turned out to be good advice too because W. A. Wilson *did* grow to be much bigger than Stewart and Shields Builders.

Jim Shields fell out with me over that. I was still based in their offices at that time and, returning to work after a holiday, I entered my office to find my secretary, Christine Moffat, sitting at a desk in the middle of an empty room. They had stripped my office of everything, with the exception of the odd file. I realised that the time had come to look around for new premises.

I managed to buy some land at Lomond Street, Helensburgh from Prow Motors. Because the land had at one time been used for allotments, there was a strict building restriction placed on it that limited what it might be used for. And because the previous owner had applied on several occasions for permission to build on the site for the purpose of repairing cars and been refused, I was able to secure the land for a knock-down price. At once I appealed to the Secretary of State and stated my intention to construct office facilities on the site – and won immediate approval to proceed. We built two-storey office accommodation there and were employing a staff of eighty by the mid 1970s. It was around this time that Mary joined me in the office.

In the event, W. A. Wilson Electrical went from strength

to strength after we broke away from Stewart and Shields Builders. The reason for our rapid growth at that time was not because Stewart and Shields had done anything wrong but because the link between us had meant that W. A. Wilson was not getting any opportunities to work for other builders because they had surmised that our allegiance was to Stewart and Shields. But as soon as other building companies saw us breaking away and going out on our own, we started to pick up more work elsewhere.

The company was still unlimited at that time and I was the sole proprietor. Then, shortly after moving into our new offices, my accountant from Wylie, Guild and McIntyre recommended that the time had come for me to safeguard the company's considerable assets by incorporating the business. I took his professional advice and instructed him to proceed with the process of incorporation. Unfortunately, however, he made a hash of it and I wound up being landed with a massive tax bill that could have been avoided had I received better advice.

That was an expensive lesson to learn – but one which I've never forgotten. I remember thinking to myself, 'It's all very well knowing the engineering side of the business, how to price jobs and knowing that you've made some money – but you're going to have to learn how to *keep* as much of that money as you can. You're only going to get so much advice from professionals, so you're going to have to learn about the financial aspects of running a business yourself.'

So I determined to make the effort to understand all the various financial matters involved in a company's operations. And I studied company finance in depth and to the point where, to this day, I regularly have running arguments with my accountants over various financial matters – and I win my fair share of these arguments.

It was around this time that I went to Wales for a short break with my brother John, who was playing on a rugby tour there. We finished the trip by going to see a Wales v. Scotland rugby match in Cardiff before heading for home. We arrived back late on the Sunday evening and John went into his house to catch his first wife in bed with another guy. John had become a father only eight weeks earlier and, acting on our mother's instructions, he immediately lifted Richard, his baby son, from his cot and took him to our mother's house across the street.

A week or so later, my mum phoned Mary in a panic. Someone had reported my mother to the social welfare department and a social worker had visited to tell her that they were going to remove the baby because she was judged to be incapable of looking after him. Mary jumped in the car and drove over to my mum's house straight away.

'I'm capable of looking after him,' Mary told the social worker. 'I'll take care of him.'

'We'd prefer that the baby was living with his father,' protested the social worker.

'That's not a problem,' said Mary. 'His father will move in with us.'

And that's what happened. When he was three months old, Richard came to stay with us – and so did John. John's wife was given access to the child and she used to visit on the occasional Sunday for an hour or so but, more often than not, she wouldn't even bother to turn up. This went

31

on for a while until she stopped visiting altogether and John won total custody of Richard. It was then that I spoke to John.

'Look,' I said. 'Scott now regards Richard as his brother. It would make it very difficult for Scott to understand if, all of a sudden, you decide you're taking Richard away.'

'That's not going to happen,' said John.

'Well, we'll adopt Richard,' I said.

Richard has always been told openly that he was adopted. Once, when he was just a wee boy, he turned to Mary and said, 'Did I come out of your tummy, like Scott did?'

'No,' Mary told him. 'You didn't.'

Richard looked at her and said, 'I didn't think so – but you're still my mum.'

4

Cruising in the Seventies

I owned ninety-eight per cent of the allocated shares of the incorporated business, with Mary owning the remainder, and that's how it remained right up until 28 May 1996, although I'd made some employees directors by then, including George Mundie (a cousin of Ian Mundie, my first employee. In fact, Ian's younger sister came to work with us some years later). Unfortunately, though, one of my directors (not George) grew greedy and, when I discovered that he'd been stealing from the company, he had to go.

Employee theft has arisen on several occasions over the course of my business career and though I've often wondered if it was because employees felt they were underpaid – even though I've always paid at the going rate or above – Mary's view has always been that employee theft has little if anything to do with salary or how employees are treated by their employer but can, instead, be explained simply by the fact that people who want to steal will steal.

One day, some years ago, my secretary Christine Moffat drew my attention to an invoice for four new tyres. She had checked the size of the tyres shown on the invoice and realised that the company had no vehicle that corresponded to that particular tyre size. When I raised the matter with the employee who had signed off the invoice, he confessed that he had put four new tyres on his wife's car and cashed it through the company. It's my experience that things like that happen all the time unless you keep a very close eye on the firm's day-to-day operations.

For example, we had been aware for some time that there was something wrong with our fuel expenses when we discovered that one of our electricians was signing for ten gallons of fuel, getting five put in the company van, getting two-and-a-half gallons put in his own car, and the pump attendant, who was in cahoots with him, was getting two-and-half gallons so that the next time he sold petrol for cash, he could pocket the difference and everything would balance.

It was particularly upsetting to find that some of the guys whom I discovered had been stealing from the company had started their working lives with me. At this time, my father had contracted cancer and I'd bought him a house beside the yard. Many of these guys had a soft spot for my dad and he had a soft spot for them. And because of that, although he was aware that they were stealing from the company – and didn't disagree that they'd have to be punished – he didn't want the police to get involved. In the event, I opted to respect his wishes and so never contacted the police.

But sometimes these things have a habit of biting back at

you, particularly in a small community like Helensburgh, and, on several occasions, I was approached by people in the street and castigated for having fired an employee for no apparent reason. I chose not to enlighten these accusers by informing them that I had fired the individual concerned because I had found him stealing. Mary would often argue that I wouldn't have been subjected to such misdirected verbal abuse if I'd involved the police at the outset and certainly, nowadays, I wouldn't hesitate to call in the police if I found an employee stealing from the company. In fact, over the last few years I've reported several incidents of theft to the police.

But firing someone is not something I take lightly. I'm a pretty hard person in many ways but I'm also very soft in others. Firing someone is a very hard thing to do because you're taking someone's livelihood away. It's particularly difficult when you have to let good employees go due to lack of work. Although I've always tried to be fair, I know that I can't satisfy all my employees all the time. But I also know that I can't make a different set of rules for each employee – a company must operate to a set of rules that encompass everyone, whilst recognising that different things motivate different people. I certainly understand that employees need to be paid a fair wage but I also found that salary was not the only thing that motivated people – I think it's important that employees feel part of something. And that's why, in the early days of the business, I'd make a habit of finishing earlier than usual on a Friday and meeting up with some of the guys in Helensburgh for a few beers and a bite to eat.

I've never been a high flier. I've always driven a nice car

and I love to go to the football on a Saturday but, other than that, although I was earning a lot of money by this time, I'd continue to go to the Rhu Inn with my usual pals and, though I could probably have afforded to buy all the drinks at the bar, I'd only ever buy my own round, so that I remained just one of the crowd.

However, I've always taken great pride in my holidays and my cars. These have been my two great indulgences in life and I'd have to confess that, when it comes to cars and holidays, I've been more than a little extravagant. I've done a lot of travelling in my time and, whenever I travel, I enjoy a bit of luxury – the best room and the best restaurant on the ship during a cruise, the best rooms in the best hotels in the cities we visit and, whenever I travel by air, I like a first-class ticket. But though I've always enjoyed indulging myself on holidays, I've also always wanted to be able to socialise freely with a mix of fellow travellers, rather than be divided artificially according to wealth.

Although my first-ever car was a Transit van and I know very little about cars, I've always enjoyed driving high-performance cars – and I've owned many over the years. A Ford estate wagon, a Cortina and then a 5 Series BMW followed the Transit. My first-ever performance car was a revolutionary new type of car at the time called a Wankel Rotary Engine NSU Ro80 and, after that, I bought my first Merc – a white 250.

A few years later, I bought a second-hand Rolls-Royce. A couple of weeks after that, I was sitting at work one day when I was paid a visit by Brian McGinley, the former referee, then working for Purdie & Kilpatrick, the photo-copier company.

'Whose is the fancy Roller parked out in the yard?' he asked.

'That's mine,' I said, proudly.

'That's my boss's old car!' he said.

In the event, I didn't keep that Rolls for very long because it didn't handle too well, so I sold it and went back to a BMW before moving on to Jaguars. After an XJ12, I bought a couple of E-type Jags but, after picking Richard up from school one day, I hit a patch of ice near St Fillans, skidded off the road and slid into a tree. The E-type's big broad tyres meant that they skidded easily on ice – and I decided to have another go with a Rolls-Royce.

I bought myself a two-tone blue Rolls with white upholstery – a beautiful car. But, when the time came to change it, I decided to go even further. The ultimate in indulgence, as far as I was concerned, was to have a Rolls-Royce custom built to your own specifications. And that is exactly what I did. I arranged for the car to be hand-built at Crewe. It took a full fifteen months to build, from order to delivery and, throughout that time, Rolls-Royce would arrange for me to be flown up and down from Glasgow to Crewe to show me its progress. It was a silver and British racing green Rolls and had cream leather seats with green piping. I picked the colour of the carpets, specified all the custom-built interior furnishings, including the walnut dashboard, and had all its gold trims done in British racing green with a gold stripe and its wheels all colour matched. I was very proud of that car.

You will sometimes see real gold custom-built Rolls-Royces, which are very popular in the Middle East, though they don't offer that service in Crewe. Rather, many of the

Arabic purchasers of Rollers send them out to a specialist company called Hoopers, which converts them to their specifications. You can always tell when a Rolls-Royce is owned by an Arab because its famous Spirit of Ecstasy or Flying Lady figurine is kneeling.

More recently I've been driving a Mercedes CL55 AMG, which is a nice, high-performance car, though I got a bit of a shock when, having paid £107,000 for it, the price I was quoted for selling it two years later, with only 16,000 miles on the clock, was only £40,000!

In the early days of building my business, I opened the yard in the morning and I shut it at night. But though I worked hard putting in the hours all year round, it was during this period that I also began to develop a taste for travelling. I've always been able to shut myself off from work on holiday – until the very last day, when I'd switch back to work mode and start to fret about what had happened since I'd been away and what problems I'd be returning to. There were always problems when I returned to work, though, looking back, I can see now that these problems were almost always caused by me. That's because, in the early days of my business, I was never a very good delegator. Although I had managers working for me who were more than capable of doing jobs and making decisions themselves, I couldn't stop myself from sticking my nose into everything they did. Although I still tend to do the same today, I've learned over the years to know when to back off.

I had some fantastic, adventurous holidays throughout that time. When I was in my thirties I went on some long-distance cruises to South Africa, South America and the West Indies. I've never been on a Mediterranean cruise in my life and I've never been on a cruise without incident – passengers jumping overboard or dropping dead. I remember one year we joined the *Oriana* at Southampton and we were sitting having an early dinner on the first evening when this guy sitting at the table next to us suddenly keeled over and dropped dead with his head straight into his soup before we'd even reached the Isle of Wight! I suppose his wife was fortunate in so far as the pilot boat was still with us, which meant that they were able to remove his body from the ship and return him to Southampton, because if a passenger should die in the middle of the ocean then they're buried at sea.

We cruised mostly with P&O, in the days when all the ladies still wore long dresses and all the men wore dinner suits, though the ship was no longer split into first- and second-class passengers with restrictions placed on where in the ship second-class passengers were permitted to go. But, though anyone could now go anywhere on the ship, if you paid more money (which I did), you had a more spacious cabin and you were able to meet and talk to anybody – which is what it's all about.

Whenever the ship moored in a port, I would always prefer to go and do something a bit different – go exploring by myself to get into the heart of a country – instead of going on the usual guided tour. I remember one cruise on the P&O *Canberra* when we stopped off to bring on supplies at Dakar in Senegal, West Africa, en route to Rio de Janeiro in Brazil. Although Dakar is French, the locals speak perfect English and, when we disembarked, I asked a couple of folk where would be the best place to visit. One guide told me about the nearby Senegal River and offered to drive us there.

We took him up on his offer and, at the riverside, stepped on to a crudely crafted canoe – little more than a hollowed-out tree trunk. Scott, who was with us, was only five years old at the time and I remember having reservations about getting into this canoe when I saw these strange white objects bobbing and floating by us as we were punted up river. Further on, I noticed, in the distance, stilts emerging from the river with little wooden platforms built on top of them and, as we sailed closer, I could see that the platforms were only a foot or so above the surface of the water. When I asked our guide what these platforms were for, he explained that this was what he had brought us to see. We had sailed into a burial ground built on the river where corpses were placed on these stilted platforms. As the corpses decayed, they were swept off the platforms and into the river. It transpired that the white objects that had floated past us earlier had been bones swept downstream from these platforms.

From Dakar we crossed the South Atlantic to Rio de Janeiro. One of the popular pastimes on that trip was a bingo-type game called 'snowball' where, each day, more money was wrapped around a ball, which grew bigger and bigger, until some lucky passenger won the 'snowball'. I distinctly remember sailing up the inland waters of Rio de Janeiro, between the towering Statue of Christ the Redeemer at the top of Corcovado Mountain on one side with Sugarloaf Mountain on the other . . . and the decks of the *Canberra* were almost empty! All these passengers had spent a fortune on this once-in-a-lifetime cruise and they were missing this magnificent view for a game of snowball!

Rio de Janeiro was a fascinating city and during our stay there we hired a minibus to take us up to the top of Corcovado Mountain at midnight, where we looked down over Copacabana beach, Ipanema beach and the whole city. It was an unforgettable experience. I remember, too, that while Copacabana beach was bordered by a string of magnificent apartments and hotels, the streets behind this glittering façade were comprised chiefly of tin shacks. A guide informed us that the traffic lights were switched off after 10 p.m. so that the traffic along Copacabana kept flowing freely because if you stopped your car, bandits would jump into action, hold you at knifepoint and demand your wallet.

After Rio de Janeiro, we sailed up the coast and stopped off at Salvador before proceeding up to Venezuela and then into San Cristobal on the Caribbean side of the Panama Canal, where I hired a car with a driver to visit Panama City on the other side of the canal. It was only on our return journey to the ship, when we had a puncture, that the driver confessed that he didn't have a spare wheel. That presented a real problem for us because we knew that the ship wouldn't wait for us. As luck would have it, we managed to get back just in time to board the ship before it set sail after flagging down a passer-by to give us a lift.

It was on one of these cruises, when we'd stopped off at Fort Lauderdale in Florida, that an item in a local newspaper about buying a property caught my eye. It occurred to me that, for all the money we were spending on cruises, we could afford to buy our own property. So it was that, in 1977, we bought our first home abroad, near Clearwater, Florida. However, after Freddy Laker, who operated one of the very first economy airlines, was squeezed out of business by British Airways, it became very expensive to travel to Florida. We had to fly from Glasgow to Heathrow to Miami to Tampa – and there were no discounts for the children – so we never really settled in Clearwater and decided to sell up.

It was around this time that I was approached by a golfing friend, Colin Robertson, who'd heard I was selling my property in Florida and enquired whether I'd be interested in a property in Portugal. Since I'd never even been to Portugal on holiday, my immediate response was to decline this offer. But when I mentioned the conversation to Mary, she expressed an interest in taking a closer look for herself and so it was that we flew out to Portugal on 8 December 1979 for a couple of days. Although the property we flew out to view was a timeshare arrangement and we quickly decided it wasn't for us, Colin introduced us to Jim Player, who has been a friend ever since and through him we found and bought our first property in Portugal on that same trip. We've had a home in Portugal ever since.

5

WAW

One of the properties Jim Player showed us had been nearing completion when its Swedish developer had fled Portugal at the time of the 1974 Carnation Revolution. I ended up buying the uncompleted property from an airline pilot and we proceeded to build our own swimming pool and grow our own orchard at the back of the villa. We kept the house for five years before deciding that the time had come to move to a larger home.

Once again, Jim Player had started showing us around various properties when, one day, he asked us if we'd ever considered buying a plot of land and building our own house. Of course, I'd already done that back home, with Westerton Villa, but not in a different country where I'd be unable to monitor the progress of any construction as closely as I would like. But though I told Jim that we had reservations about building our own home in Portugal, nevertheless, as it turned out, that was exactly what we did.

A couple of days later, we spotted an ideal plot of land, so I approached another friend I had in Portugal, Clive Batchelor, an architect who had served his time with Baxter, Clark and Paul. Clive advised me not to buy the plot because, as it was rustic land – equivalent to our green belt – his view was that I would never get permission to build a property on it. In the event, I ignored Clive's advice and decided to take a gamble on buying the land. What Clive didn't know was that I had a few other connections in Portugal that I hoped might be able to help me out with regard to getting the necessary permission.

I had a very close friend on the council out there called José Margado, who had worked for the Bank of Borges in Lisbon for many years and was also one of the directors of the football club at Loule. On one of my previous visits to Portugal with Celtic, I'd been able to use my contact with José to gain access to the local football stadium for the Celtic players to train on the pitch. Much to Clive's surprise, a few weeks after asking José if he could help me out, I received permission to build my own home on the seven acres of land I'd bought – for only £13,000. So I commissioned Clive to draw up some plans and duly set about constructing the house, closely monitoring the progress of the building project myself.

It was a beautiful big, open-plan villa with a swimming pool. We moved in on 15 September 1986 and stayed there for almost twenty years. For several years we spent six months of the year in Portugal and six in Scotland, though never six consecutive months. We used to spend May and June in Portugal then come home in July and August when the heat became too intense and the Algarve became too busy with tourists. But we've had a place out in Portugal for so long that I can walk around Almancil today and there will be more people that know me than if I walked around Helensburgh.

We eventually sold our villa, regretfully, on 15 December 2004 after a fire, which had broken out in it three years previously, had broken Mary's heart. The fire had erupted one Easter when we were at home in Kilmalcolm. I remember Mary coming off the phone in tears. Anna, our housekeeper, had called from Portugal to say that the house was in flames and was surrounded by fire engines. We caught the next available flight out and were devastated when we saw for ourselves the full extent of the damage.

Ironically, for an electrical contractor, the cause of the fire had been an electrical fault. I'd had a large fridge-freezer built into the kitchen which Anna had switched on that morning but, in the afternoon, she'd noticed that it didn't appear to be working. She went outside to check the circuit-breakers before returning to the kitchen to open the door of the fridge-freezer and it exploded. It seems that a gas had been leaking from a compressor at the rear of the fridge and it had ignited. Fortunately Anna was unhurt but the fire caught the curtains and, because the villa was open-plan, it quickly spread throughout the whole house. The heat must have been intense because the damage was extensive. The concrete ceiling was cracked where the steel frame had twisted under the severe heat – and the windows had completely melted. Eventually, we had the insurance all sorted out and I spent a lot of time and money putting the house all back together – but Mary could never settle in it after the fire and so we decided to put it up for sale.

It was only a couple of years after I'd bought my first property in Portugal that I moved home from Westerton Villa to Rhu Lodge. Firth Brown, the company which owned the Forge steelworks – now the site of The Forge shopping centre – had bought Rhu Lodge in 1978, ostensibly to entertain overseas guests. But when the steel-works folded a couple of years later, Rhu Lodge came up for sale. I happened to be in Alan Berry's office one day – the architect who had drawn up the plans for Westerton Villa – and some photographs of Rhu Lodge that were lying on his desk caught my eye. When I asked him about the impressive building in the photographs, Alan informed me that Firth Brown was in the process of closing down the Forge and, because a lot of workers were getting paid off, the company wanted to sell off the lodge discreetly because not many people even knew that it existed. It seems that the property had never really been used for entertaining overseas guests. Rather, it had been used by company directors as somewhere to take their mistresses. When I told Alan how impressed I was with the quality of its modernisation and internal fittings, he suggested that I should submit an offer to buy it. I scoffed at the very idea. I could see immediately from the photograph that the property was way out of my league.

'What d'you think it's worth?' asked Alan.

'Well, to me it's only worth what I could afford to pay for it,' I said, jokingly mentioning that I could probably scrape together around £130,000–£140,000 to buy it. Alan then spoke to Firth Brown's financial director and, two days later, I was asked to submit an offer in writing. I was initially reticent to do so because I really didn't think my offer had any hope of being accepted but Alan advised me to put in an offer anyway. I'm glad I did because it was accepted and the money I made from the sale of Westerton Villa paid for Rhu Lodge.

I picked up the keys to Rhu Lodge two days before my mother was buried.

I remember stepping out of the ironmonger's on Sinclair Street in Helensburgh, when I heard my mother shouting, 'Here, big fella, I hear you've gone and bought yourself a big house up in Rhu!'

'Who told you that?' I asked, annoyed. I've always been a private person. I like to keep some personal matters to myself and I didn't particularly want many people knowing my business.

'Well, that's what I've heard,' she said. It transpired that John's mother-in-law had told her. But as it turned out, my mother was never to see the house.

Mary had bought my mum a pair of Moorland fur boots for Christmas but they must have been a bit too small for her because the tight fur had damaged one of her toes and her doctor had arranged for her to have an operation at the Vale of Leven Hospital to have an ingrown toenail removed. I remember being in the utility room at Westerton Villa when I saw Mary standing at the door between the utility room and the kitchen and I could tell from the look on her face that something terrible had happened.

'My mother's dead,' I said.

'I've just had a phone call,' said Mary. 'A nurse had just

gone to her bed to check up on her after the operation – and found her dead.'

I'll never know what went wrong. My mother had been fit and well for her age. She used to walk to Rhu from Helensburgh every day.

I moved into Rhu Lodge in 1982. The property dates back to the early nineteenth century and has been owned by the Duke of Argyll and Princess Louise, Queen Victoria's daughter. At one time, it was also owned by Noel Coward. Located at Rhu Point, the house has views out over Gareloch. Princess Louise used to travel from her estate in Bishopton to catch the ferry over to Rosneath Castle but, if the tide was unsuitable for sailing, she would spend the night at Rhu Lodge.

Not long after we moved into Rhu Lodge, the McGinleys, family friends of ours from Kirkmichael, moved into the neighbouring property. Converted from the lodge's stables, the McGinleys' home still has rings on the wall from when the horses were tethered there. The McGinleys are very close friends of ours, to the extent that there are nine in the family and I'm often referred to as the tenth McGinley.

After my mother and father died, Neilly and Rita McGinley grew very close to me and I confided in them about everything. Neilly, who survived an extended period as a Japanese prisoner of war following his capture in Singapore, is eighty-seven now and I still regularly ask him for advice. We had a gate put in the fence that separated our houses and I used to go over every night after work for a wee dram and a blether with Neilly. Our friendship has grown stronger as time has gone by and, whenever the chips are down, you can guarantee that one of the McGinleys will always be the first at our door to see what they can do to lend a hand.

I remember that, not long after we moved in, Bill Cullen of Clyde Properties was keen to showcase Rhu Lodge on *Home Show*, a property programme broadcast on STV presented by husband and wife team Viv Lumsden and Alan Douglas. I told Bill that I had no problem with the house being filmed, provided that I was not interviewed and was not mentioned in the programme as the owner. Bill spent a month or so trying to persuade me to participate in the programme but I steadfastly refused. I've always preferred to keep some things private, so I arranged to leave my keys with friends so that the property could be filmed while we were away in Portugal.

Shortly after my return, I walked into the executive lounge at Parkhead ready to watch a game of football only to be greeted by a chorus of friends and associates ribbing me about my house which they'd seen on television. I was furious.

'How did you know it was my house?' I demanded to know.

'Your car,' was the answer.

I've always had a fondness for a fancy car and, at that time, I was driving my custom-built Rolls-Royce. Of course, I'd left it sitting in the yard beside the house while I was away in Portugal and the *Home Show* cameraman had deliberately swung the camera around from the house to zoom in on the car. My personalised number plate 'WAW 820' (which Mary had bought me as a birthday present –

my middle name is Alexander, after my dad) appeared in full view in the centre of the screen, as plain as you like for all to see!

We had many happy times in Rhu Lodge and lived there from 1982 until 1997.

6

Making a Million

The 1980s proved to be a very successful decade for the business. With the company going from strength to strength, I appointed financial advisers Service, Miller & Company to look after my personal financial affairs. One day in 1982, Mac Service suggested that I should consider investing in the recently introduced Small Self-Administered Pension Funds, which required Mary and me to compile a list of our assets for insurance purposes. This list was drawn up by Murdoch Hodge of R. A. Clement & Company, my accountants at that time. It was at a meeting to discuss the value of these assets that Murdoch turned to me and asked, 'Did you know you were a millionaire?'

'No!' I replied, taken aback.

'Well, here's the evidence,' he said, showing me his valuation of my assets.

I think I had little more than tuppence in the bank at that time – though it would seem that I had substantial assets – and that proved subsequently to be a less than ideal financial arrangement. The one piece of financial advice I'd give to anyone is to make sure that you have some savings so that you can get your hands on money at short notice in the event of the need arising unexpectedly. One thing my old man used to say to me was, 'You can't beat putting your money into bricks and mortar.' But while many fathers give their children that advice, if you should ever find yourself in financial difficulty, then it can prove difficult to sell bricks and mortar quickly – and if prospective buyers learn that you're seeking a quick sale, then you can be sure that they'll be seeking to purchase your property at a bargain price.

During this period I'd become friendly with Duncan Fletcher, who has subsequently gone on to become the very successful electrical contractor Forth Electrical (FES). In those days, Duncan and I were submitting quotes for social housing projects, competing head to head against the biggest companies in the industry, and we decided that, between the two of us, we could win many of these contracts because we were substantially cheaper than our bigger competitors. Later on, Duncan landed the opportunity to undertake some commercial contracting work for the Sheraton Hotel in Edinburgh and opted to focus his business increasingly on the commercial sector, whilst I opted to remain focused primarily on the housing sector.

But although the business kept developing during this period, we found ourselves in the frustrating situation where, although we were submitting the best tenders to builders, we were still not winning the contracts. Dutch auctions started to become more common around this time.

The construction industry has always had a proportion of people who are 'on the take'. We call them 'the brown envelope brigade'. We've never been a company that would get mixed up in that kind of dodgy dealing. We'll entertain clients, take them to the football and to the golf – though that's frowned upon in the public sector now too – but we've never paid someone in order to win a contract. I've never become involved in that and never will. I always remember something that my father used to say to me: 'You know Billy,' he said, 'a secret's not a secret if two people know.'

That's when I decided to become a main contractor rather than a subcontractor, retaining the electrical work and subcontracting various other trades. We did that very successfully from the early 1980s through to the mid 1990s when we became involved in civil engineering.

The 1980s were also the period when I started to follow Celtic. When Scott was still very young, family commitments made it less easy for me to follow Celtic, though I'd been able to continue my close involvement with Rhu Amateur Football Club, to the extent that I was made an honorary member in 1982. I invested a tremendous amount of time and money in Rhu Amateurs, including building a pavilion with changing rooms at the ground. Although the club never owned the ground, which belonged to Dumbarton County Council, Rhu Amateurs had sole rights for its use on a Saturday and for training on Tuesdays and Thursdays. The club also applied for and received a licence to sell alcohol, which helped it from a fund-raising perspective, though, with the benefit of hindsight, was perhaps not the best way for an amateur football club to proceed.

Having enjoyed some fantastic success in the 1960s and early 1970s, when the team had been regularly winning leagues, the 1980s were a time when Rhu Amateur Football Club started thinking about how to recapture those past glories. I approached Bobby Lennox, a friend of mine, who was then a coach at Parkhead, Billy McNeill being the manager, to see if he could assist Rhu in any way. Bobby and I came to an agreement whereby W. A. Wilson Electrical Contractors would sponsor him to coach Rhu Amateurs and provide him with a car for his services. That arrangement proved to be of great benefit to the club. Not only did the players benefit directly from some quality coaching, but the news that the team was receiving training from none other than Bobby Lennox spread like wildfire throughout the football community, earning the club some credibility and valuable publicity.

Some years later I was approached by Celtic to see if I'd be interested in buying the new scoreboards for Parkhead, so I accepted an invitation from Daktronics, the manufacturer, to travel to America to see the scoreboards in action for myself at an international golf tournament. The scoreboards for Parkhead ended up costing me about £380,000 but the idea was to put some revenue back into the club with a view to rebuilding the team.

Some time later, Bobby Lennox arranged for me to meet up with Liam Brady, Celtic's manager at that time, who asked if I'd be able to supply the team with a minibus to drive them to and from Parkhead to the training ground. I remember some business associates remarking that they'd seen my business advertised on Celtic's team-minibus. The fact of the matter, however, was that it was my bus – not Celtic's. I owned it.

Yet, despite various investments I've made in Celtic over the years, I've never owned a share in Celtic Football Club myself though I did buy the minimum amount of shares for my two boys.

I remember that Mary and I were sitting around the pool at our villa in Portugal one morning with Bobby Lennox and his wife Kathryn, just relaxing in the sun, when Anna, my housekeeper, came down to say that there was a phone call for Bobby.

'Who was it?' I asked him on his return to the pool side.

'It was Stevie Chalmers on the phone,' he said. 'Apparently I've been fired.'

'You're kidding.'

'No. Stevie says he's read in the paper that I've been let go.'

That was how Bobby learned that he'd been fired from his coaching post at Celtic.

I'd also become involved in helping out Dumbarton Football Club during this period. I'd been sponsoring their shirts for a while and then, when Murdo Macleod was paid off by Hibs and Dumbarton needed a manager, I stepped in to pay Murdo's wages. I thought that this was the right thing to do because Dumbarton was a local club and I believe that sometimes you have to give something back to the local community.

Although I'm a Celtic fan, over the years my friends have invited me to Rangers' games. Duncan Fletcher, for example, has facilities at Ibrox and I've accepted the odd invitation to watch an Old Firm game there as one of his guests – though I tend to wear a pocket-less raincoat on such occasions so that I can applaud Celtic underneath my raincoat without anyone seeing me!

I remember one day Celtic were playing Rangers at Ibrox and Duncan had invited me along to the Willie Thornton suite for a meal and a few drinks before going out to watch the game. A small party of us were standing chatting and having a drink when a guy called Bill Mather, who'd been running late, came to join us. No sooner had he ordered his drink than he flung his arms over a couple of the guys' shoulders and announced, 'Isn't this great? All Rangers' supporters together!'

I remember the look of concern on Duncan's face that I would take offence.

'I'm afraid you've got it wrong today,' I said, turning to the latecomer. 'I'm an out-and-out Celtic supporter!'

Well, he didn't know what to do with himself or where to look. Of course Duncan stepped in quickly to defuse the situation but it's my belief that there's no use in pretending to be something that you're not. After the game, we were sitting having some coffee when Duncan handed everyone a gift – a Rangers FC tie.

'Thanks Duncan,' I said. 'That'll do me fine for holding up my trousers.'

That was an example of some gentle ribbing between friends but there's some unpleasant bigotry at large in the west of Scotland and it's not confined to the football terraces at Ibrox and Parkhead. Over the years, I've encountered a couple of incidents of bigotry in my business life that I've found disturbing.

For example, I had a friend who was the district architect in Clydebank and whom I'd worked alongside for many years when he was at the county council as a young architect at Dumbarton. I remember he phoned me one day to ask if I was planning to go to Joe Burke's funeral and, if so, could I give him a lift. Joe Burke had owned a business called Lennox Electrical in Dumbarton before becoming an electrical clerk of works with Clydebank Council. So I picked up my friend at Clydebank and we drove out to Jackie Stewart's garage to the fork in the road where one route leads to Helensburgh and the other goes straight on to Balloch. I'd automatically gone into the Helensburgh lane, probably because I was living in Helensburgh at that time, and I remember him saying to me, 'Oh, Billy, you're in the wrong lane. This funeral's out in Alexandria, at St Ronan's – Joe was one of *them*.'

I turned round to him and said, 'What are you talking about, one of "them"? I'm one of "them"!'

I never won another contract in Clydebank after that.

A while later, one of my employees went to Clydebank Council offices to ask why we weren't winning any contracts.

'Look, Jimmy,' was the reply, 'it's hard enough getting work for our ain kind without worryin' about others.'

Another unpleasant example of bigotry occurred when we won the tender for a project to modernise council houses in Larkhall and John received a call from the district architect at Hamilton District – now South Lanarkshire – who enquired if we'd be prepared to withdraw from the contract because the tenants were furious that we'd won the job and were threatening to burn down the caravans used for temporary accommodation while the houses were being upgraded. I refused point blank to countenance withdrawal.

'Under no circumstances,' I said. 'That's the council's problem, not mine.'

On another occasion, I'd bought a factory in Cumbernauld, refurbished it and invested heavily in equipment to manufacture UPVC windows. At the peak of production, we were churning out 700 windows a week, chiefly for the social housing sector. But although we were based in Cumbernauld and had invested a considerable amount of money in our factory there, we never once won a job in Cumbernauld. I mentioned this one day to the service manager with Strathkelvin, who said to me, 'You'll not get any work out of Cumbernauld, Willie. You've got no chance; you kick with the wrong foot for up there.'

Some people claim that sectarianism has disappeared but, sadly, in my experience it's still going strong.

7

The Heart of the Matter and an African Adventure

By the late 1980s, many builders and property developers in Glasgow had started to invest in security door entry systems for tenement buildings and my business became heavily involved in this market. Although a couple of companies subsequently developed specially shaped steel doors offering enhanced security, at this time we were still working with timber doors, which meant that the joiner was able to dictate the speed at which an order could be fulfilled. As I sought control over the production process, I decided to forge a link with a joiner and so I broached the subject of a merger with a local company in Helensburgh called J. Allan Osborne Joiners.

It was just as we were about to start a meeting in my boardroom with Allan and two of his co-directors to discuss a merger of the two companies that what felt like a tidal wave suddenly surged up inside me. Unable to catch my breath and feeling as if I was going to drown, I excused myself from the room and went to the toilet to try and calm myself down. But when I returned to the meeting and the same thing happened again, I panicked.

I apologised, explaining that I had been taken unwell and would have to leave the meeting, then went outside to drive to the doctor's surgery. But when I opened the car door, I found that I was too frightened to sit in the car, so instead I set off along Princes Street, heading for the doctor's surgery on foot. My consternation must have been apparent by this time because when I arrived at the surgery, the receptionist took one look at me and asked the other patients in the waiting room if anyone had any objections if I could jump the queue and be seen by the doctor straight away.

'What's the problem?' asked the doctor, as I entered the consultation room.

'I think I've just had a heart attack,' I said.

'And I suppose you've just run from your yard all the way here after a heart attack?' said the doctor. 'I don't think so. I tell you what I want you to do: *calm down.* I want you to arrange to be taken home and I want you to pour yourself a whisky and relax. If you feel you want to go to bed then do that. And when surgery's closed I'll come and see how you're feeling.'

So that's what I did but my anxiety continued and my self-confidence started to drift away from me, to the point where I was regularly attending the McAlpine Hospital, eventually ending up in the hands of Dr John Kennedy, the principal cardiologist at the Western Infirmary. Finally, after many tests, Dr Kennedy called me in for a consultation.

'Willie, there's absolutely nothing wrong with your heart,' he told me. 'But I know that you're still convinced there is and I think that your belief is so embedded psychologically that the only way I can prove to you that there's nothing wrong with your heart is to let you see *inside* your heart. So I'm making an appointment for you at Ross Hall Hospital, where they will do an angiogram that will let you see your heart working normally.'

So I was admitted to Ross Hall for a couple of days and then hooked up to a catheter through my leg and into my heart where they pumped a fluid which enabled me to see my heart beating regularly, just as it should. The staff explained to me what I was seeing and showed me that everything was as expected of a healthy heart. The next day, Mary arrived at the hospital to take me home. We were driving towards the roundabout at Hillington, just off the M8, when I turned to her and said,

'You know, there's some kind of con going on here.'

'What d'you mean?' she asked.

'The pictures of that heart they showed me back there in the hospital,' I said. 'It wasn't mine, you know. That was somebody else's heart they were showing me. They were trying to trick me.'

I didn't know it at the time but I'd lost the plot.

I was advised to take some tablets to calm my nerves but I refused. During my mother's battle with alcoholism, a doctor had prescribed Valium and she had become addicted to it.

'I'm not going to end up like my mother,' I said.

'Well, if you don't take the tablets you've been prescribed, then you're going to suffer,' said my doctor.

But I never did take the tablets.

Although we went on holiday to Portugal during this time, I would have panic attacks at the thought of having to board the plane home. The following year, Mary arranged to drive me to Portugal rather than fly but every few miles I had to cover my eyes in abject terror at the cars passing by. It was a dreadful time. As far as I'm concerned, a mental illness is worse than a physical illness – and I've had experience of both, even though I always kept myself physically fit and regularly participated in sport. I've been a swimmer all my life, I played amateur football as a youngster and I rowed for Loch Lomond Rowing Club for five or six seasons in my twenties with Martin Malley, a pal from my days living at Kirkmichael.

Eventually my GP reached the conclusion that he had to get me out of the hands of the medical profession.

'You're going to have to learn how to relax,' he said. 'You need to speak to either a psychiatrist or a psychologist.'

'Well, I'm not going to see a psychiatrist,' I said. 'So we'll try psychology.'

I was referred to Ros Taylor, a clinical psychologist who, at that time, also presented the weather forecast for STV and wrote a newspaper column. Ros showed me how to relax and taught me how to recognise my symptoms. I was still experiencing pains in my chest but she taught me that I was creating the pains myself, by hyperventilating. I would get a panic attack, my lungs would tighten and I would mistake the pain for a heart attack. Ros cured me within a year. But, though I'd been unable to go to work for all that time, the business continued to thrive.

In the event, the proposed merger with J. Allan Osborne

Joiners never transpired. Instead, we resolved the production issue with security doors by establishing DCF, a
joinery business, with someone who had served his time
with me and whose father had been a site agent for R. D.
Robertson, one of the first companies I'd worked with. We
split the ownership of the business fifty-fifty but that relationship was not fated to last because I discovered that my
business partner was not keeping me fully informed about
all the activities of the business – I'd appointed Paul
Clancy, my accountant, as a director of the company whilst
I remained a shareholder and Paul had discovered that
there was work being done by the company that was going
unrecorded – and so I removed myself from that business.

It was after a round of golf with some friends at the club at
Vilamoura in Portugal in the late 1980s that we met up
with some guys from a mining company called
Cementation who invited us to South Africa to play in a
golf tournament. A party of us flew out to Johannesburg
early the following February, with myself as the non-
playing captain, and I just fell in love with South Africa
from the minute the plane landed. I had expected the
whole of Africa to be barren and scorched – but this place
was luscious and green!

   After a day or two in Johannesburg, our hosts at
Cementation arranged for us to play a couple of rounds of
golf at Sun City so we hired a small private plane to fly us
there. We sat in this tiny, rickety plane and, because we
weren't travelling at any great altitude, we could clearly
see all the hills around us and I remember being tapped on
the shoulder by Donald McIntosh, who was sitting behind

me. When I turned around to see what he wanted, he pointed and nodded over to Mary, who was sitting reading in the seat across the aisle from me.

'What is it?' I asked him.

'Look closer at the book Mary's reading,' he said.

So I did. The book was upside down. Mary was the first to step off the plane and the first thing she said was, 'I'm not going back on that plane.' And she didn't.

A couple of days later, when we were due to return to Johannesburg, our hosts had decided that the plane was inadequate to carry all the golf clubs on board and had made arrangements for a wagon to come up from Johannesburg with a trailer attached to the back to drive the clubs back while we flew back. But, rather than take to the skies again, Mary got herself up at five in the morning, travelled back in the wagon with the clubs and met up with us later that day in Johannesburg Airport!

The next stop on our tour was Cape Town, which was absolutely marvellous. From there we hired a Combi and drove through the Transky, through Mossel Bay and Port Elizabeth, right into Durban. That was a real adventure, passing through tiny African villages, scattered with mud huts. It was at one of these villages that we stopped off to refuel and check the oil. When we lifted the front passenger seat to access the centre panel to dip the engine in this Combi, we discovered several coins which must have fallen out of some previous passenger's pocket. I remember the petrol pump attendant couldn't take his eyes off this money – they were nearly popping out of his head. And I'll never forget the look on his face when we told him to take the money – you'd have thought we'd given him half the world!

It's a pity that visitors can no longer travel through the Transky but much of it is now closed off to tourists because it's so dangerous.

I loved South Africa so much that no sooner had we returned home than I decided to return on holiday the following year and to take the boys with us this time. So the following Christmas we left for Johannesburg. It was there that Scott paid a visit to some family friends who had emigrated to South Africa a few years before. A couple of days later we flew down to Durban and, having spent one afternoon out sightseeing, we returned to the hotel to be informed by the concierge that there had been a telephone call and a message left for Scott at reception.

Scott returned from retrieving the message with a big grin on his face, though he remained unforthcoming about what it was about.

'What are you doing getting messages in Durban?' I said. 'You'd better tell us what it's all about.'

'Well, while I was visiting our friends back in Johannesburg, I decided to apply for a job,' he confessed. 'I've got an interview. The company has said it's prepared to fly me from Durban to Johannesburg and fly me back after the interview.'

So when we got to Durban, Scott hopped on a plane back to Jo'burg then arrived back the next day to announce that he'd got himself a job!

Scott came home to Scotland with us at the end of that holiday but only for a few weeks, before flying back out to

South Africa in early February, supposedly only for a six-month stint. In the event, of course, it lasted much longer than six months. When he was still there the following Christmas, Mary and I decided to go over for a month to pay him a visit.

We rented accommodation at Santon, near Bryanston golf club, and spent some time with Scott, though we began to notice that he never seemed very keen for us to visit him at home. I began to suspect that there was something not quite right so when he had to stop off to pick up some items from his apartment one day, I drove him there, then followed him into his house to find that he'd been living in a dark and dingy hovel – the bedroom was entirely bare, excepting a mattress in the middle of the floor.

I decided right there and then that, if he was intending to stay in South Africa any longer, I would buy him somewhere decent to live.

And that's how we wound up buying a brand new house at 5 Summercroft Close, Bryanston, in Santon, part of a complex of eight houses, arranged to form a secure 'fortress' and surrounded by razor wire – unfortunately security was an issue out there at that time – and set about building ourselves a swimming pool. Scott lived there for a couple of years before moving on, at which time we rented it out before selling it twelve years later in 2004.

During that time, whenever we went to South Africa, we'd always travel down to Langa township in Cape Town, one of the areas that were designated for black Africans during the apartheid era, and Mary would hand out all the items of clothing she'd bought to distribute amongst the most needy – dozens of pairs of trainers and numerous jeans and shirts. It can be heartbreaking at Langa but I've got a local contact called Jimmy Jimta – a taxi driver from the Transky who moved down to Cape Town – who drives us down to Langa from the Vineyard Hotel at Newlands. Langa can be quite intimidating for any visitors who don't know quite what to expect from a township. It was constructed to accommodate a certain amount of people but probably houses ten times the population for which it was originally intended – and the obvious poverty there can be distressing.

But, although I like to get involved in hands-on charitable work and have done so for many years, I've never considered it important that anybody should know about it. Rather, I've always thought that what's most important about charitable giving is that it's the recipient who benefits, not the donor. And I've always been wary of people who make charitable donations and then publicise the fact because I think they're effectively using their charitable donations in order to gain publicity. If they can afford to give a donation and the sum involved is no material loss to them yet they make a point of announcing the fact, then they're simply creating publicity for themselves from it and, to me, that's not right.

A favourite act of charity that I have supported over many years has been to fly a family with a terminally ill child out to Disney World in America for a two-week holiday, with the proviso that the recipient family would not have been able to afford to fund such a trip themselves. This was one way that we felt we were able to directly benefit people in need. And, with the help of some friends – a priest, my accountant Charles Barnett at PKF and Mary

McGinley, a manager at the Royal Infirmary – we've been able to fund these trips anonymously.

Charles Barnett also helped me make another anonymous charitable donation in 2004. His firm had invited me to the Hottest Night of the Year at the Hilton Hotel – an annual charitable event organised by Glasgow curry king Charan Gill. Tired at the end of a busy week, I made my excuses and left for home straight after the meal, just as the comedian Andy Cameron was about to start to compère the raffle. The following morning, I was travelling to work when the telephone rang. It was Charles Barnett.

'Are you sitting down?' he asked me.

'I'm in the car,' I said.

'Well, you won the star prize last night,' he said.

I couldn't believe it. 'Oh? And what *is* the star prize?'

'You won the car!' he said.

John McGuire of Phoenix Honda had donated a Honda car to raise funds for the Hottest Night.

'Andy Cameron had pulled out the winning ticket, announced that it belonged to someone sitting at table twenty-nine and promptly put it in his top pocket without revealing the winner's identity,' said Charles. 'So, of course, all the remaining guests at table twenty-nine – myself included – thought that one of *us* had won the prize, forgetting that you had already left!'

When Andy Cameron finally announced my name as the winner of the star prize, Charles had to make his way up to the stage to collect it on my behalf – only to be met with cries of 'You're not Willie Wilson!' as he did so.

The next day I spoke to Mary McGinley at the Royal Infirmary, who has a contact at the Macmillan Nurses, then phoned Charles to request that he make arrangements for the car to be donated anonymously to the Macmillan Nurses. When Charles made contact with John McGuire and informed him of my intentions, John decided to convert the value of the car into money and give it as a donation on my behalf to the Macmillan Nurses.

That's what charitable giving is all about.

My granny, Maggie Nugent

My grandpa, William Wilson

My dad and my uncle John

My mum as a bus conductress

My mum and dad's wedding, 3 October 1938 – left to right, Agnes O'Hare,
Alec (my dad, aged twenty-seven), Annie Nugent (my mum, aged twenty-three) and their best
man, my uncle Patrick Nugent

Me at six months old

My brother John at five months old

A school photo, taken at St Barbara's – I'm in the second back row, fourth from the left

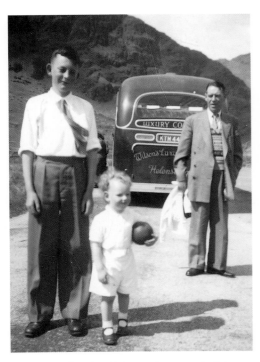

Me, my brother John and my uncle John

Me with my mum and dad

Our wedding with, from left to right, my dad, Alec, Jim Shields, who was our bestman, me, Mary, Hugh Walsh, Maureen Malley who was our bridesmaid, Margaret Walsh and my mum, Annie.

My mates at our wedding – from left to right, they are my brother, John, Jim Gillespie, Billy Goodall, Johnnie McQueen, Jake Orr, Terrence Shields, David Shields, Jim Shields, me and Martin Malley

Mary and I got married on 24 June 1967

My dad and me at Scott's christening, 1968

Mary's dad, Danny, Mary, my dad, Alec,
and Scott, aged about three months

My mum, Annie, Mary and Scott,
aged about two and a half, at Laggary Road

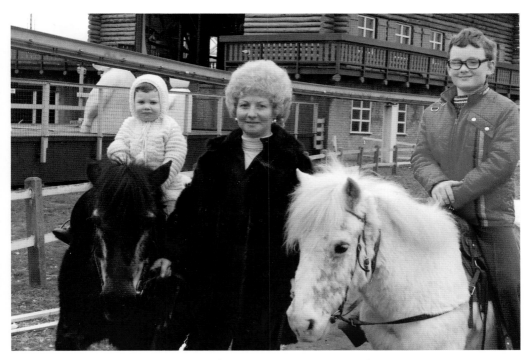

Mary with Richard and Scott enjoying pony rides, 1977

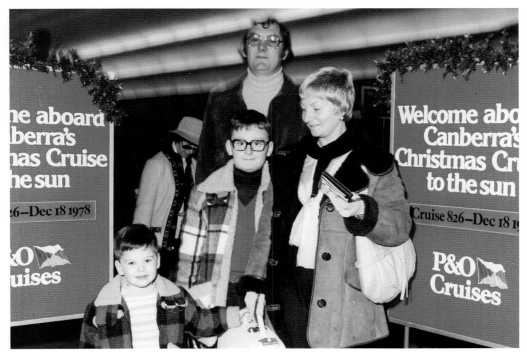

Mary and I boarding Canberra with Richard and Scott in 1978

Mary and I are dressed for dinner during the 1978 cruise

My blue Rolls-Royce outside the W. A. Wilson Electrical building in Helensburgh

My custom-built Rolls-Royce outside our home in Portugal

Mary and me on our 1980 cruise

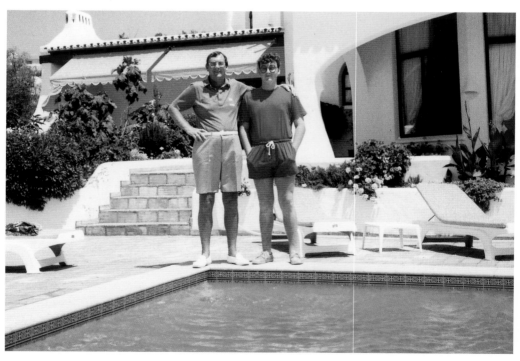

Scott and me at the pool of our home in Portugal

Our house in Rhu

Mary in Portugal with our dogs Beamish and Zoë in 1993

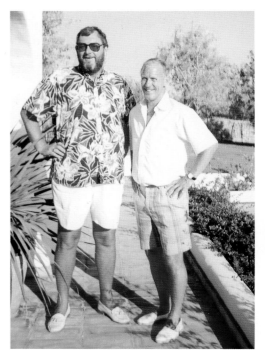

Me with Bobby Lennox in Portugal

Our grandson Michael proudly wearing his Celtic top

Me and Michael in Dublin in 2005

Mary with our grandson Michael in 2002

Our grandson Connor

John, Scott and Richard help me to celebrate my fiftieth birthday

Richard, me, Scott and John at Scott's wedding in 2000

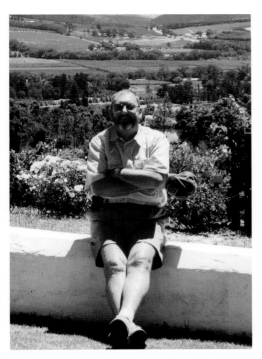

This is me in South Africa
on the Wine Route in 2001

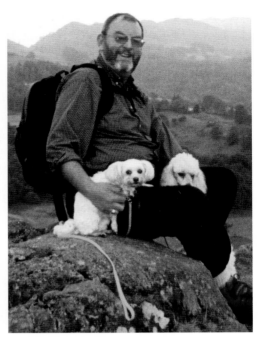

And here I'm doing some hill walking
in the Lake District also in 2001

The new building housing the headquarters of WWW Electrical Ltd

Me with Jim Alexander and Danny McIntosh in Portugal in 2005

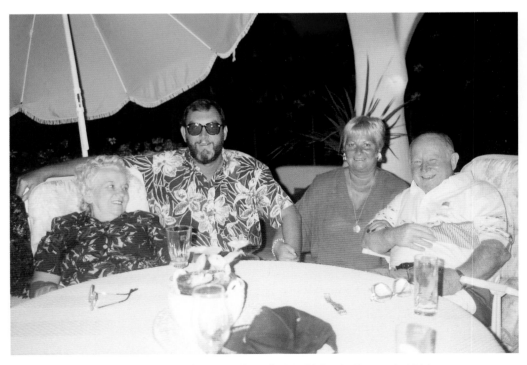

Me and Mary with Rita and Neilly McGinley in Portugal, 1991

8

A Quinta, Australia and a Stroke of Bad Luck

In 1988, I got wind of a rumour that a new road was going to be built linking Portimao on the west of the Algarve with Vilareal on the east. My house was in Val Formosa on the road towards Loule, through which this road was earmarked to be laid. I realised that this would become the main approach road to the motorway for such neighbouring towns and villages as Almancil and Vilamoura and so I bought an old bar called The Dutch Inn, which sat on the roadside, with the intention of turning it into a filling station when the new road was built.

But, when it turned out that the filter road on to the motorway was not at the location that I'd thought, I was left wondering what to do with the property. In the meantime, I continued to run it as a bar. A year or so later, I got a phone call late one Sunday night from my accountant, Paul Clancy, who had been preparing the accounts for the bar. According to his figures, the bar had lost a total of

£18,000 over the last accounting period. This made him immediately suspicious because, as far as we were concerned, it had been trading profitably.

Mary booked a seat on the first available flight to Portugal the next morning where she ordered a taxi from the airport straight to the bar, walked in and told the staff to put on their jackets and leave, then locked the bar behind her. Then she phoned John Hatton, a friend of ours, and asked him to come and change all the locks on the doors. John arrived with a lorry to remove all the stock from the bar, which we stored in the garage of our house. It was when we took account of all the stock that we discovered that we had more than had been recorded in the accounts. We found out later that the bar manager had been ordering stock and, instead of receiving discounts, was receiving a crate of whisky free of charge, which he was flogging himself, without going through the books.

It was then that I decided to convert the bar into a restaurant and commissioned an architect to draw up designs to have the whole place modernised. The changes were extensive – and expensive. They included building a new kitchen and a new frontage and, because we were constructing another storey on top of the existing structure, we removed the roof and put in a ring beam that would carry the weight of the new floor, as well as putting reinforced concrete pillars into the existing walls.

The modernisation took place during the winter of 1990/91 and was scheduled for completion before Easter. But, when we went out to visit the site in February, I realised that, if the construction continued at its current pace, it was never going to be ready in time for Easter so I decided to stay in Portugal to supervise the modernisation project myself.

I already knew that the Portuguese love a beer and so one of the things I did to get the construction workers on my side – and hopefully speed up the project – was to fill an ice-cream freezer unit with a couple of crates of beer every morning and I'd hand out an ice-cold beer every night to each worker on site before they finished up for the day.

But I began to notice that they had a certain way of doing things which, to my mind, was causing unnecessary delays. For example, they would only mix enough sand and cement in a mixer to fill one wheelbarrow at a time instead of mixing up much more of it and laying it out on a board from where they could take more as and when they needed it, as construction workers would do back home in Scotland. Although I discovered that the reason for their way of working was that the Portuguese climate meant that the cement dried quicker out there, I made some enquiries with friends in the construction trade back home, who let me in on some trade secrets about how to keep the cement sufficiently moist, such as adding washing-up liquid to the mix!

I'd also noticed that the tilers were working side by side and so, thinking that an element of competition might speed things up a bit, instructed them to lay tiles in different corners of the floor and come together in the centre. I had all the floors laid out in azulejos, a locally made clay tile which I'd had made the year before and placed in baking houses to dry out in the sun.

In the event, *A Quinta* – Portuguese for 'farmhouse' – did

manage to open as a restaurant in time for Easter in 1991. The décor is beautiful and traditional Portuguese. When I put on the new roof, I re-used all the original farmhouse tiles and augmented those with others sourced from nearby old buildings of a similar type. I must have spent around £250,000 on converting the building but it was worth it. The architect and the builders did a wonderful job and, to this day, it remains a very popular restaurant in Portugal.

I sold *A Quinta* for a tidy profit to Mark Ralph in May in 2004, having rented it to him a couple of years before. Although another couple – Roger and Gaye Evans – put in a higher offer (to the extent of £50,000) for the restaurant, Mary insisted that, since we'd already made a handsome profit and since it was Mark who had built up the restaurant business over the last few years, we should sell it to him.

A couple of months after the deal had been signed, Paula Carnavarro, my lawyer, rang up to say that Mark had raised a query about the contract. In truth, I'd been expecting her call. In Portugal, every plot of land is allocated a number and every building is allocated another number and I'd discovered when I'd originally bought The Dutch Inn that it had two plot numbers – one for the building itself and another for the car park – and *A Quinta's* car park (in which I'd invested substantially in landscaping) is bigger than the building itself. It had already occurred to me when I had sold the restaurant to Mark that his lawyer had not seemed to realise that he was only buying the building and not the car park as well.

So when Paula Carnavarro phoned to enquire about this, I told her that I still owned the car park.

'Oh, but Mark thinks that he's bought the restaurant *and* the car park!' she said.

'I'm aware of that,' I said, 'but he hasn't.'

'And according to the papers, there appear to have been two different owners. Is that right?'

'That's right,' I said, 'W. A. Wilson General Contractors Pension Fund and Willie and Mary Wilson. I arranged it that way so that I only had to pay tax on one of the properties.'

'But Mark bought the restaurant thinking it included the car park in all good faith . . .'

'I know,' I said. 'And I'd be happy to help him out but the problem is that I now have a tax problem. So I'm willing to sign over the ownership of the car park to Mark if the additional tax liability that I'm due on this is taken care of.'

So that's what happened.

In the afternoon of Christmas Day 1993, Mary and I set off on a long-haul trip to Australia and New Zealand – a part of the world I'd never been to before. We flew into Singapore and spent three days there before continuing to Sydney. We spent a week in Sydney before moving up the coastline to Port Douglas to visit the Great Barrier Reef. After that, we flew to Brisbane and spent some time there before flying out to Fiji.

It was while we were in Fiji that we met up with some people who were about to embark on a week-long Blue Lagoon cruise around the islands and we decided to join them. It was a very small ship with only around eighteen passengers and a modest crew who doubled up as waiters and entertainers in the evening, and we saw some tremendous sights.

On our return to Fiji, we stayed for a few more days before going on to New Zealand. We flew into the North Island and stayed in Auckland. We also visited Rotorua, with its famous geysers, and the Bay of Islands. Although New Zealand was fascinating, it was while we were there that I suggested to Mary that, rather than continue on our planned round-the-world trip by flying to America and coming home that way, we return instead to Australia.

The reason for our change of plan was that I'd been reading about the Indian Pacific Railway and I fancied the idea of travelling on it, so we booked ourselves tickets for the rail journey in Auckland, flew back to Australia, stayed the night in a hotel in Sydney and joined the train the next morning. The train journey took us through about five different time zones – from Sydney to Adelaide, right through the vast Nullarbor Plain and into Perth – and by the end of it we were both pretty exhausted so we decided to skip our planned visit to Hong Kong and instead return home to Scotland.

We arrived home from that trip at the tail-end of January and no sooner had we set foot in Scotland than we flew out to Portugal with a party of friends for a special Burns' Night Supper in Zena's that we'd organised with Roger and Gaye Evans, who had a complex there. Douglas Dalgleish, a well-known lawyer with Brunton Miller and ex-chairman of Dumbarton Football Club, helped assemble a great line-up of entertainment, including a presenter from the BBC, who acted as master of ceremonies and performed a special toast to the sardine instead of a toast to the haggis, Gordon

Hanning, the singer, and an accordionist. We also had a piper from Portimao. Everyone made an extra-special effort, with all the ladies wearing white blouses with tartan sashes and tartan skirts and all the men in kilts or black ties.

I'd arranged for the haggis to be flown out from Scotland and met up with Roger in the afternoon to go over the arrangements for the party that evening. Amongst the topics we discussed was how we would go about piping in the haggis but we were oblivious to the fact that Roger's Portuguese chef – who could speak only a smattering of English – had been eavesdropping on our conversation.

The evening duly went off without a hitch until all the guests were seated at their tables and the haggis was piped in. No sooner had the haggis been served than it became immediately obvious that something was awry.

Mary turned to me and whispered, 'What's wrong with the haggis?'

'I don't know,' I said, 'but I've never seen haggis served like this before.'

It wasn't until the following morning that we discovered that Roger's Portuguese chef had overheard our conversation about piping in the haggis, had got the wrong end of the stick and had put all the haggis through a piping bag and squeezed it like a paste on to the plates! Tom Shields, the diarist for the *Glasgow Herald*, somehow got wind of this story and duly had fun at our expense by reporting it in the paper the following week.

One Saturday afternoon, shortly after returning from Portugal, I went to see Celtic play Hearts at Tynecastle with my brother John and Scott and a couple of friends and I began to feel very tired. About a year before, one night at around eight o'clock, I'd been in a meeting with John in my office, standing and leaning on the back of a chair when, out of the blue, I felt what I can only describe as a sudden loss of power. And then it happened again. I didn't say anything at the time but decided to head home. After that night, I didn't get the sensation again so I didn't think any more of it but, in retrospect, I can see that it had been a warning – a warning that I didn't heed.

When I still felt tired the following morning, I decided to stay in bed instead of going for my usual morning swim. At that time I was swimming every day at Cameron House Hotel, Loch Lomond, at seven o'clock in the morning Monday to Friday and at half past eight in the morning on Saturdays and Sundays.

Mary helped me prop the pillows up in bed and I settled down to watch the TV while she went through to run herself a bath. The last thing I heard was the bathwater running and then I must have conked out.

According to Mary, I'd asked her to contact Neilly, our neighbour, for help, though I've no recollection of this. Whilst I'd fallen unconscious, Mary got in touch with Neilly, who phoned his daughter Mary at the Royal Infirmary for advice. Because she already knew that I'd had a history of high blood pressure, she advised us to get in touch with a doctor straight away. Apparently a doctor came out and immediately advised that I be transferred to the Vale of Leven Hospital. It transpired that I'd suffered a minor stroke – a clot of blood had been trapped in my head.

When I left hospital, I was concerned about what would

happen if I ever had another stroke. This dented my confidence a little and made me reluctant to drive. I also decided to take some time off work. Unfortunately, during my absence from work, the business took a turn for the worse, the seriousness of which I was not able to discover until it was already too late.

9

The Worst Day of My Life

I was still absent from work when one day John asked me to accompany him to the Thistle Centre in Stirling, where we were undertaking some civil engineering work for John Laing Construction. When I arrived on site I noticed this giant crane being used to lay massive sewer pipes under the M9 – and then I noticed that it had our company name on it. I knew right there and then that this was an expensive mistake.

I've always had a gift for knowing when something's not quite right in business. Bobby Lennox is a friend of mine but, if I played football every day for ten years, I'd still never have the same football skills as Bobby Lennox – just as Bobby Lennox will not necessarily have my gift for running a business. Everyone has their own strengths and weaknesses and, as soon as I saw that crane at the Thistle Centre, I realised that we had become involved in projects that were too big for us to handle.

Almost from start-up, my business had been buoyant

but, after my stroke, I began to notice a change in the amount of cash coming into the company. I had always operated with any excess cash from the company going straight into a deposit receipt account at the bank, so that it was readily available in times of need. I made a point of never making any very large investments and the financial arrangements I put in place meant that I could pull any funds back out of the deposit receipt account with only three days' notice if required. Throughout the early 1990s I'd always had a considerable amount of money sitting in this deposit receipt account – never any less than £1 million – but I had to draw on some of that money and put it back into the company in 1994. And by early 1995, all of it was back in the company.

It was at this point that Mary, who was aware of these financial problems and was also aware of various monies that had been spent on equipment by the company without my knowledge during my absence from work through illness, decided to invest £550,000 of her pension back into the company.

I informed my bank manager about my unease concerning the company's financial situation and enquired if he could recommend a firm of accountants for financial advice. I purposely did not want to go through my own accountants, or question Paul Clancy, my in-house accountant, as they had only recently produced a set of management accounts for the company and I was seeking a different opinion. My bank manager recommended that I appoint one of the big four accountancy firms to review the accounts and, because I had used KPMG on a previous business project in Portugal, my bank manager made arrangements for them to contact me.

The following February, Jim Thornton from KPMG based himself in our office and pored over our accounts, reporting directly to Blair Nimmo, his line manager, and charged us an extortionate fee for the privilege – £5000 a week, or £20,000 a month! This went on for about five months until I decided to call a halt to it and phoned my bank manager to arrange a meeting, only to be told that he was about to phone me anyway to suggest the same thing.

By this time, I'd started to question Paul Clancy, my own accountant, and had asked him if he'd been hiding anything from me. The truth was that there had indeed been some financial matters that had been concealed from me but the most annoying thing for me was to learn that my auditors had simply seemed to accept my own accountant's figures rather than conduct a rigorous, independent audit.

A series of meetings with my bank manager followed until I was hauled up to the Bank of Scotland's head office in St Vincent Street, Glasgow – a beautiful office with solid oak tables and a deep pile carpet – I'm over six feet tall but, when I walked across that carpet, I must have looked only about four feet tall!

When a senior banker from Edinburgh asked me where I thought the business would be financially in the next twelve months, I explained that I would be hard pushed to say since the regionalisation of the local councils that was underway at that time had meant that, rather than electrical contracts being put out to tender, the councils' own direct works departments were undertaking most of that work in-house until such time as the regionalisation process was complete. That meant that there were fewer tenders to bid for, which was particularly significant for our firm, given our heavy dependence on public sector spending on upgrading and modernising social housing stock. The banker responded by saying that he would be prepared to finance the company through this period of uncertainty, provided that I would be prepared to underwrite a personal guarantee for a loan.

'Well, I'll need to think carefully about that,' I said.

'What d'you mean?' he asked.

'Well, I don't know how many new contracts I'm going to win, so I'll need to think long and hard about making a personal guarantee.'

'We need to move quickly if we're going to resolve this,' said the banker.

'I accept that,' I said, 'but I'm not going to provide a personal guarantee without careful deliberation because if I don't win the new contracts, then I stand to lose a fortune.'

At that point the meeting was adjourned until the following day, with the banker requesting that Mary, as a two per cent shareholder, be present at the next meeting. I refused that request.

'There's no way I'm going to expose Mary to this,' I said. 'Mary is kept fully informed about these proceedings but she'll not be coming to the next meeting.'

That meeting had been arranged to take place at eleven o'clock the next day. I'd travelled with my bank manager to all the previous meetings, so it seemed strange to me that he made no travel arrangements for this particular meeting. I was taken aback on entering the bank's boardroom to be confronted by a large number of people – including my own bank manager – and immediately decided to cut the meeting short.

Mary and I had discussed the matter in detail the previous evening and had arrived at the decision that we were not prepared to plough any more of our personal money into the business because, in the event of it going awry, we could easily wind up penniless. So that's what I told the Bank of Scotland. I'll never forget the incredulous look on the face of the senior banker from Edinburgh when I told him my decision. He nearly fell off his chair!

'You're surely not prepared to let thirty-five years of business end like this, are you?' he asked in amazement.

It was then that I was able to call upon the valuable lessons I'd learned from studying accounting and financial matters, as well as from years of experience running my own business. The banker had assumed that I would accept his conditions for support but what he hadn't realised was that all these meetings had made me stronger and I had come to the conclusion that I could not afford to allow my heart to overrule my head on this matter.

'D'you think this is easy for me?' I asked. 'This is a very difficult decision to make but I've made up my mind – I'm not putting any more personal money into the business.'

There was now a lot of tension in the room.

'In that case, I don't know how we're going to deal with this situation,' said the banker.

'I know exactly how you're going to deal with it,' I said. I pointed to my own bank manager sitting on the other side of the table and said, 'Next week he's going to tell me that our overdraft is being reduced. And you'll reduce my overdraft to the point that I can't work any longer. That's what you've got to do.'

Although nobody spoke, nobody denied that this was

the very action that would be taken. Finally, the banker broke the awkward silence and said, 'This is bad timing. It's a bank holiday weekend and we're closed tomorrow and Monday.'

'Well, there's no point discussing this any further,' I said. 'I've told you my decision. There's no more money going into the business from me, so whatever you decide to do now is up to you.'

I received a call from Blair Nimmo at KPMG at nine o'clock in the morning on the following Tuesday.

'This is a courtesy call to inform you that we'll be arriving at your office within the hour,' he said. 'The bank has appointed me as your receiver.'

It was my turn to almost fall off my chair. I was outraged.

'I've employed your company for five months and paid you £100,000 – and you've been appointed as the receiver? That's a clear conflict of interest!' I protested.

But my protestation met with a stony silence.

An hour or so later, Jim Thornton and one of his female colleagues from KPMG marched straight into my office, as if they didn't know me, and assumed control. The first person to be summoned to the boardroom was me. So I entered my boardroom and a woman, whom I'd never met before, addressed me as if I were a naughty schoolboy, instructing me to get my jacket and leave the building immediately then phone in and make an appointment to come in and remove my personal possessions at a later date.

I was furious.

'I've run this business for thirty-five years – and I've had people who've worked in here for me for over twenty-eight years,' I said. 'This is the worst day of my life! My staff are going to be losing their jobs, at least some of them are going to hate me and blame me for that predicament but I'll be the last person to leave this office today because, whatever my employees might think of me right now, I'm going to be right here to thank them personally for all the work they've done for me over the years. *That's* how it's going to be.'

At that point, Jim Thornton intervened to defuse the situation. 'That's fine, Willie,' he said. 'We'll agree to that.'

So I stayed for the rest of the day and spoke with many of my staff to explain the situation until, on the stroke of five o'clock, a joiner appeared and started to change all the locks on the doors. It was utterly degrading.

The receivers retained my surveyor, Calum Blair, and produced a financial statement detailing what the company was owed and what money they expected to recoup. In my opinion, they deliberately undervalued the company's assets to paint it in the worst possible financial light because they knew there would be debtors and, by making the firm's financial affairs appear worse than they were in reality, the receivers made the situation favour themselves. Indeed, I seem to recall Calum Blair telling me that, at one stage, the receivers told him to stop recouping money owed to the company.

'But surely I have to work in the best interests of the creditors?' he protested.

'Yes but there's more money coming back into the company than we thought there would be,' they replied.

And when I made an offer to buy back my own building, the receivers refused to sell it to me. Instead, they sold it to the local authority, Argyll and Bute Council, for less money than I had offered. When the receivers then auctioned off the company's remaining assets, people I'd thought were colleagues descended like vultures, picking over the pieces, buying my cars and various items of equipment at rock bottom prices . . . the whole process was degrading.

But that was a decade ago and W. A Wilson General Contractors still remains in receivership today, with around £500,000 in the bank, never having been made bankrupt. That's because the receiver cannot legally liquidate the company but would have to appoint a liquidator to do so. And, because Mary is the company's biggest creditor – the bank debt was only £185,000 and was settled on the first day while the Inland Revenue and most other creditors had their debts settled early on in the process – she can effectively prevent the company being put into liquidation. In theory, what should happen is that the receiver should wind up the company and hand what's left back to us but, in practice, he is not legally obliged to do that and so we would need to make a legal claim to force the issue. In the meantime, I keep a close eye on the situation – but you'd be shocked at the interest that's being earned by that sum of money lying untouched in that bank account!

Receivers can get up to all sorts of dirty tricks but the one thing they cannot do is hide receipts. A couple of years after going into receivership, I approached MacRoberts solicitors to express my concerns about KPMG's appointment as my receiver, which I still regarded as a blatant conflict of interest, given that I'd been paying them in the months leading up to the receivership to assess the company's financial affairs. It was then that a solicitor informed me that, no longer than three months after my initial complaint about a conflict of interest, the Clydesdale Bank stipulated that if a company invites an accountant in to look at its accounts, then the bank would not subsequently appoint that accountant as a receiver for that company. That has since become standard practice so that this conflict of interest no longer arises.

I also queried the solicitor about the financial statement produced by the receiver for W. A. Wilson General Contractors, which showed none of the assets from our window factory, which we had wound up in an attempt to reduce the burden of debt. This intrigued the lawyer.

'Was your window factory a separate company?' he asked.

'No, it was a wholly owned subsidiary,' I said.

'I bet you I know what the receiver's done,' he said. 'All the creditors will be looking for financial information relating to W. A. Wilson – I bet the receiver's recording W. A. Windows' accounts separately.'

So we checked and, sure enough, all the financial information relating to W. A. Windows appeared separately, showing clearly that the factory had been sold, with separate sums of money appearing in an account where no creditors of W. A. Wilson would be searching.

In my experience, receivership is a dirty business and I'd never want to be involved in that process again. My company going into receivership was definitely the worst day of my life – seeing all these people I'd worked alongside for years losing their jobs, leaving nothing but empty desks behind to be auctioned off at bargain basement prices.

But, in time, I was to learn that there's life after the death of a company.

10

Life After Death

The entire blame for the company falling into receivership lay on my shoulders. Whilst I believe that it wouldn't have happened had I not been absent from work due to my illness, in retrospect I can see that I should have had tighter checks and balances in place within the company. I had allowed a certain leniency to creep into the management of the business, for example by authorising any two directors to sign off a cheque when, on reflection, perhaps I should have insisted that one of the two directors must always have been me. That way I would always have known what money was being paid out by the company. Under normal circumstances, if I'd had managers in place that were capable of assuming the full responsibility of their positions then the company might have survived but, on reflection, I can see that I had promoted some individuals to positions beyond their capabilities and had let my heart overrule my head.

That was a mistake and nowadays I sign off every

cheque personally but it taught me an important lesson – when you are at the head of a business of a certain size, you can't afford to let it all revolve around yourself. You have to be clever enough to know that you should employ people cleverer than yourself rather than people who know less than yourself because, as long as you own the shares, it's your company. In W. A. Wilson General Contractors everything revolved around me and I made all the decisions. It was always 'my way', which meant that, when I fell ill, it was 'nobody's way' and there was no rudder to the boat.

I was at a real low after the receivership. One of the things that particularly troubled me, more than my own dented pride, was knowing how hard it was going to be for some of my employees. I was really worried for them because, essentially, I'm a people's person. I'm ruthless with employees when they don't do what they're supposed to do – but I'm fair.

I had hardly left my office for eight hours when some clients with whom I'd been working on projects phoned to say that they wanted me to carry on and complete the contracts under another company name. One wholesaler lost £80,000 when we went into receivership but he opened an account for me the very next day. I'd been doing around £1.5 million worth of work a year with that wholesaler and perhaps one reason for the support I received from him and other wholesalers was that, once I'd met with the bank and had reached a decision about what I was going to do, I phoned around some wholesalers and told them that I thought that my company might not survive, so that if they had delivered any stock to our yard, then they should consider sending around some vans to retrieve it. So the day after we went into receivership, several wholesalers, without hesitation, gave me credit and that in itself spurred me on because it made me realise that these guys had confidence in me and they understood the risks involved in running a business.

I'd thought that all my wholesalers would want to crucify me. I suppose you always tend to look at the worst possible scenario – but it doesn't always turn out that way. In the event, I'm proud to say that every one of our wholesalers continued working with me after the receivership and I encountered no trouble sourcing materials whatsoever. I think that says something.

But once we'd completed all the unfinished contracts that had been underway at the time of the company going into receivership, Mary and I decided to call it a day and pursue other interests. We drew down our pensions and moved out to Portugal with a view to settling down out there. We played golf in the morning, strolled around the village and then relaxed around the pool in the afternoon – but I soon grew tired of that and realised that retirement wasn't for me.

Whenever I went down to the village in the morning, I'd invariably bump into someone I knew who was out there on holiday and who would invite me for a beer. Of course, as they were on holiday, a pint or two of lager at eleven o'clock every morning is not a matter of concern but I wasn't on holiday – I was in Portugal with a view to retiring there – and it wasn't long before I started wanting to nip down to the village for a beer in the morning, regardless of whether or not someone had invited me to join them for a drink. It was then that I realised both that this was habit-forming – and I didn't want to end up an alcoholic like my mother – and that I couldn't retire to Portugal.

'We'll need to go home,' I said to Mary.

We lived in Kilmalcolm at this time, having bought Wilmar Villa, a new house in Cala's Auchenbothie Estate. We'd just built this beautiful new conservatory for it and one day we were sitting enjoying the view when Mary turned around to me and said, 'Billy, you'll need to get a job.'

'Why?'

'Because you're driving me nuts!' she said.

'Why's that?' I said, surprised.

'Because you're getting under my feet – and I've got to get on with my work!'

'But who am I going to work for?' I said. 'I couldn't work for anybody else. I've always been my own man.'

So I phoned my brother John, who'd been asking me for some time about when I'd start up a new business, and told him that I'd decided to get back into the saddle. It was just the news he'd been waiting to hear.

I then spoke to Calum Blair, who had just accepted an offer of a position in another company, having set up shop as a freelance, working out of a small office he had rented in Paisley. So I phoned Calum's landlord and arranged to take over Calum's lease. Next, I went to see Arthur Lawson at McArthur Stanton solicitors and, in order to get back up and running quickly, he arranged for me to buy an 'off the shelf' company and convert its name. Unfortunately that caused a bit of unnecessary bad feeling amongst some former employees when it confused the managing director of one of our wholesalers.

When you buy a company off the shelf, although you convert its name and effectively start again, the company still retains its original registration date and financial accounting period. This confused one wholesaler who had seen the accounts and then put word around the trade that I'd had this other business in place for six months while W. A. Wilson General Contractors was going into receivership. He got it completely wrong and it caused some avoidable resentment amongst former employees who suspected, mistakenly, that I'd deliberately put W. A. Wilson General Contractors into receivership whilst I simultaneously had this other business operating alongside it. Fortunately, that confusion has since been cleared up.

The new business, WWW Electrical Contractors, started on 12 July 1999, the start of the Glasgow Fair. The original intention was to return to our core business of electrical contracting and to steer clear of getting involved in the larger civil engineering side of the business that had caused all our earlier financial difficulties.

We started out doing some small contract works but it wasn't long before I got a call from a friend of mine, Ian Donaldson at Scottish Homes.

'I hear you're back in business,' he said. 'We've got a couple of big rewiring projects for 550 houses in Balornock that I thought you might like to tender for.'

'Thanks for thinking of us, Ian, but this new company has no track record,' I said.

'I realise that,' he said, 'but there might be a way around that.'

'What's that?'

'I've already spoken to Alistair Wylie of Campbell

Construction Group, who are on our tender register,' he said. 'If we send the tenders to him, Alistair's prepared to pass them on to you and you can price them to him, just as if you were a subcontractor.'

So we submitted tenders and ended up winning the contracts. In our first year of business we turned over £730,000. By 2005 that turnover had grown to over £7 million.

One of my managers recently had a conversation with the purchasing manager at Edmundson Electrical who told him, 'When someone like Willie Wilson has had a bad setback in business, two things usually happen – either the next business fails very quickly, or it grows to become much stronger than the first business. It's definitely the latter that has happened with WWW.'

And he's right. This business is stronger than the first because I've learned from my mistakes – and you never stop learning in business. From my mid forties into my sixties, I've amassed a substantial amount of useful business knowledge. That's not to suggest that every iron in the fire is always hot – you get knocks but you get used to that because that's the type of thing that happens in business.

I love the challenge of business and I love tendering for work. I would say that there's not too much about tendering for electrical work in the social housing sector in the west of Scotland that many people could teach me – not because I'm cleverer than everyone else, but because I'm one of the oldest still working in the industry and I know it inside out. I know what it takes to do a job, I know what the client wants and I know all the potential pitfalls involved in a job, and putting all that knowledge together means that we are able to satisfy our clients by delivering projects on time and within budget.

A couple of years after starting up, we relocated into new rented accommodation in Drumchapel. The original idea had been to keep the business a modest size, just big enough to earn a decent living from it, but it wasn't long before I realised that, whether we liked it or not, this business wasn't going to remain small for long. Having been in business before, I knew that we were faced with a simple choice – either the business would not develop at all, or it was going to grow – and rapidly. I also understood that, if the business was going to remain small, then, because of the nature of the tendering process, there could be long periods without any work at all because, the smaller a business is, if it misses out on tenders, the more often it's left without any work at all. Conversely, the larger a company is, the more tenders it submits and the more work it wins.

Deciding to expand the company, I realised that our premises in Drumchapel would be too small and decided to build our own offices. The previous year, Alistair Wylie had invited me over to see Campbell Construction Group's new premises that he had built in Cambuslang. It was while I was there that I noticed a neighbouring plot of land that had been built up with rubble and stone. When I enquired about it, Alistair told me that the rubble had been placed there to compact the ground and that he owned the land. I didn't broach the subject that day but, a few months later, I enquired whether he'd be prepared to sell the land to me. Although he declined initially, a few months later he called and said that the timing was now right and that the

97

plot was for sale. I agreed to buy it, provided it was totally freehold.

When I saw the business start to grow, I decided that I wanted my own piece of land and that I wanted to own my own building. Some business people like to rent and others like to own but I had plans in store for this building. I planned to use it to secure an income for my family. We built Camas Long House, our new office, and moved in on 15 April 2004.

11

The Surgeon System

Once I'd recovered from the initial shock of my first company falling into receivership on 28 May 1996 and realising that there was life after death, I decided to get my head down and get on with things. I'm not a negative thinker. I can get down for a short period but then I think, 'What's all this feeling sorry for yourself? Get out there and get on with it!' So I put myself right back into the thick of things business-wise and that's partly why – from 1999 to the present day – the growth of the business has been considerable. The figures that have been achieved by WWW have been superb. Indeed, we've never had a break-even year – because we've been profitable from year one.

In November 2001, I attended a golfing trip and conference in Portugal as a guest of Holland House Electrical. On the return journey we changed flights at Gatwick Airport and Ernie Finnie of long-established Ayr-based electrical engineering contractors John Finnie & Son invited a group of us to join him for lunch at a Scandinavian fish bar as we waited for our connecting flight. It was as we were washing down salmon with a fine Muscadet that Ernie announced that this would be the last year that he'd be joining us on this trip.

'Why's that?' I asked.

'Because I'm getting out of the trade,' he said. 'I've decided to sell my business if I can and, if I can't find a buyer, I'm going to shut up shop anyway.'

My ears pricked up when I heard this, though I didn't say anything at the time. But when I got home I immediately decided to do a bit of research into the business. Once I'd gathered some background information about the company, I made contact with Ernie Finnie again.

'Ernie, I know we had a bottle of Muscadet at that lunch,' I said, 'but you made an announcement . . .'

'That's right,' he said, 'and I can confirm that I'm definitely selling the business.'

'Right,' I said, 'in that case, I'd be interested in buying it.'

So, the following February, I instructed Charles Barnett of PKF accountants and David Chaplin from Anderson Fyfe solicitors to investigate the business for me and I ended up buying Finnies – together with its Hayters subsidiary – on 15 May 2002 for £130,000.

As soon as I looked at Ernie's accounts, I could see a couple of areas where some savings could be made. For example, Ernie had been running a fleet of sixteen vans – and he only had around sixteen employees. The accounts also showed that the value of this fleet had been devalued to about £13,000, which meant that, in theory, that was all I would pay for it. In the event, I decided to keep eight of the vans and sell off the other eight – for a total sum of £13,000 – which meant that I ended up with a fleet of eight vans free of charge.

It was little things like that which helped us turn around the performance of the business, during our first year of ownership, from having operated at a £140,000 loss into generating a £245,000 profit. That was a remarkable turn-around but, in all honesty, it wouldn't have been too difficult for most experienced business people to achieve – if they had the guts to go in and tackle the problems head-on, which meant having to lay off some employees. But there were staff on the payroll at Finnies who were not contributing anything to the company – there was too much labour, with too much supervision, and the whole structure of the firm was out of balance.

A couple of years after the acquisition, Ernie Finnie had a business meeting with my son Scott, whom he'd not met before.

'I've got to tell you one thing,' Ernie said to Scott, 'I've never met anyone in business as *hard* as your father – but I've also never met anyone in business as *honest* as your father. Your dad was a hard man to deal with on a business level – but he was very fair.'

The acquisition of Finnies gave WWW a tremendous boost because it brought with it some very lucrative commercial contracts that helped establish our name in the commercial sector. We continue to operate from Finnies' premises in Ayr, which we rent from Ernie Finnie. Meanwhile, I've had our company pension fund re-registered under WWW Electrical Contractors, rather than the former company name of W. A. Wilson Construction. This means that our head office building at Cambuslang is owned by our pension fund and that the company pays the pension fund a rent which will pay for the family's pension – while the building itself will always remain in our hands. As well as owning several other premises, our pension fund owns fifty-two per cent of the Barras Enterprise Trust, the board of which, in addition to myself, comprises Christopher Dunn of Dunn & Moore and representatives from Scottish Enterprise.

I'd been suffering from prostatitis – inflammation of the prostate gland – for a few years when, in 2003, just before we were heading out to South Africa, I began to feel partic-ularly uncomfortable and exhausted. I paid a visit to my GP, who prescribed some medicine, but I noticed in South Africa that I wasn't feeling any better. I kept that to myself for a while but, after the holiday, when I eventually told Mary, she immediately phoned the doctor and arranged another appointment for me. My GP instructed his nurse to give me a blood test and I received a phone call a day or so later to say that my PSA (prostate-specific antigen) count was very high, which indicated that I had a problem but didn't confirm anything in itself.

I had private medical insurance so my GP advised me to make an appointment with a doctor at the McAlpine. I arranged to see Dr Laurence Walker that same afternoon. He told me that he wasn't particularly concerned about the PSA count on its own but, on examining my prostate, he suspected that it was misshapen and so arranged for me to return for an MRI (magnetic resonance imaging) scan the next day. The only trouble was that, the following day, I discovered that I was just too big to fit into the scanner! In the event, they put me in upside down – feet first – and I had to lie there with my hands clasped behind my head for forty minutes. When I came out I couldn't put my arms down – they'd gone stiff!

The scan confirmed that I had prostate cancer and Dr Walker arranged for me to have a biopsy at Ross Hall Hospital. Prostate cancer is measured in various stages – T1, non-palpable, T2, nodule and T3, extracapsular (outside the prostate capsule). Mine was classified as T3 as my prostate capsule had burst on one side. Although Dr Walker recommended surgery, my GP advised me to seek a second opinion.

'Why d'you say that?' I asked.

'Look, Willie,' he said, 'this is a major operation. There are many organs that have to be moved aside to do this operation – your nerves for your legs run alongside your prostate – and your prostate sits right underneath your bowel and your bladder. That's why I would recommend seeking a second opinion.'

So I phoned my friend Mary McGinley at the Royal Infirmary and she spoke to Professor Cook, the principal there, who recommended I speak to Mark Underwood at Ross Hall for a second opinion. But before I met Mark Underwood, I was given an appointment to go in and see Dr Dodds, an oncologist at the Western Infirmary, who was adamant that I should not undergo surgery.

'If you go for this operation, you'll be back in the Western Infirmary six months later needing radiotherapy,' he said.

'Look,' I said, 'I'm confused now. I'm getting conflicting

103

advice. I'd like to speak to my GP and arrange for him, myself and Mary to meet with you, Laurence Walker and Mark Underwood and we can all discuss the best way forward.'

It was agreed at that meeting that the best way forward was to start hormone treatment immediately, as well as a course of radiotherapy for eight weeks. I continued to work throughout that period of radiotherapy treatment by leaving the office early to go to the hospital then heading straight home to bed. I never lost a day off work during that time. I saw Dr Dodds every two months and, over the course of the next year, my PSA blood count fell from eleven down to only 0.005.

The hormone implant treatment involved attending my GP's surgery every three months for three years to have a pellet of a female hormone, that prevented me from producing testosterone, syringed into my stomach. The long, thin royal jelly slow-release pellet discharged the hormone over a three-month period. Prostate cancer feeds on testosterone, so the theory is that, if the hormone is able to stop testosterone being produced, it would also stop the growth of the cancer. One of the side effects was that I lost some of the hair on my arms, as well as some muscle tone, through muscle deterioration. A few people commented on how thin I was becoming but, though I'd lost some weight because of the treatment, I laughed off such comments by saying that I'd given up eating chocolate biscuits.

The implant treatment was painful but, after the first time, I chose not to have a local anaesthetic because it numbed my leg and meant that I couldn't drive home. Initially, I drove to Glasgow for treatment, rather than attend my local GP's surgery, because I didn't want any locals gossiping about my condition but eventually I discussed the matter with my local GP and I now attend his surgery to receive the treatment.

Although my cancer was diagnosed in March 2004, Mary and I chose not to tell the family at the outset because of the initial confusion about the best way to treat it. I thought it would be better to wait until the treatment was decided upon before informing them. I told Scott in June when he was over on a visit from Ireland for his wife's uncle's retirement party in Edinburgh. He was angry at me for not having told him earlier – and I knew that that would be his reaction – but I knew too that, after his initial anger, when I was able to explain the reason for not having informed him earlier, he would understand.

The three people I told immediately were Mary, Neilly and my brother John. We had just committed to moving into our new head office building when I received my diagnosis. The timing couldn't have been worse and my initial thought was that we either needed to find someone else to help John run the business or we'd have to think about selling up.

John had made it abundantly clear to me that he didn't consider himself to be cut out for the job of managing director. His strengths lie elsewhere in business – and both he and I are well aware of that. And it makes life much easier for me to know that John isn't one of those guys who try to kid themselves that they are capable of doing something that they are just not cut out to do. I'd had my fingers burned once before because of this very problem and, ultimately, I blame myself for putting certain people in positions of responsibility in the company for which they were unsuited. That was one reason behind the failure of my first company.

It was around the time of the failure of W. A. Wilson Construction that both Scott and Richard went to London to work. Both of them have always had a keen interest in the structural rather than the mechanical side of the business and, after a few years working in London, they both wound up working in Dublin, where there was an economic boom in the construction sector throughout much of the mid 1990s.

Scott's introduction to Ireland had been when he'd accompanied me on a trip there with Celtic Football Club, then managed by Lou Macari, when former footballer Sean Fallon was awarded the freemanship of Sligo. I was closely involved with Celtic at that stage and travelled almost everywhere with the club. We stayed in Donegal and Scott fell in love with Ireland. A few years later he moved to Ireland to work and then he got married there. Richard soon followed, attracted by the job opportunities and the generous salaries on offer.

It was always my intention that Scott would take over the business. I didn't know it at the time but Mary approached Scott, who was working in Ireland, to see if he'd consider coming back to Scotland to work at WWW. Knowing how I like to run a company, which differed from his own preferences, Scott was initially reticent to do so.

My thinking has always been that company directors should take only a modest salary out of the firm and, if it becomes profitable, then they are entitled to a considerable dividend or bonus – but only if the company can afford it. As far as I'm concerned, directors are only entitled to dividends and bonuses once the company has sufficient funds to provide them and they should not take a large salary before knowing how good, bad or indifferent the trading year has been. I understand that key employees must be rewarded with a competitive salary – and I fulfil that part of it – but my view is that the company owners should not take money out of the company if the funds are not already there to justify them doing so because that is tantamount to taking money from the till before you've put it in; so all WWW directors have a modest salary, though that's not to say that they don't do well for themselves – because they do very well.

Perhaps understandably, Scott, as a young man with a young child earning a large salary in Ireland, didn't find that way of thinking particularly appealing. Before my diagnosis, I'd suggested to Scott that he should consider coming back to work in the firm by pointing out that, although we couldn't match the salary he was earning in Ireland, the cost of living in Scotland was not as high as it was in Dublin. But although my arguments failed to convince Scott, I was pleasantly surprised when Mary told me that Richard was returning from Ireland to help out at the company. I knew too, though, that coming to work for the firm would require a steep learning curve for Richard because, while he is very capable and a marvellous letter writer, he is not particularly interested in money management.

One of the positive contributions that Richard brought to the company was to establish monthly directors' meetings which helped expose various aspects of the firm's operations that could be improved upon. For example, we discovered through these meetings that we were hiring small tools to deliver projects when it would have been less expensive to buy them outright. So these meetings led us to establish various management processes and procedures to ensure that the business operated more cost-effectively.

Nevertheless, because of Richard's relaxed attitude to finance, I had to tell him that I had no short-term plans to make him a director of the company – and I know that he found that odd as he had thought that becoming a director of the firm was what he'd been working towards.

WWW is fortunate because it is presently self-financing but if, at some stage, we want to build up the company at a quicker pace, perhaps by acquiring another firm, then we will most likely need to borrow funds from a lender. In the old days – when I first started up in business and my bank manager was Sam Graham at the British Linen Bank – bank managers would watch closely how their business customers lived their daily lives. They would know when and how often their customers went to the cinema and they would know whenever they bought an ice cream – and they would instinctively know if their customers could afford to buy a business. And that was how they would decide whether or not to lend money in support of a business venture. The theory of bank managers in the old days was, 'If a business customer can't look after his own money, then how can I possibly expect him to look after the bank's money?' I share that same outlook. I used to pump that message into my directors all the time.

'When you become a director in my company, you'd best

remember that how you live your own life will be getting watched closely,' I said.

That continues to be the case and that, combined with the fact that I told him that I couldn't see him becoming a director, probably had something to do with Richard's decision to leave the company and return to Ireland to work as a civil engineer. Having just returned to work from a Christmas holiday in America, Richard informed me that he was handing in his notice.

'When do you plan to leave?' I asked.

'I was going to wait till May,' he said.

'Just give me the normal notice period,' I said. 'If you've already decided that you're leaving then your heart's not in the job.'

In retrospect, I see that I could have handled that better, because I know that Richard was doing his best to help out the company.

Then, in May 2005, Mary received a call from Scott who said that he was coming over from Ireland to work. I've always felt that Scott is very much like me – he reminds me of myself at his age, though, like Richard, I can see that his financial acumen is not yet fully developed. And while Scott is very keen to expand the business quickly, my view on business growth is that, if there is a sum of money available to be invested in expansion, then only a proportion of that sum should be put towards a speculative new business venture – and that proportion should be sufficiently minor so that, in the invent of the new business venture turning sour, it could afford to be lost without affecting the existing business. I believe that you can have too many branches growing out of a business – and these branches can grow thin and break off too easily. In my view, a business is better off with five big stout branches than numerous small and thin branches.

I'm determined to pass on to him all the lessons I've learned about running a business. To this end, Scott was appointed joint managing director of WWW at the end of 2005 and is working alongside me to learn the ropes at first hand before I retire. I call it the 'surgeon system' – a newly qualified surgeon always works alongside an experienced surgeon for a few years before being allowed to carry out an operation by himself. That's a good system and I'm using it in my business to help manage Scott's take-over.

I've no concerns about Scott's work ethic and the effort he puts into the business – and I'll certainly never need to teach him anything about marketing – but I want him to see at first hand how I go about making certain financial decisions. I'm guiding and advising him and there's no doubt that you do learn quicker when you're building up your own business from scratch than trying to learn from someone else – but we now know where we are and we know where we're going and the business is going from strength to strength.

12

Contemplations on the Future

Although I had owned a chalet, which we used as a summer holiday home, on the south shore of Loch Earn for over thirty years, it was to be 2004 before we set up our permanent home in St Fillans on the north side of the loch, having moved from Glen House at Clachan of Campsie in East Dunbartonshire, where we'd lived since 2001. But though I'd been interested in buying our home in St Fillans three or four years earlier, someone else had snapped it up before me. It was a couple of years later, in 2004, that a friend enquired if I was still interested in buying a house in St Fillans and, when I assured him that I was, he mentioned that he thought one was about to come on to the market and that he would keep me informed.

Hardly a week passed before we received a phone call and our friend told us that a house had indeed come up for sale at St Fillans and, as it happened, it wasn't just any house but the very house we'd been interested in buying a couple of years earlier! So we approached the owner and proposed an arrangement whereby we would match the figure he was seeking from the property – provided it received a good valuation report from the surveyor – if he would keep it off the open market. In the event, the owner agreed and we were finally able to secure our permanent home in St Fillans.

One of the great attractions of the village is its location by the lochside. Over the years, we spent as many week-ends as we could at St Fillans, where we walked the dogs, bought a speedboat to take the boys water-skiing and did some fishing. I've always loved fishing – it's a great sport. I often go fly-fishing and harling for salmon on the River Tay at Upper Red Gordon, a beat owned by Alan Dunnet, who owns Holland House Electrical Supplies and Ferguson Shipyard.

And, as soon as I'd secured the house at St Fillans, I decided to have my own boat built so I could go fishing on Loch Earn – which might not be one of the best locations in Scotland for fishing but I can testify that sitting in a small boat in the middle of Loch Earn, drinking in the scenery of the surrounding mountains, is indeed one of the best places in the world to be. Jock Tait, the ghillie on the Upper Red Gordon, put me in touch with a timber boat builder called John Robertson.

John built me a nineteen-foot clinker boat in twelve weeks. He delivered it in March 2005 and we launched it shortly after we moved to St Fillans. It has its own mooring right outside the front door of my house. My brother John and I trawl up and down the loch in it most weekends. It gives us a great chance to get away from things and take some time out on our own. I called the boat *Shulla II*, after our first ever dog – a Labrador.

As a family, we've always had dogs. When the boys were wee, we were keen walkers and we always had Labradors or retrievers. But, since the boys have grown up and left home, we've opted for smaller dogs. When we lived in Portugal, we had two Dalmatians called Beamish and Zoë. We currently have three poodles, Bobby, a blind orphan, Bailey, who has white fur, and Fruin, who has black fur and is a real character, and two Maltese terriers, Ben and Glen – and we love them.

In November 2005, I arranged to have a check up at my doctor's surgery as I'd started to feel a terrible pain at the base of my spine which was becoming unbearable. I mentioned to my GP that I'd become very thirsty of late and had been drinking a tremendous amount of water – I was drinking around two litres of water each night and couldn't keep away from the soft drinks' dispenser in the office throughout the day. My doctor decided to test me right there and then for diabetes and his diagnosis revealed that I have Type 2 diabetes, which is treatable with tablets and a change of diet rather than insulin.

It transpired that the pain I'd been suffering was being caused by the movement of a tumour towards my spine, causing lumbar compression, which has since led me to lose the power of my legs. I was admitted to Ninewells Hospital in Dundee at the beginning of January 2006, where I was given nuclear medicine: a bone scan, a CT (Computed Tomography) scan and an MRI scan, after which the doctors decided upon a course of radiotherapy treatment with the aim of shrinking the tumours to the point where they would disappear completely. I was transferred from Ninewells to Crieff Hospital a couple of weeks later for physiotherapy treatment and was soon being transferred from my bed to a chair so that I could work on strengthening the upper part of my body and be able to operate a wheelchair myself. I've got various exercises which I do every day to rebuild my strength and I'm hopeful that I'll be able to regain the power of my legs one day – though I'm told that this will be a long haul. But I'm contented. I understand the situation I'm in and I'm dealing with it. I'm feeling very positive. I know exactly what's happening around about me and I feel in control.

What I've now embarked upon is a building project to adapt my house so that it will accommodate a wheelchair – and I'm project managing this from my hospital bed. Because of my knowledge, interest and experience in the building trade, I've been playing a full and active role in all the discussions about the various changes to be made to the house. And I've been running all the meetings from my hospital room, which has been dubbed the 'battle command centre' by the architect!

Scott and I are now joint managing directors of WWW and recent months have shown that this arrangement is working out perfectly. My disability is physical, not mental, and I'm still actively involved in managing day-to-day business affairs. Scott and I discuss business matters together all the time and I've effectively become his journeyman – the only difference being that, instead of learning a trade, Scott is learning how to be the managing director of a thriving business.

Once I've regained my health, I plan to work two or three days a week on business affairs in an advisory capacity. I'll certainly not consider retiring altogether. Our plan for the future of the business is to augment the volume of work we have established throughout Scotland with work south of the border. That's the main corporate goal for 2006 and already we've won a substantial five-year social housing contract in Newcastle. I'm convinced that the future growth of the firm lies south of the border – though our company headquarters will always be at Camas Long House in Cambuslang, Glasgow.

I've never taken a salary out of WWW Electrical Contractors – it wouldn't be in my interest to do so because of my pension arrangements – and I don't need it anyway because when my first company went into receivership, both Mary and I drew down our pensions. So whenever someone asks me what motivates me, I answer that it's certainly not the money – because I don't have a salary! What I do have is a dividend – though even then I sometimes waive it.

We recently established a fund from the company to be put into a self-administered pension scheme – not for Mary or me, but for our family. It's their time now. I've got everything I need. I don't have a mortgage. Mary and I own our own house. We own our own cars and we've both got substantial pensions which means that we can afford to go on holiday whenever we want to and we can afford to go out for a nice meal if we want to – the simple things in life.

It's now time for Scott and Richard so that they can provide for their sons. That's the way it goes. And I've got two grandchildren. Richard's wee boy, Connor, is seven years of age but he was born in London and lives in Pretoria in South Africa which means that, unfortunately, I don't really see much of him. I'm fortunate in that I do get to see Michael, Scott's son, who is four years old – and Michael's my pride and joy.

Reflecting on my life to date, I realise that there's nothing I wish I'd done differently. I've managed to achieve most of the things that I've wanted to achieve in my life. And I consider myself a success: I've got to, considering the education, or lack of education, I had. If there's one thing that my career proves, it's that you don't necessarily need academic qualifications to succeed in life. If you have some common sense then you can do very well for yourself.

I've always been a very determined guy and I've always enjoyed what I do. I've had a happy life. It's achievement that brings happiness – and especially achieving success in business second time around. I've no doubt that success tastes sweeter second time around. The first time you taste success, you wonder if you've just been lucky but, the second time around, you know that the success is down to you. There are no great secrets to my success – I've always known exactly where I was going and how to achieve it. And I take pride in the fact that, despite my success and the wealth I've achieved, I've always kept my feet on the ground. I've always remained the same old Willie Wilson.

13

In Other Words . . .

Archie Cassells has known Willie Wilson for around thirty years. Willie has always purchased his electrical materials from the electrical wholesaler Archie used to work for. Over the years, their relationship grew from a business acquaintance into friendship. When, having worked for a quarter of a century for electrical wholesaler Rexel Senate, Archie was reluctant to accept an offer to relocate to a new position within the company, he opted to take a redundancy package instead and accept Willie's offer to join him at WWW Electrical Contractors, which had then only recently been founded. Archie is now WWW's general administration manager.

'WWW has never looked back since the day it was founded,' said Archie. 'And our friendship has never altered. Whether as an employer or as a friend, Willie's a superb guy in every aspect.

'I first made his acquaintance through business and we'd often meet up at various functions. Willie had a box at

Parkhead and he'd extend regular invitations to my firm to attend matches and, over the years, my company would hold various corporate golf outings, which Willie would often attend. In those days, W. A. Wilson was Rexel Senate's biggest account in Scotland.

'I've yet to hear somebody say a bad word about Willie. He's very highly regarded within the industry – and that doesn't happen very often when companies go bust and start up again. But the growth of WWW over such a short period of time has been remarkable. It's been a dramatic growth and it's all been down to Willie. He's always been the driving force and, with Willie currently absent through illness, it's like three directors are absent from the company – that's how hard it is to replace him.

'The whole electrical industry in Scotland knows Willie. If he goes to a trade function and there are 600 people in the room, then you can bet that at least 400 of them will know him – and Willie will know the other 200! That's the kind of guy he is. He's a big presence and is known all over Scotland in the electrical industry. Whenever you go anywhere with Willie, he usually holds the centre of attention. If you were at a table of eight at a business dinner, invariably the conversation around the table would revolve around Willie.

'He's been all around the world. For a guy from such a humble background to achieve what he's done in his life is remarkable. He's led the life of half a dozen men. I've not led half the life that Willie's led. He's a great employer and a great friend – and you can't say much more than that.'

Jim Gillespie is the regional director of Rexel Senate, with responsibility for Scotland. He has known Willie for the best part of twenty years, at first as a customer then, latterly, as a friend.

'Willie's a very down-to-earth man with no airs and graces,' he said. 'Both Willie and Mary are very good company. We've been to a few football matches together over the years and I regard them both now as friends rather than customers. My company had a box at Highbury, Arsenal's ground, for many years and we used to have regular trips down there with some of our valued customers and their wives for a weekend in London. Willie's daft on his football, so he and Mary were regular guests.

'As a customer, Willie's been loyal to Rexel Senate over the years and when he fell on hard times in his business life, he was very honest in his dealings with us as a company – and with me personally – and I've always appreciated that. That honesty meant that we were only too happy to support him when he started his new business venture. Willie's a well-known figure in the trade and a well-known character within the industry – with customers, contractors, suppliers and wholesalers.'

Although Father Paul Friel has known of Willie for most of his life, he only got to know Willie personally over the last few years – especially during the last year, when, in his capacity as a priest, he has been helping Willie through his recent illness.

'My late father worked for Willie for around ten years,' he said. 'He'd known Willie's parents from Helensburgh and had known Willie when he was a young boy. My father had been at Parkhead several times as a guest of Willie and, more recently, I've met up with Willie at various locations in Europe when we've both travelled to see Celtic play in France, Germany and Spain in recent years.

'I know Willie as a very generous man who has made various kind charitable donations – donations that he never likes to speak openly about or seek credit for. He's always struck me as the kind of guy who has dealt well with his wealth and success. He's widely travelled and has achieved much, having come from such a humble background. I don't think he's ever lost sight of his roots. Despite his many achievements, he's managed to keep both his feet planted firmly on the ground.

'He seems to be coping with his latest illness remarkably well, partly by maintaining an active role in his business interests. From what I see, he's confronted his recent illness with courage and great fortitude.'

The McGinley twins, Mary and Kathleen, grew up in Kirkmichael, Helensburgh around the corner from Willie, though, since Willie is ten years older than they are, they didn't know him particularly well at that time. What they did know was that Willie was an electrician who had gone on to start up his own business.

'He enjoyed a reputation as a good employer – someone who worked his staff hard, knew the game inside out and rewarded his employees well for their efforts,' recalled Kathleen.

'A good friend of ours, George Mundie, started his time with Willie and went on to become one of his managers. And one of our cousins was married to a guy who served his time with Willie and went on to become a tradesman

and a gaffer. Through these friendships and family rela-
tionships, we learned that Willie was a hard-working and
demanding employer – but that he was also a good
employer.'

One of the twins' first proper meetings with Willie
occurred many years later when they bumped into each
other on an aeroplane to Portugal.

'We were flying out with a friend on holiday while Willie
and Mary were flying out with friends to Rhu Monte, their
villa in Almancil,' said Kathleen.

'We were staying at a village called Montechoro when
one night we bumped into Willie and his pals sitting
having a drink outside a restaurant. When we accepted
Willie's invitation to join his party for a couple of drinks,
we discovered that they'd decided to pay a visit to
Montechoro, only to lose their car keys, leaving them
stranded in Montechoro while their wives remained in
Almancil. To this day I'm not sure whether the car keys
were lost intentionally or not!'

The McGinleys moved to Rhu on 25 May 1988 (the
twenty-first anniversary of Celtic winning the European
Cup) only to discover that their new next-door neighbours
were Willie and Mary. It didn't take them too long to get
reacquainted, initially through Scott, who was home alone
that first summer whilst his parents were in Portugal.

'My sister Mary and I first caught up with Willie in the
Rhu Inn on the day he ordered his brand new green Rolls-
Royce – what a car *that* was,' recalled Kathleen.

'We got chatting and I remember Willie asking, "Does
yer faither like the fitba?" From then on, our dad, Neilly,
was regularly afforded VIP status, being collected from the

121

house by Willie and driven to Celtic Park in the Roller, where he was wined, dined, watched the match and met up with Celtic stars past and present before being driven home again by Willie. One year, when Willie was away on holiday, he arranged for Paul Clancy, his accountant, to take our whole family to the box to see a game on New Year's Day, an Auld Firm derby at Parkhead. That was really something special – even though Celtic were gubbed that year!

'A whole new life opened up for our dad. Willie would always be dropping in for a wee blether with my mum and dad – to the extent that he ended up building a gate in the fence between our houses. Willie would come home from work, park his car then nip through the garden and into our house for a chat to our mum and dad for half an hour, have a wee Glenmorangie and put the world to rights until Mary phoned to tell him that his tea was ready.'

Mary McGinley suggested that a possible reason why Willie and Mary got on so well with her own parents was the fact that, by then, they had both lost their own parents and, in some respects, Neilly and Rita McGinley filled the role as an older influence in Willie and Mary's lives.

'I think they felt the loss of their parents,' she said, 'and that some of the things that Willie did with my dad, he'd have wanted to do with his own – but he never got the chance.'

The first holiday the families shared together was when Willie and Mary invited the McGinley twins and their parents to join them for a week's holiday at their villa in the Algarve.

'We had a great week,' said Kathleen. 'Willie and Mary

went to such great lengths to make sure that my mum was comfortable in the heat and everything was laid on for us. They really spoilt Mum and Dad and Willie took a lot of pleasure in showing them all his favourite restaurants and places to go in the Algarve. But we didn't eat out all the time. We had barbecues too and Willie would don his chef's hat whilst Mary served up the drinks. Willie's a real action man – he can't sit still for five minutes. Even if you're lounging by the pool, he's always pottering around sweeping up leaves, keeping himself busy.'

The two families, together with Bobby and Kath Lennox, also holidayed at Kelly's Resort Hotel in Rosslare, Co. Wexford, Ireland, a holiday that Willie enjoyed so much that he returned in 2005 with his son Scott and his grandson Michael. In 1997, the twins and their parents undertook a holiday tour of Ireland with Willie and Mary, visiting Ashford Castle, Cashel House Hotel in Conne-mara, Ballymalloe in County Cork, Kinsale and the Lakes of Killarney. And Willie, John and Neilly followed Celtic throughout the team's remarkable European campaign in 2002/03.

Ever since becoming friends with Willie and Mary, the twins and their parents would often go out for a meal to cele-brate a special birthday. For example, the twins and Neilly joined Willie and Mary at the Mount Juliet Hotel in Kilkenny for Willie's sixtieth birthday and at Cameron House at Loch Lomond for Mary's surprise fiftieth birthday celebration.

In one particular year, a week or so before the twins were due to take their parents over to Ireland for a short break, Willie and Mary invited them all out for a meal in Colgrain Farmhouse on the outskirts of Helensburgh. As they were

123

in the habit of meeting up for a meal together before or after a holiday, the twins thought nothing more of it. But no sooner had they ordered their drinks at the bar than one of their brothers emerged from the toilet – only to be followed by every single member of their family!

'Willie and Mary had organised this extra-special fortieth birthday bash for us and we were totally gobs-macked,' said Kathleen. 'They had made it a very special night for us – one that we've never forgotten.'

Another special birthday shared by the families was Richard's twenty-first.

'I remember that Richard had just been presented with a new car for his birthday – as Scott had been for his twenty-first a few years earlier – and those of us sitting around the table were reminiscing about the various twenty-first gifts we'd received,' said Kathleen.

'Willie's wee brother, big John, announced that he'd got a divorce for his twenty-first!'

Richard's birthday present was a Toyota RAV, bought by Willie from the garage that Kathleen ran with one of her brothers in Helensburgh.

'Willie was always looking to strike a bargain whenever he bought a car from me,' said Kathleen.

'That's the businessman in Willie – he's built his business through his expertise in purchasing power. Willie wouldn't buy a boiler from the cash-and-carry warehouse if he could buy it cheaper direct from the manufacturer. In fact, he'd travel to Milan to buy the boiler direct from the warehouse – and he was the same with cars. We might be close friends but that didn't stop him from nailing me to the ground to get the best deal he could!'

Hard-nosed in business, certainly, but Willie showed himself to be kind-hearted too. He proved that when he approached Mary McGinley, then head of the paediatric unit at Rottenrow Maternity Hospital with close contacts at Yorkhill Hospital, about funding a trip for a terminally ill child, together with his or her family, to visit Disneyland in Florida.

'Willie gave me strict instructions that he should remain anonymous,' said Mary, 'and he arranged everything – from the transport to the airport, the flights, the hotel and spending money. And he did that on several occasions.'

Then, several years ago, Willie contacted Kathleen about making a donation to the St Vincent de Paul Society, the international Christian organisation that helps the needy with which the twins are involved through St Joseph's, their local church in Helensburgh. The sum donated by Willie enabled the society to undertake immediately various projects which it would have otherwise been unable to progress for some time.

'Similarly, when Willie and Mary sold their home in Portugal – and when they moved to St Fillans – they donated to the society very good quality bed linen and towels and arranged for various items of furniture and domestic appliances to be distributed to the needy,' said Kathleen. 'They've always been very generous – but in a quiet way.'

The twins have known Willie and Mary throughout both the good and the bad times.

'The failure of his first business was a very tough time for Willie and he took it very badly,' said Kathleen. 'But, before you knew it, he'd bounced back and rebuilt another business empire.

'Willie kept his prostate cancer confidential for a long time partly because he didn't want it affecting his business. We visited him in November 2005 and, although he had a sore back, he was reluctant to visit the doctor. When he did, he discovered that his cancer had spread but he's been as brave as a lion throughout his treatment and has kept himself busy with project managing the conversion of his house for when he gets out of hospital.'

'Willie has been very unfortunate with the type of cancer he has – it's paralysed him from his waist down – and he's always been such a big strong man,' said Mary. 'He's a big man in every sense of the word – big in stature and a big-hearted, outgoing guy. He's always been a great blether of a man. He's always interested in everything – even in things that aren't necessarily in his line of work. He has a genuine interest in people.'

'He has a natural rapport with people – it's a gift he has,' agreed Kathleen. 'He's genuinely interested in people – a real people's person. He's a man's man as well. When our brother Pat had to retire through ill health some years ago, Willie was very good at taking the time to sit down and talk to him. He was a great support to Pat. Willie has never felt awkward about visiting a family member of ours who had fallen ill – he just considers such visits as what he should be doing.

'Willie's shared his personality with every patient on his ward at Crieff Hospital, where most of his fellow patients are psycho-geriatrics, while he's still as sharp as a tack. To see just how courageously he's dealt with his illness and the situation within which he currently finds himself – a total contrast to the kind of life he's led – is a real mark of the man.'

Ultimately, the Wilsons' and the McGinley twins' relationship is closer to that which exists between family
members than friends – and Kathleen McGinley has a
theory why that should be so.

'Willie and Mary have had their ups and downs in their
lives that they've shared with us and we've had our ups
and downs in our lives that we've shared with them,' she
said. 'That's what makes them more than just friends –
they're like an extended part of our family.'

Postscript

'What's New?'

Willie Wilson was a bright spark who lit up the lives of his family and friends. That spark finally went out at Crieff Hospital on Saturday, 15 July 2006 when, three days after celebrating his sixty-third birthday at home with his family, Willie eventually succumbed to the illness he had battled against with such courage, dignity and determination.

Father Paul Friel began Willie's funeral mass, held in a crowded St Fillans Roman Catholic Church in Crieff on the following Thursday, by welcoming all in attendance, noting that some of the congregation had travelled from Portugal and Ireland, before affirming that this was a time of sadness, a time of forgiveness, a time of thanksgiving but, above all, a time of hope.

Temporarily wrong-footing some members of the congregation by referring to Willie as 'Billy' throughout the mass, Father Friel mentioned that Billy had told him several weeks earlier that he had fully reconciled himself to God. Recalling Billy's likeability and legendary generosity as a host, Father Friel cited as an example the hospitality box at his beloved Parkhead which Billy purchased with the intention of using it as a venue to entertain clients and business acquaintances. More often than not, however, the box was populated by friends – though the line distinguishing friends from clients, colleagues and business associates was frequently blurred where Billy was concerned.

Father Friel recalled an occasion when several wives of Billy's regular guests wondered aloud why it was that their husbands would invariably return home from a visit to Parkhead a little the worse for wear, only to be given the excuse that this was simply because there were no measures on the drinks served in the hospitality box. Billy vowed to rectify the matter. At the very next game at Parkhead, measured drinks *were* introduced, only for Billy's guests to return home to their loved ones after the game in a more advanced state of intoxication than ever before!

Father Friel revealed that Billy had planned his own funeral down to the very last detail and had made a particular request. 'Paul,' he'd said, 'I'd like you to call me Billy at my funeral because my mother and Mary always called me Billy.'

Following a reading by Mary McGinley from the second letter of St Paul to the Corinthians ('God loves a cheerful giver'), Angus McAulay paid tribute to the amazing intellect and 'encyclopaedic mind' of his late friend who had travelled so far and wide, gained extensive knowledge and developed strong opinions on a vast range of issues.

Commenting upon Willie's brilliant eye for detail and impressive memory, Angus recalled that, whenever, during the course of a discussion, he made a comment that contradicted something he'd said years earlier, Willie would spot it right away and interject by saying, 'Hold on, gaffer . . .' before delighting in highlighting the glaring inconsistency. Angus said that he knew he would not be the only member of the congregation who would miss hearing Willie's familiar catchphrase, 'What's new?'

At the conclusion of the mass, the congregation left the church to weave its sombre way over to the neighbouring Crieff cemetery, each of its members wrapped up in their own private reminiscences. It was the hottest July in Scotland on record and, beneath a threadbare blanket of low grey clouds, the greens and browns and muted mauves of the hills of Willie's much-loved Perthshire melded into a scene of breathtaking beauty to bestow an everlasting tranquillity to his final resting place.

As Willie's remains were lowered into the ground by his sons, his brother, relatives and closest friends, his beloved Mary, surrounded by more family members and friends, looked on, forming a desperately sad tableau, aching with resonance. Then, as if on cue, a gentle rain began to fall. But, though beads of rain began to spatter the booklets that had been handed out at Willie's funeral and to which many members of the congregation still clung, the quotation on the booklet's cover – chosen by Willie himself – remained unblemished. It read, 'Our Loved ones have gone no further from us than to God and God is very near.'

For those whom he loved and for those who loved him, big Willie Wilson feels very near still. And, if they listen closely to their hearts, they can still hear his echo asking, 'What's new?'

131

GARY GIDDINS

SATCHMO

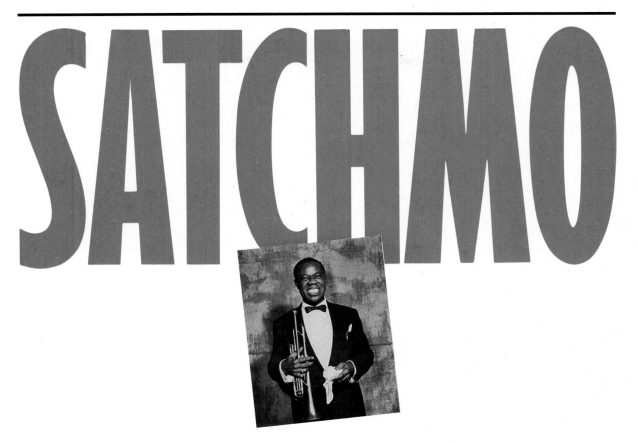

PRODUCED BY TOBY BYRON / MULTIPRISES

A DOLPHIN BOOK
DOUBLEDAY
NEW YORK LONDON TORONTO SYDNEY AUCKLAND

Louis Armstrong demonstrated the kind of mouthpiece he wanted by taking a designer into the bathroom and having him feel the inner curve of a toilet bowl. The custom-made mouthpiece was presented to him in 1965 by the Giardinelli Company. *(page 1)*

On September 14, 1967, Armstrong appeared on a television show called *All That Brass*, taped in New York. *(pages 2-3)*

Armstrong backstage during rehearsal for a concert in France in February 1959. It was part of a grueling European tour that had begun in January and ended June 22, when he suffered a serious heart attack after a concert in Spoleto. *(page 4)*

All That Brass, 1967. *(page 5)*

Clarinetist Edmond Hall and drummer Barrett Deems of the All Stars back Bing Crosby and Louis Armstrong in "Now You Has Jazz," from the movie *High Society*, 1956. *(pages 6-7)*

Armstrong played Wild Man Moore in the movie *Paris Blues*, in which Duke Ellington also appeared. Armstrong's scenes were shot in December 1960. The following April, he and Ellington finally met in the recording studios for two fruitful sessions. *(page 8)*

A Dolphin Book
Published by Doubleday, a division of
Bantam Doubleday Dell Publishing Group, Inc.,
666 Fifth Avenue, New York, New York 10103

Dolphin and the portrayal of two dolphins are
trademarks of Doubleday, a division of
Bantam Doubleday Dell Publishing Group, Inc.

Design by Gates Studio

Library of Congress Cataloging-in-Publication Data
Giddins, Gary.
    Satchmo / by Gary Giddins.
       p.   cm.
    "A Dolphin book."
    ISBN 0-385-24428-2 : $24.95 (est.)
    1. Armstrong, Louis, 1901–1971—Pictorial works.   2. Jazz
musicians—United States—Biography—Pictorial works.   I. Title.
ML410.A75G5   1988
785.42′092′4—dc19
[B]
                                            87-34001
                                          CIP
                                          MN

ISBN 0-385-24428-2

Printed in the United States of America
First Edition
December 1988

Responding in 1949 to a "Blindfold Test," in which he was asked to rate unidentified records with one to five stars, Louis Armstrong said:

"I couldn't give anything less than two stars. You want to know why? Well, there's a story about the sisters who were talking about the pastor, and only one sister could appreciate the pastor. She said, 'If he's good, I can look through him and see Jesus. If he's bad, I can look over him and see Jesus.' That's the way I feel about music."

I loved and respected Louis Armstrong. He was born poor, died rich, and never hurt anyone on the way.

—*Duke Ellington*

The Abbot gazed at the boy who stood before him. He had intended to scold him, but as he looked at him, his expression sweetened. "Why did you stop my child?" he asked. "You abandoned the vision in the middle. One mustn't do that. He's a prophet, and prophets must be revered."

—*Nikos Kazantzakis*

To the memory of Louis Armstrong.

And to my family—Alice and Bill, Donna and Paul, Lee and Jennifer, Helen and Norman and Ronnie, and the Green-Eyed Wonder.

And to the family of jazz, particularly the "illegal" Prague Jazz Section—its leaders Karel Srp and Vladimir Kouril, their fellow defendants Vlastimil Drda, Milos Drda, Csmir Hunst, Tomas Krivanek, and Josef Skalnik, and their countless supporters—whose courage in the face of lunatic persecution reminds the world that Louis Armstrong's legacy is an art of unconditional freedom and that oppressors of every stripe will always fear it.

Contents

"on the fields below"

"The folks all singin'"

"soft and low"

"Now the pale moon's shinin'"

Preface

Some books and articles call him Daniel Louis Armstrong. No one seems to know where the Daniel came from. Armstrong said it wasn't part of his name, and his baptismal certificate backs him up. You can start a fight over how he was addressed by friends. The Louis faction ("Hello, Dolly, this is Louissss, Dolly," the man sang) can get downright rude about those who pronounce it Louie. He wasn't French, they point out. But many friends and at least two wives called him both. The safest and by far the most common form of address was Pops, which is how he addressed everyone else—though in letters he would refer to male friends as "my boy" and to himself as "your boy." As a kid with a large trumpet player's mouth, he earned many nicknames, including Dippermouth or Dip, Gatemouth or Gate, and Satchelmouth or Satch. The last, unwittingly corrupted by a British journalist (Percy Brooks), survived as Satchmo. Insiders will tell you that no one ever called him that. No one but the man himself, who loved the name, and a hundred million fans who loved him.

Through much of *Satchmo*, Louis Armstrong speaks in his own voice in previously unpublished words.

Of Armstrong's many accomplishments, the least recognized is his prolificacy as a writer of autobiographical prose. He was by far the most expansive musician-writer jazz has ever known: In addition to the famous memoir of his youth and an earlier book so heavily ghosted as to be spurious, he wrote more than two dozen magazine pieces, ranging from "Why I Like Dark Women" for *Ebony* to a monthly column on jive talk for the *Harlem Tattler* to a travel piece for *Holiday* to a review of Alan Lomax's *Mr. Jelly Roll* for the *New York Times Book Review*. Yet most of his writing was not intended for public scrutiny during his lifetime. In addition to hundreds of chatty letters, he wrote hundreds of pages of an autobiography intended for posthumous publication. He was unschooled in spelling and grammar, but he had an ear for language and could express himself with enviable clarity in trim, speechlike cadences. Tallulah Bankhead wrote in 1952, "He uses words like he strings notes together—artistically and vividly." She was referring to his conversation, which was peppered with an inventive brand of slang, but the observation holds for his prose as well. Usually, he typed single-space and fast. Sometimes he would write dozens of pages at a clip in an always legible and authoritative hand. He favored yellow typing paper and pens with green ink.

In England c. 1968.

Resting in the 1940s. (*facing page*)

With Belgian writer Robert Goffin, 1934.

Louis married Lucille Wilson in 1942. (*facing page*)

He was never too far from a typewriter. (*overleaf*)

One might have thought that the letters incorporated in Max Jones's and John Chilton's *Louis* (1971) would create interest in a whole volume of them. But perhaps it was too soon. Armstrong was adored throughout the world, yet his unself-conscious candor made many people uncomfortable. His joyful presence became a mask that interviewers, especially American telechat hosts, were wary of lifting. Journalists invariably refrained from asking tough or even interesting questions, in spite of—or because of—Armstrong's willingness to respond honestly. Protective friends and editors, suffering from the effects of a Victorian education that Armstrong never had, frequently purged and prettified his writing.

Of the two books published under his name, the first, *Swing That Music* (1936), in many ways a fascinating document, has the distinction of being the first volume by or about a jazz musician (unless you consider Paul Whiteman a jazz musician), but was so bleached by a zealous ghostwriter—probably Horace Gerlach, who contributed the Music Section—that it's unreliable as biography or history. It disappeared soon enough. The justly renowned 1954 memoir *Satchmo: My Life in New Orleans* (hereafter *My Life*) is—despite the editor's prissy if generally sensible tidying up of a rapidly composed yet coherent manuscript—largely faithful to Armstrong's typescript, including inadvertently misspelled names.

Still, *My Life* was intended as the first in a series (a second volume was announced at the time of publication); it was based on the first 120-plus pages of a longer text that Armstrong continued to work on for years. Armstrong's long-standing manager and closest professional associate, Joe Glaser, is said to have terminated the published account with Armstrong's arrival in Chicago in 1922, because at that point he began to recount his problems with the law, a consequence of his lifelong fondness for marijuana, and the mob, which attempted to control his career. Armstrong frequently spoke of the larger text. He told Dan Morgenstern that he was mincing no words and that publication would have to be delayed until after his death; he read to Jack Bradley and others an excerpt on his belief in the curative value of pot that Bradley says had everyone present doubled up with laughter. Yet seventeen years after Armstrong's death, the manuscript has not been found. Neither Queens College, which recently acquired the Armstrong archive, nor the executors of his estate admit knowledge of the manuscript's whereabouts. A close friend of Lucille Armstrong's and an administrator of the estate, Phoebe Jacobs, suggests the widow may have destroyed it.

In 1974, Mrs. Armstrong told me, "Louis gave his writings to Joe Glaser, and I never saw them again." She also said she and Glaser were unhappy about the way *My Life* was edited and that "the second part" had been left out.

Other manuscripts, however, have turned up. In addition to numerous letters, some of them several pages long, they include the typescript for *My Life* (working title: *The Armstrong Story*), and two series of documents separated by more than twenty-five years. The first is a group of notebooks, written in 1944 for the Belgian writer Robert Goffin, who published a biography of Armstrong three years later but made little use of the material Armstrong sent him. Goffin's book is rough going, with its heavy dose of platitudinous politics, made-up dialogue ("Dey gwine down tuh Congo Place"), and countless misstatements, yet it relates facts about Armstrong's childhood that, though ignored by subsequent biographers, are confirmed by Armstrong's writings and my own research. When Goffin died, the notebooks were acquired by the Institute of Jazz Studies at Rutgers University.

The second manuscript, found among his papers, is far more remarkable. It consists of 129 pages written in longhand between 1968 and 1971 and falls into six sections. The most revealing is also the most troubling: a fifty-three-page memoir entitled "Negroe Neighborhood," in which Armstrong rails against the New Orleans blacks who failed, in his opinion, to stick together to improve their lot, and sings the praises of a Jewish family that gave him his first job at age seven, encouraged his singing, and enabled him to purchase his first cornet. Bitter, repetitive, achingly candid, and sometimes contradictory, it is an obsessive *cri du coeur*, unlike anything else he wrote. The second piece, a twenty-two-page open letter written after his second stay in the hospital, has the familiar ring of the irrepressible Satchmo. It tells of his conversion of all Beth Israel's nurses to his preferred physic, Swiss Kriss; his courtship of his wife Lucille; and his admiration for the great entertainer Bill Robinson. "New Orleans" amounts to a literary experiment: a forty-two-page dialogue that emerged as Armstrong copied a 1968 letter from someone he knew in the Colored Waif's Home, adding comments as the letter triggered them. It is a uniquely vivid montage of a vanished era and is published here in its entirety in the Appendix.

In addition, there are three short pieces—another attempt to retell the story of "Louis Armstrong and the Jewish Family in New Orleans, La. The Year of 1907"; "Barber Shops," a valentine to Corona, Queens;

Armstrong typed hundreds of chatty letters while on the road. This one was to Bill Russell, who wrote the chapter on him in Ramsey and Smith's *Jazzmen*, 1939. The postcards were to their neighbor Lassie Smith Joseph and to Zutty Singleton—the last was never mailed. (*facing page*)

and an unfinished, deeply moving letter to all his fans, who he feared he would never again see. For obvious reasons, I hesitated to use some of the controversial material. But not for long. Louis Armstrong was censored all his life by people who thought they knew his mind better than he did. They censored his books, attempted to gag him when he took one of the bravest stands on civil rights of any black entertainer in the 1950s, banned one of his records, and possibly destroyed or suppressed his autobiography. "To be great," Emerson said, "is to be misunderstood." Armstrong was misunderstood throughout his career. The more we know of him, the better we can reckon the man and his

Louis purges his horn, 1950s.
(*facing page*)

Note: The Armstrong passages from previously unpublished sources are designated *Archive* (the 1968–71 material), *Goffin* (the 1944 notebooks), and *My* (the typescript for *Satchmo: My Life in New Orleans*). When typing, Armstrong like to punctuate sentences with three or four periods (the old Walter Winchell style); I've removed them because they were likely to get confused with my own use of ellipses. The only editing I've done is the minimal kind any writer expects as courtesy—chiefly spelling and punctuation. Armstrong, who traveled with a well-thumbed dictionary, did not consider misspelled words "colorful."

The
ENTERTAINER
As
ARTIST

O N E

Genius is the transfiguring agent. Nothing else can explain Louis Armstrong's ascendancy. He had no formal training, yet he alchemized the cabaret music of an outcast minority into an art that has expanded in ever-widening orbits for sixty-five years, with no sign of collapse. He played trumpet against the rules, and so new rules were written to acknowledge his standards. His voice was so harsh and grating that even black bandleaders were at first loath to let him use it, yet he became one of the most beloved and influential singers of all time. He was born with dark skin in a country where dark-skinned people were considered less than human and, with an ineffable radiance that transcends the power of art, forced millions of whites to reconsider their values. He came from "the bottom of the well, one step from hell," as one observer put it, but he died a millionaire in a modest home among working-class people. He was a jazz artist and a pop star who succeeded in theater and on records, in movies and on television. Yet until he died, he traveled in an unheated bus, playing one-nighters around the country, zigzagging around the world, demanding his due but never asking for special favors. He was an easy touch and is thought to have handed out hundreds of thousands of dollars to countless people down on their luck. Powerful persons, including royalty and the Pope, forgave him a measure of irreverence that would have been unthinkable coming from anyone else. Admirers describe him as a philosopher, a wise man, someone who knew all the secrets of how to live.

But few people knew him well, and many of those who were most possessive about his art were offended by his popularity. The standard line about Armstrong throughout his career, rendered in James Lincoln Collier's 1983 biography, goes like this: Louis Armstrong was a superb artist in his early years, *the* exemplar of jazz improvisation, until fame forced him to compromise, at which point he became an entertainer, repeating himself and indulging a taste for low humor. In his 1981 Armstrong discography, Hans Westerberg notes that he "was generally despised by critics and jazz purists during the last decades of his career." *Despised!*—the word sounds jarring, overbaked. Louis Armstrong despised? Yet, in fact, he was beset by damning reviews for nearly forty years. He was excoriated for playing pop tunes, fronting a swing band,

Duke Ellington is in the control room (rear) as he and Louis listen to a playback from the great recording session of April 1961. (*overleaf*)

Dressing room, c. 1945. (*preceding overleaf*)

appearing with media stars, sticking to a standardized repertory, engaging in vaudeville routines, making scatological jokes, mugging, entertaining. When he knocked the Beatles from their number 1 perch in 1964 with "Hello Dolly," the last record by a jazz musician or (excepting Frank Sinatra) a prerock artist ever to top the charts, the jazz community was ambivalent.

Seventeen years after his death, he made the charts again, with a song cut in 1967, "What a Wonderful World"—the only track in the movie *Good Morning, Vietnam* to get a new life. According to statistician Joel Whitburn, who uses ratio and sales figures to simulate pop charts going back to the 1890s, Armstrong's first "hit" was "Muskrat Ramble": number 8 in 1926. No other singer comes close to spanning sixty-two years on the charts. One can't imagine a single contemporary of Armstrong's in the 1920s—Al Jolson? Bing Crosby? Gene Austin?— enjoying the same degree of success six decades later. Armstrong's undying popularity is as significant a tribute to the timelessness of his music as is the undiminished purity of such epochal masterworks as "West End Blues" or "Potato Head Blues." A jazz aesthetics incapable of embracing Louis Armstrong whole is unworthy of him, and of the American style of music making that he, more than any other individual, engendered.

Armstrong was an artist who happened to be an entertainer, an entertainer who happened to be an artist—as much an original in one role as the other. He revolutionized music, but he also revolutionized expectations about what a performer could be. In the beginning, he was an inevitable spur for the ongoing American debate between high art and low. As his genius was accepted in classical circles around the world, a microcosm of the dispute took root in the jazz community, centered on his own behavior. Elitists who admired the musician capable of improvising solos of immortal splendor were embarrassed by the comic stage ham. One reason, surely, is that critics were frustrated (far more than Armstrong ever was) by the fact that relatively few of his fans knew just how profound his stature was. How many of those who joined Benny Goodman's swing caravan in the thirties or rocked to Chuck Berry in the fifties or savored the increased vibrato that became fashionable in the brass sections of symphony orchestras knew the extent to which they were living in a world created by the famous gravel-mouthed clown? How many appreciated what Miles Davis meant when he said, "You know you can't play anything on the horn that Louis hasn't played—I mean even modern," or Bing Crosby, when he dubbed

Armstrong "the beginning and the end of music in America," or Virgil Thompson, when he wrote that his "improvisation would seem to have combined the highest reaches of instrumental virtuosity with the most tensely disciplined melodic structure and the most spontaneous emotional expression, all of which in one man you must admit is pretty rare"?

Eddie Cantor and Bert Williams of the Ziegfeld *Follies*, 1917.

Perhaps because it elicits concentrated emotional and carnal responses, music often makes us pietists and hypocrites. Having experienced great music, we are torn between promulgating it and protecting it from the great unwashed. Armstrong would have none of that, and his career superbly demonstrates the democratization of an art conceived, as he insisted, "in the cause of happiness." He is the only major figure in Western culture who influenced the music of his time equally as an instrumentalist and singer. His popularity enabled him to shatter countless racial obstacles, while his manner undermined Europhile assumptions about the way an artist was supposed to present himself. He advocated and perfected purity of tone and obeisance to melody; patented the rhythmic gait known as swing; transformed a polyphonic folk music into a soloist's art; established the expressive weight of blues tonality; proved the durability of harmonic improvisation. But he also relished the tradition of humor that had grown out of the black archetype in minstrel shows and had become a mainstay of black entertainment throughout the first two decades of his life. In 1938, he paid tribute to such monologists as Bert Williams (whose records he collected) with his Elder Eatmore sermons.

Constance Rourke observed in *American Humor* that two of the three primary nineteenth-century American theatrical archetypes—those of the Yankee and backwoodsman—were shy of emotion, indulging at best in "mock melancholy." In the third, minstrelsy, "emotion was near the surface, surging obscurely through the choruses and walkarounds, but this was always communal, never individual . . . individual emotion was sponged out." This despite the "strong individualism" of actors who subverted minstrelsy's ritualism. Yet she also noted that while Negro humor shared with the other archetypes a sense of "comic triumph," it remained unique on two counts: It developed "conscious" satire, and it recognized the absurd, which Rourke described as "an unreasonable headlong triumph launching into the realm of the preposterous."

To separate Armstrong the sublime trumpeter from Armstrong the irrepressible stage wag not only curbs a magnanimous artist to satisfy a misguided appeal to Kulchur, but underestimates the absurdist humor that informs his serious side. His ability to balance the emotional gravity

In the movie *Every Day's a Holiday*, 1937.

of the artist with the communal good cheer of the entertainer helped enable him to demolish the Jim Crow/Zip Coon/Ol' Dan Tucker stereotypes. In their place he installed the liberated black man, the pop performer as world-renowned artist who dressed stylishly, lived high, slapped palms with the Pope, and regularly passed through whites-only portals, leaving the doors open behind him. Americans loved Armstrong, and he counted on that love to do what only the greatest artists are prepared to do—show the world to itself in a new light. By the late 1940s, fashions changed and many blacks and not a few whites took offense at his clowning, equating it with racial servility. But an Uncle Tom, though he may stoop to conquer, consciously demeans himself. Armstrong would have considered ludicrous an attempt to equate his style of entertainment with self-abasement. He was as much himself rolling his eyes and mugging as he was playing the trumpet. His fans understood that, but intellectuals found the whole effect too damn complicated.

Significantly, Armstrong disdained black entertainers who went along with the minstrel tradition, still rife in the 1920s, of using burnt cork. Which is one reason he so admired dancer Bill "Bojangles" Robinson:

> To me he was the greatest. He didn't need blackface to be funny. Comedian + danger in my race. Better than Bert Williams. I personally admired Bill Robinson because he was immaculately dressed—you could see the quality of his clothes even from the stage, stopped every show. He did not wear old raggedy top hat and tails with the pants cut off, black cork with thick white lips, etc. But the audiences loved him very much. He was funny from the first time he opened his mouth till he finished. So to me that's what counted, his material is what counted. *(Archive)*

Armstrong loved working with great entertainers, including Bill Bailey and the legendary team of John Bubbles and Buck Washington (at piano). State Theater, Hartford, 1945. *(facing page)*

Armstrong loved sharing the stage with Robinson and mourned the fact that there could never be another like him. He'd have hated the idea, but his success was one reason Robinson's style soon appeared antiquated. The thing that Louis put onstage with unequivocal self-confidence, bordering on macho arrogance, was a personal magnetism that transcended every trace of racial inferiority. You can see it in his earliest film appearances. In 1932 he made a short called *Rhapsody in Black and Blue*, in which a hen-pecked husband falls asleep and dreams

Rhapsody in Black and Blue, 1932.

he's king in a heaven in which Armstrong performs at his command. The husband is the stereotypical lazy black, stereotypically performed and guaranteed to make a modern audience squirm. That's nothing compared to what Armstrong is asked to embody. The whole deck is stacked against him. First, he's garbed in a leopard skin; second, he's ankle deep in soap bubbles; third, he performs "You Rascal You" and "Shine" ("I take troubles all with a smile . . . that's why they call me Shine"). None of it holds him back. He transcends the racist trappings by his indifference to every sling and arrow. The director/writer is trying to tell the audience one thing. Armstrong is telling it something entirely different—he's doing it not only with the magnificence of his music, but with his physical muscularity, his carriage, his boding sexuality ("comedian + danger"), the look in his eye. Blacks understood this in the 1930s and made him a national hero. When styles changed and black audiences abandoned him, Armstrong was wounded and he never got over it. In 1969, in a moment of uncharacteristic self-pity, he complained of being called "a white folks' nigger" and retorted, "Believe it. The white folks did everything that's decent for me. . . . They never let us down with their attendance and their appreciation." On every level of his art/entertainment, Armstrong combined musical inspiration with a beguiling knowledge of the anomalous. The result is manifested in obvious ways: in his use of nonsense syllables—scat singing—to replace or supplement the lyrics of a song or to facilitate vocal improvisation; in song titles that celebrate sex or pot or food, usually in slang too inside even for most musicians; in the humor that deflates the sentimental pretensions of pop songs; in the stage routines that persistently undermine the seriousness of his own art, so that vainglorious brilliance is balanced by an indecorous wit that establishes casual mutuality with the audience. Yet his familiarity with the absurd runs deeper still, producing the fundamental detachment or irony that allowed him to transfigure the music of his day.

When Armstrong came on the scene, an entertainer would look at lead sheets and choose the songs he liked or felt were right for his style. Blacks quickly realized that song-pluggers and producers were not going to offer them the best material and learned to make do by creating their own or by transforming the chaff. As in so many other areas, Armstrong led the way. At first he played the so-called traditional repertory, a portfolio of originals to which he contributed many classics, including "I Wish I Could Shimmy Like My Sister Kate" (which he sold for fifty dollars), "Muskrat Ramble" (which he allowed Kid Ory to claim), "Struttin' with Some Barbecue" (one of several pieces he allowed his second wife, pianist Lil Hardin, to claim), "Weather Bird," "Wild Man Blues," "Cornet Chop Suey," "Don't Forget to Mess Around," and more. Then he began recording pop songs, good and bad: lovely ballads, trite novelties, Cuban and Hawaiian songs, and anything else the traffic would allow. He took it all, having known apparently from the beginning that no song could diminish him and that he could lift most songs far beyond their earthly calling. Though he appreciated quality—he quickly established himself as a loyal and matchless interpreter of Fats Waller and Hoagy Carmichael—he was undaunted by junk.

Armstrong personified a strangely new idea in music, one that became axiomatic when Trummy Young outlined it in a song: " 'Taint What You Do, It's the Way That You Do It." At his best, Heifetz is as good as his material. Armstrong stands above his. This phenomenon would seem to posit a colossal musical ego, able to digest all songs, in the spirit of noblesse oblige. Except that it won't work unless the performer is willing to get into the dirt with his material and have fun with it.

When Armstrong takes a first-class song like "Stardust," he discards everything a conventional performer would seize. Using mild embellish-

Louis's number in *Doctor Rhythm*, "The Trumpet Player's Lament," was cut from the generally released print and apparently has not survived. 1938.

ment and bold improvisation, he rephrases, restates, amplifies, and finally re-creates the melody. He is equally unintimidated by the lyric, which he turns into a pastiche of words and moans. That song, which most performers find difficult to sing straight, is in Armstrong's hands the starting post for an emotional statement far more potent than the original. He is no less compelling on a relatively trite piece, for example "Lazy River," in which he interrupts the record to observe, "Boy, am I riffin' tonight," then makes good his promise with a mind-bending glissando that still has trumpet players shaking their heads in wonder. Nowhere is his irony more breathtaking than in "Laughin' Louie," in which he discards the rum tune after a few measures, addresses the other musicians in the role of a laughing buffoon, and then plays an unaccompanied melody—recalled, he says, from his youth—of immutably stark and haunting beauty. What manner of man is this Laughin' Louie who can play music to make the angels weep?

T W O

In distinguishing between the artist/entertainer that was young Armstrong and the entertainer/artist he became, you have to take into account the changing identity of his audience. His earliest audiences, in New Orleans and Chicago, were made up of fellow performers and fans drawn from insular communities that evolved with the new music. In those days, when he was shy and somewhat apprehensive about striking out on his own, Armstrong proved himself by pleasing his colleagues. After tearing his mouth apart with high-note displays of virtuosity, he came to realize—with the help of a powerful manager—that there was a much larger audience that expected more and less of him: more personality, less grandstanding. He eventually grew relatively indifferent to the musicians onstage with him. He took no part in hiring or firing band members, expecting them to back him up in a creative and professional manner. He had turned his focus to the other side of the footlights, though—like all real artists—he continued to satisfy himself first.

Armstrong knew the difference between a comic duet with his foil Velma Middleton and a perfect rueful chorus of "Black and Blue," which he was likely to do at the same concert. He also knew that a thin line separated the two, since the abiding job was to please the audience, a

In Europe, 1933. (*facing page*)

mandate he took very seriously. Like Shakespeare, he wasn't so much ahead of his time as he was plugged directly into it. For two hundred years, idiot scholars with a class problem have tried to prove that Shakespeare couldn't have written his plays because he wasn't well educated or politically connected. Perhaps if Armstrong's genius were preserved only in scores and on records, some future scholar might try to prove that the man who virtually invented jazz and swing, who put blues improvisation and the vernacular voice on the map, could not have been an untutored black kid from Jane Alley. It must have been somebody trained in the subleties of phrasing, intonation, and harmony. Picture the headline in the *Times:* Professor Emmeff Offers New Armstrong Theory, says there were two men, the first died mysteriously in the early 1930s, was replaced by an impostor hired by a venal manager to fulfill fifty years of signed contracts.

Yet what made Armstrong an innovative entertainer was his ability to show how the same impulses and techniques that went into the early masterpieces could become the lingua franca for a music of universal appeal. The artist, however, always governed the key musical choices: what notes to play and how to play them. An indefatigable propagandist for playing straight melody and seductive rhythms, he was never so hidebound by fashion or his success that he stopped developing. If the later Armstrong was incapable of the complex rhythmic bravura of the 1927 "Hotter Than That," the devilish imp of the twenties could not have produced the resplendent mid-register lyricism of the 1955 "Blue Turning Gray Over You." Armstrong never declared himself an artist or an entertainer. But in 1932, when applying for a passport, he gave his occupation as "actor and musician." Although he had appeared in two or three short films by that time, he had not yet done any acting per se. He undoubtedly used the term in the same generic sense that every vaudevillian, minstrel, and cabaret performer of the day did. Music was his art, as dancing was Fred Astaire's and joking was Jack Benny's. They were all actors. From the time he sang for pennies in a boys' vocal quartet in the streets of New Orleans, Armstrong was a showman as well as a musician.

Which is not to say he didn't know who he was. He seems to have known what he could do long before he did it, and he carried himself with the dignity and assurance of a man fully aware of the magnitude of his accomplishment. He knew he was the best, knew he was the only genuine king of swing, knew it and (when a young gunslinger or an

Armstrong poses with two aides-de-camp (Professor Sherman Cooke on the left) at the end of a photo session in Chicago, 1931. (*facing page*)

Cheers, c. 1940

Buddy Bolden (second from left, rear) and his band, 1905. (*facing page, top*)

Louis Armstrong and the All Stars. Left to right: Jack Teagarden, Earl Hines, Barney Bigard, Cozy Cole, Armstrong, Arvell Shaw, Velma Middleton, 1950. (*facing page, bottom*)

overpromoted white celebrity musician forced his hand) proved it—not with talk, but with his trumpet. But unlike those critics who would have had him play chamber jazz for aficionados all his life, he recognized the obligation of a gift that could bring his music far beyond its original coterie. The caveat that held "My Bucket's Got a Hole in It" to be better jazz material than "Body and Soul" because it embodied old (read: folk) traditions never impressed him. Yet he remained steadfast in his devotion to the principles he learned in New Orleans and defended them with controversial fervor in the bop years.

In a 1948 discussion in which Barney Bigard said, "You got to move along with the times," Armstrong replied: "I'm doing something different all the time, but I always think of them fine old cats way down in New Orleans—Joe and Bunk and Tio and Buddy Bolden—and when I play my music, that's what I'm listening to. The way they phrased so pretty and always on the melody, and none of that out-of-the-world music, that pipedream music, that whole modern malice." That statement, with its unconscious echo of Charles Lamb's "the measured malice of music," was widely quoted by the modernists as proof that Armstrong had fallen into a rut. They missed the irony as well as the poignancy of his plea. Here was ol' Satchmo declaring solidarity with a tradition that had virtually excommunicated him fifteen years earlier for going modern. Targeted from both sides, Armstrong sometimes bellowed back. Usually, he kept his own counsel and looked straight ahead—at the audience.

If Armstrong was as accepting, generous, and loving as his friends, acquaintances, and musicians claim (no man personified better the credo *Homo sum, et humani nihil a me alienum est*), he was also proud and competitive, sometimes fiercely so, easily miffed when another musician foxed him onstage. Everyone in his life, including four wives, knew that the trumpet came first. He lived life as he pleased, which meant constant work and lots of play. He was a sensualist who smoked pot daily, devoured rich, simple foods (he often signed his letters "Red beans and ricely yours"), drank heartily (he liked bourbon and slivovitz, a plum brandy), and enjoyed the company of countless women. Still, he always hit the gig on time and played to the peak of his amazing energy. The attorney Charles L. Black, Jr., a white Texan who was part of the team that litigated *Brown v. Board of Education*, has traced his journey from "good old boy" Austin to the Supreme Court to an encounter with Armstrong's music at a whites-only hotel in 1931. He wrote of that evening: "Louis seemed—as was guessed, I believe, of Paganini—under

Satchmo the Great with Leonard Bernstein, 1957. (_facing page_)

demonic possession—strengthened and guided by a Daemon. [He] played mostly with his eyes closed; just before he closed them they seemed to have ceased to look outward, to have turned inward, to the world out of which the music was to flow."

In the course of talking to dozens of people who knew and worked with Pops or simply heard him and were changed forever, I came across two ideas repeatedly. The first was this: What you saw was what you got—he was every bit as bighearted and open and genuine as he seemed onstage. The second, relating to the later years, described a transforming magic that occurred right before he walked into the spotlight. I was lucky enough to experience it firsthand. In 1968, as an undergraduate in charge of college concerts, I arranged for Armstrong to play at a convocation at Grinnell College in Iowa. He never knew about two incidents that marred the occasion for me and seem now to delineate the bastard place jazz occupies in America's cultural life: Nearly two dozen intellectuals and artists were on campus to participate in a series of discussions and to receive honorary degrees, yet the college refused to award one to Armstrong; outside the gymnasium where he performed, a handful of students picketed because they wanted a rock group.

The band arrived and repaired to the gym locker room to dress. I had never seen Armstrong before and was determined to shake his hand. I chatted with his pianist, Marty Napoleon, who told me Pops was isolated in the back with his doctor but would be happy to see me before they went on. He talked about how great he was and what an honor it was to travel with him—you'd have thought they'd just started together, but Napoleon had already been on the road with him two years. (He talks the same way about Louis today.) Suddenly, there he was, an old man in a loose tuxedo, his brown coloring tinctured with gray, his eyes slightly rheumy, the scar on his upper lip (which had been rebuilt with grafts a decade before) alarmingly raw. Doc, a congenial white-haired man, walked him to a bench, and he sat there looking downcast. Napoleon introduced me to Doc (Dr. Alexander Schiff), who brought me over to the bench and said, "Pops, this is Gary Giddins. He produced the gig and would like very much to meet you." He put out his hand and stood, his eyes brightening and his smile rising like the sun. "Hello, Pops," he said. A jolt ran through my arm, though his grasp was slack. I mumbled something, wanting to embrace him and tell him how much his music meant to me, but was restrained by how fatigued and fragile he looked. He peered out at the gym, and I thought: This is just another one-nighter . . . in Iowa. Why does he still bother?

S.S.-32

A few seconds later he said he was ready, and I walked out front to watch the show. Between the locker room and the steps leading up to the stage was the space of a few feet cast in shadow by stark lighting. Each musician disappeared into it before attaining the stage. As Armstrong emerged into the light, arms slightly raised, palms out, he appeared transfigured. The ashen color was gone, the eyes blazed, the smile blinded. When he sang, he engaged the crowd eyeball to eyeball. When he blew trumpet, he kept his eyes open, but the pupils rolled upward as though he were no longer in the room. His huge tone was as gold and unspotted as ever. Each musician had a feature number, at which time Armstrong walked into the shadows to rest. He would return glowing with energy.

I've often thought that had I been a critic then, I might have disdained the same old same old: the inevitable "Indiana" opener, the excessive drum solo, the chick singer, "Hello Dolly." But maybe not. The set worked. And when Armstrong was onstage, nothing else mattered. He carried the weight of his own myth in all its grandeur, but it was the myth made human—made possible.

T H R E E

How better to start an American myth than with a flag-waving birthday: July 4, 1900. The man who established America's preeminence in the world of twentieth-century music is ushered in amid roman candles and a couple of killings in the first year of the new age—or so he told us. But it isn't true. The alleged date of Louis Armstrong's birth, like that of the Battle of Hastings, is a bit of information that everyone seems to know. Armstrong himself was steadfast about it, even filling in details of the Independence Day action he said he learned from his mother. Many scholars doubted him, figuring the year was correct but the month and day were chosen later—impoverished blacks in that era often chose July 4 when they didn't know the actual day. After all, Louis enjoyed no annual birthday celebrations as a child. In his 1983 biography *Louis Armstrong: An American Genius*, Collier wrote, "There is not a single document to prove that Armstrong even existed until he was eighteen years old," and then adduced a birthdate of 1898, on the grounds that a couple of contemporaries thought he was older and because a 1918 draft form

Good evening, ev-ery-bo-dy. Anytime, anywhere. (*facing page*)

47

Certificate of Baptism

Sacred Heart Of Jesus Church
138 South Lopez Street
New Orleans, Louisiana 70119

This is to Certify

That   Louis Armstrong

Child of   William Armstrong

and   Mary Est. Albert

Born in   New Orleans, La.

on the   4   day of   August   19 01

was

Baptized

on the   25   day of   August   19 01

According to the Rite of the Roman Catholic Church

by the Rev.   J. M. Toohey, C.S.C.

the Sponsors being   J. M. Toohey,

Catherine Walker

as appears from the Baptismal Register of this Church

Date   6/27/88   Vol.   3   Pag.   347   No.   70

SEAL   Rev. C. Richard Nowery, CSC

The certificate of baptism authenticating Armstrong's true birthdate was signed by the Reverend C. Richard Nowery in June 1988.

The page from the baptismal register for the Sacred Heart of Jesus Church, written in Latin, shows that Louis Armstrong was the illegitimate son of William Armstrong and Mary Albert. He was born August 4, 1901, and baptized three weeks later. (*facing page, top*)

The 1900 census report for Jane Alley lists the family of Isaac Myles, Mayann's cousin. (*facing page, center*)

The 1910 census report for Perdido Street shows the Myles family living next door to Armstrong's. Louis Armstrong, the last entry, is listed as Mary Albert's eight-year-old son. He would turn nine in August. (*facing page, bottom*)

shows the registrar started to write July 4, 18—, then crossed out the 8 and wrote 1900. Collier assumes that Armstrong shaved two years to avoid the draft during World War I, which makes no sense. The Selective Service Act of 1917 drafted men between the ages of twenty-one and thirty; when it was amended in September 1918, at which time Armstrong registered, the age was lowered to eighteen. Armstrong made himself no less vulnerable by declaring himself eighteen than twenty. In any case, there *are* earlier documents, and they show that he altered his age for the same reason most adolescents do—to appear older, not younger.

Louis Armstrong was born August 4, 1901, in a ramshackle house on a squalid block-long lane in New Orleans called Jane Alley, between Perdido and Poydras streets. His mother, either fifteen or sixteen years old at the time, was Mary Albert, who had come to the city from the sugarcane fields of Boutte, Louisiana; his father, who abandoned them shortly after his son's birth, was William Armstrong, whose family may have come from St. Charles Parish. On August 25, three weeks after he was born, Louis was taken to the white Sacred Heart of Jesus Church, on Lopez Street, to be baptized. He wrote that his father's mother, Josephine, a Catholic who raised him during his first four or five years, took him to church that day, but it was probably a white neighbor named Catherine Walker, who cosponsored him with the Reverend J. M. Toohey. Since his mother, to whom he returned to live at age five, was Baptist, it's unlikely he ever worshiped in a Roman Catholic church again. The baptismal register certifies his birthday and the names of his parents. Additional confirmation of his age is found in the 1910 census record for the 1300 block of Perdido Street, which lists a family of three at a rooming house at 1303 Perdido: Thomas Lee, the twenty-four-year-old "head" of the house, who gave his occupation as laborer on a schooner (Louis mentions him as one of several "stepfathers" in My Life); Mary Albert, his twenty-five-year-old "companion," who gave her occupation as laundress; and Louis Armstrong, her eight-year-old son. The census was taken April 22 or 23, 1910, so Louis would have been nine in August.

Why did he make himself out to be older? In 1918, Louis's career as a musician was beginning to take off. Kid Ory invited him to replace King Oliver in his band, and Fate Marable wanted to recruit him for an orchestra that made interstate tours on a Mississippi steamer. A year earlier, the United States Navy had shut down Storyville, the notorious red-light district of New Orleans, and it's likely that officials were

69.
Martine.

Die XXV Augustii A.D. 1901, ego baptizavi Dominicum natum die XV Augustii 1901, ex Antonio Martine et Rosa Garlo. conj.

Patrini:— Henricus Rando et Matilda Rando.

J. M. Toohey, c.s.c.

70.
Armstrong.
(niger, illegitimus)

Die XXV Augustii A.D. 1901, ego baptizavi Gulielmum Ludovicum natum die IV Augustii 1901, ex Gulielmo Armstrong et Maria Est. Albert. conj.

Patrini:— J. M. Toohey et Cattarina Walker.

J. M. Toohey, c.s.c.

71.
Rogora.

Die XXV Augustii A.D. 1901, ego baptizavi Joannam Lydia natam die XXX Junii 1901, ex Adolpho Rogora et Maria Gerosa, conj.

Patrini:— Carolus Gussone et Fiore Gerosa.

J. M. Toohey, c.s.c.

cracking down on the remaining dives. Cabaret owners may have had doubts about hiring a minor, and even if things remained loose in New Orleans, the same might not be true of places like Davenport, where the steamboat docked. Perhaps the responsible Marable asked him to get proof of age. It was also in 1918 that Louis married the young prostitute Daisy. The one place a black seventeen-year-old could get "proof" he was eighteen was the local draft board. Armstrong wrote:

> Early 1918 came in. And with the flu sickness kind of letting up, and the United States finally getting after the Kaiser and his boys in fine fashion, and the last draft call [conscripting] 18 to 45 years olds, which fit me just right, I went on down to the draft board and registered. I sure was a proud fellow when I could feel back there in my hip pocket and feel my draft card, expecting to go to war any minute and fight for Uncle Sam. Or, *Blow* for him. (My)

Collier doesn't believe Armstrong really wanted to fight, and neither do I. He avoided physical violence all his life, as well as anything that would keep him from his music. Moreover, he admits in *My Life* that he took a job he detested, driving a coal cart from 7 A.M. to 5 P.M., to ensure a deferment. He most likely left the draft post feeling "proud" because he had proof in his pocket that he was a man, and could play nights at Henry Matranga's honky-tonk on Perdido Street. Perhaps he chose July 4 for its patriotic ring, or because it was customary for boys who didn't know their birthdate to use it, or because he had more than an intimation—this is confirmed by several musicians who knew him in 1918—of his future greatness and had the wit to pick a date that everyone would remember. Even so, for a man to walk into a draft board at seventeen and declare himself of age, he must have been exceedingly confident the army wouldn't call him. Either that or he actually considered joining up—perhaps to "Blow" with a military band. (Word must have reached New Orleans about the black 369th Infantry Regiment Band, led by Lt. James Reese Europe.) As for the clerk mistakenly writing the date 18—, he'd have gotten used to writing it; most of the new draftees were nineteen or twenty.

The new birthdate stuck. It served him well in Chicago, when he went to work with King Oliver at the Lincoln Gardens in 1922, showing he was over twenty-one. When Joe Glaser took over his career, he

Homeboy Louis with his mother (Mayann) and sister, Beatrice (Mama Lucy), c. 1920. (*facing page*)

recognized it as a press agent's dream and burned it into the public mind. Armstrong himself was utterly attached to the date—he clings to it in all his personal papers, even his photo albums, in which snapshots are captioned, e.g., "This was 1937, when I was 37 years old." When Armstrong wrote *My Life*, he insisted that the street where he was born was James Alley, not Jane Alley, "as some people call it." He didn't live there long and that's how he remembered it. In later years, jazz historians showed him he was wrong. When he sketched his youth in 1969 in a memoir titled "Negroe Neighborhood," he wrote *Jane Alley* in block capitals twice, but he held firm to his famous birthdate. The memoir begins with a solitary third-person reference, possibly to certify his true name (no Daniel). He refers to his mother, here and elsewhere, alternately as Mary Ann and Mayann:

> Louis Armstrong was born July 4th 1900, in the Back O' Town JANE ALLEY section in New Orleans. Mary Ann [was] the mother of two children who she raised and supported all by herself. We did not have a father. They must have separated soon after we were born. Mama Lucy (my sister) nor I can recall seeing him. Anyway Mayann, that's what everybody called her, worked hard to see that we had food and a place to sleep. We moved from Back O' Town JANE ALLEY into the Third Ward (into the city), located at Franklyn and Perdido Streets, where the Honky Tonks were located. A row of Negroes of all characters were living in rooms which they rented and fixed up the best way they could. We were *All* poor. The privies (the toilets) were put into a big yard, one side for the men and one side for the women . . . The folks, young and old, would go out into the yard and sit or lay around, or the old folks would sit in their rockin' chairs, etc. out in the sun until it was outhouse time . . . Everything went on in the yard. I remember one moonlit night a woman hollared out into the yard to her daughter—she said (real loud), "You, Marandy, you'd better come into this house, laying out there with nothing on top of you but that thin nigger." Marandy said, "Yassum." *(Archive)*

Some say that Armstrong never had a childhood, others that he never had anything else. All his life he worked hard and played hard. The deprivation of his early years left its mark: After he became an international celebrity, he would astonish other musicians with his genuine gratitude for such amenities as a limousine or posh hospitality. In all his published writings, he remains uncomplaining about those early years. Here is a man who saw life from the gutter up and learned to accept it all. Jane Alley was an area so ridden with violence and vice it was known as the Battlefield. For many of his friends, pimps and whores and gamblers and razor-wielding badasses were role models. Armstrong, of course, was different. In order to create music of the spheres you have to be able to hear it, and Armstrong heard it as a siren call leading him out of hell. One has to believe that the generosity-bordering-on-obsession with which he took his music to the masses reflected his own pragmatic confidence in its healing power. Raised in a house of cards in the middle of a gale, he credited music and his mother's love and wisdom with getting him through. He accepted with equanimity the possibility that Mayann, who left him in the care of his grandmother until he was five, may have worked as a prostitute:

> My mother went to live in another fast neighborhood, down on Liberty and Perdido (a cheap storyville section—what I mean by that is the prostitutes did not receive as much pay for their time as the whores did down in Storyville). Whether Maryann was selling fish (HUSTLING) I could not say. If she was, she certainly kept it out of sight. One thing, everybody from the church folks to the lowest gave her the greatest respect, and she was always glad to say hello to anybody, no matter who. Come what may, she figured. And with it all, she held her head up at all times. Nothing excited her. What she didn't have, she did without. She never envied no one, or anything they may have. I guess I inherited that part of life from Mayann. (My)

Mayann inherited part of her outlook from an upbringing in the country, an isolated Creole area about seventy miles west of New Orleans off Route 90. The riverfront is a strip about forty miles long, with vestigial plantation buildings and flat cane fields that were once patrolled by peacocks instead of dogs. Today the area is dominated largely by oil interests that have polluted the water and added carcinogenic horrors to the natural ones endured by a people situated between swamps and the river, and beset by floods and disease. In back of the riverfront part called Luling is Boutte (pronounced Bou-tee), a small community,

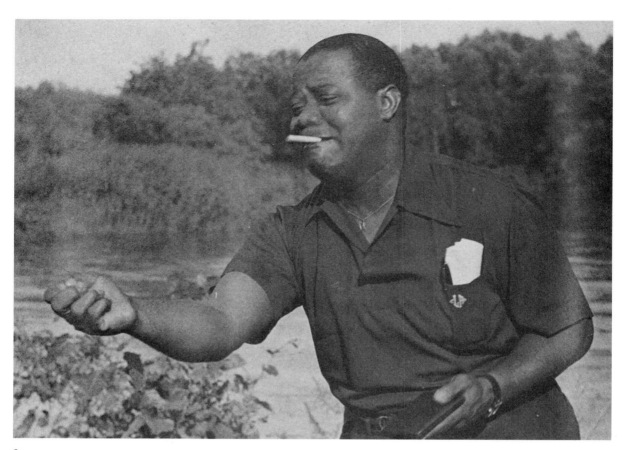

which, in Mayann's time, was connected to the front by the vast sugarcane plantations. (The largest of these, ironically, was the Ellington Plantation, now the site of a Monsanto complex.) Every kind of Creole mix could be found there, and at the bottom of the heap were the "black blacks," like Mayann, who had the fewest opportunities and were generally the last to leave.

Boutte-born Eddie Edwards, who in 1983 created the Louis Armstrong Foundation in New Orleans to tutor gifted children, says, "Everyone dumped on the black blacks, even the blacks, and if you were black black you had no idea of what the white world was like. Mayann left with absolutely nothing, and the only alternative she had to being a field worker in the country was being a servant in the city. Arriving in Jane Alley meant she started out at the very bottom. Creoles were more educated, they had schools out here and could speak English and French, but the blacks in New Orleans were working-class. They had nothing but the live-and-let-live spirit of the country where your survival was imperiled every day by floods, disease, and worse."

How much time Armstrong himself spent in the country is not known. He didn't write about it or, more significantly, title songs after it. But he had a favorite story that he occasionally told his concert audiences, including one in Chicago in 1962:

Louis and Mama Lucy in New Orleans, 1940s.

> I was telling' about the time when I was a little bitty boy in my mother's hometown of Boutte, Louisiana. I was about five years old, cute little ol' thing, too. Mayann, my mother you know, she said to me one morning, "Son, run down to the pond and get a bucket of water for your mama." And I cut out for that water, and Mayann dug me when I come back without the water and pooooh, boy! She said, "Boy, where is that water?" I said, "Well, mama, there's a big old rusty alligator in that pond and I didn't get that water." She said, "Oh, boy, go get that water. Don't you know that alligator is scared of you as you are of him?" I told her, "Mama, if he's scared of me as I am of him, that water isn't fit to drink."

On another occasion, when he told the story at a record session, he prefaced it by saying that as a kid "we lived in a little town called Boutte, Louisiana." Some of the older residents can still recall Mayann's

mother working in the fields, and some familial contact must have been maintained because Louis's sister would drive out at least as late as the 1960s. Edwards believes Boutte offered a lifeline that helped ensure Louis's independence in the corrupt city.

Mayann probably met Willie Armstrong in the city, and it was her cousin Issac Myles, a forty-three-year-old laborer living with his wife, Francis, and four children at 723 Jane (according to the census record of 1900), who found her a place to live; after June 1900, she moved next door to the Myles family, at 719, where Louis was born. When Louis turned five, he was returned to his mother's care. On that day, he encountered Jim Crow and jazz, and was confronted with the Dickensian responsibility of helping to care for his sick mother and baby sister, Beatrice (known since childhood as Mama Lucy), born two years after him during a brief reconciliation between Mayann and Willie.

The neighborhood woman who brought him back to Jane Alley on the streetcar scolded him when he obliviously sat in the white section. He asked her what the signs in the other area ("For Colored Patrons Only") said, and was told, "Boy, don't ask so many questions, sit down damnit!" (My) He recalled that it was at his first reunion with his mother that she advised him to take a physic every day, a habit that became an obsession and the subject of much of his earthy humor. In the 1969 memoir, he compared the "pure" food he ate in the home of Jewish neighbors with the tasty but "heavy" food at home ("I loved the way she used to cook those Cat Heads—P.S. bisquits and molasses. Dee-licious. Yea, make you lick your fingers"), and explained the need for homemade herbal laxatives:

Dining between shows, 1936.

> Their food was always pure—the best. I noticed whenever I ate with them I would even sleep better. Much different from the heavy foods Mayann, Mama Lucy, and me had to eat. I had the stomach ache all the time. Mama Lucy suffered with some kind of fits. One of those big names they called it. She damn near died. Mayann told Mama Lucy and me, since we have to eat this heavy kind of food because we couldn't do any better, too poor, we will just have to make the best of it. [She said] the food that you all eat today you must take a good purge and clean your little stomachs out thoroughly. They will keep the germs away. We both gave Mayann our word that we would stay physic-minded for the rest of our lives. (Archive)

The chef approves Barney Bigard's culinary skill, c. 1953. (facing page)

He attended school and church sporadically, ran errands, sold rags
and coal, cleaned graves for tips, sang on the street in a vocal quartet
for pennies. He also got into fights, and into trouble with the law for
hustling stolen newspapers and discarded food. He claims he heard the
legendary trumpeter Buddy Bolden at the end of his career, in 1905 or
1906, playing in front of Funky Butt Hall (Kenna's Hall), near his
home. It should probably be pointed out that Armstrong's neighborhood
was nearly a mile west of Storyville. Numberless writers have tended to
place every Orleanian honky-tonk and whore's crib in the much
romanticized area set aside by Alderman Story's ordinance of 1897.
Armstrong occasionally tried to correct the misconception but ultimately
acceded to the myth. Still, contrary to recent biographies, he never
lived in Storyville, which was shut down in 1917, and he almost certainly
never played there while the ordinance was in effect. The honky-tonks
he frequented (see Appendix)—including Spano's, Savocca's, Ponce's,
and Henry Matranga's, where he got his first important job as a musician—
were in the area where he lived, near Perdido Street. "Gee, that
neighborhood had a lot to offer," he would later muse without a trace
of sarcasm. He could, of course, be sarcastic as hell about other aspects
of the Old South:

The other white nationalities kept the Jewish people with fear constantly. As far as us Negroes, well I don't have to explain anything. Am sure you already know. At ten years old I could see the bluffings that those old fatbelly, stinking, very smelly dirty white folks were putting down. It seems that the only thing that they cared about was their shotguns, those oldtime shotguns which they had strapped around them. So they got full of their mint julip or that bad whiskey the poor white trash were guzzling down like water, then when they got so damn drunk they'd go out of their minds, it's Nigger Hunting time. Any Nigger.

They wouldn't give up until they would find one. From then on, Lord have mercy on the poor darkie. Then they would torture the poor darkie, as innocent as he may be. Then they would get their usual ignorant Cheshire Cat laughs before they would shoot him down like a dog. My my my, those were the days. (*Archive*)

The intersection near Louis's boyhood home: Perdido and Liberty Streets.

My Life is not quite the we-were-poor-but-happy idyll many people remember it as. Between the lines and sometimes in the lines are indications—albeit watered down, compared with his unpublished writings—of violence and misery, nightmare episodes exacerbated by his abiding resentment of the absentee Willie, and of other neighborhood men who abandoned their responsibilities. Through it all, he was brought up to be independent and to think for himself. "My mother had one thing . . . and that was good common sense and respect for human beings, yea. That's my diploma. . . . I was taught to respect a man or woman until they prove in my estimation that they don't deserve it." Mayann and Uncle Ike Myles were so determined not to let him wallow in self-pity that they even described slavery as just another obstacle to be overcome:

> Mayann and Uncle Ike had a little touch of slavery, because their relatives before them came up right in it. They said the slaves acted dumb and ignorant, kept malice and hate among themselves so the whites took advantage of it—especially when they were full of their mint julips. They couldn't keep a secret among themselves. They would make plans among themselves and one Negro would double cross them by sneaking back and tell the white man everything they had planned to do. Quite naturally they would make him the head nigger. At least for the time being anyway . . . Slavery was just like anything else. B.S. (*Archive*)

The extent to which his double education—brutish in the streets, fortifying at home—colored his observations of the adult world is apparent throughout the frequently acrimonious memoir of 1969, written during an apparent bout of depression brought on by his stay in the hospital. At times Armstrong sputters with rage:

> We never did try to get together and show the younger Negroes such as myself to try . . . with just a little encouragement I could really have done something worthwhile. But instead we did nothing but let the young upstarts know that they were young and simple and that was that. Never a warm word for doing anything important came to their minds. My nationality (Negroes) took advantage of my mother because . . . Mayann gave birth to Mama Lucy and me. She had to struggle with us until we grew up. After grabbing a little schooling and a job at a very young age, I myself will never forget. I will try to forgive.

They were in an alley or on the streetcorner shooting dice for nickels and dimes, etc. (mere pittances) . . . gambling off the money they should take home to feed their starving children or pay their small rents, or very important needs, etc.

Mama Lucy and I used to go out to Front of Town when we were very young—among those produce places—where they would throw away spoiled potatoes, onions into a big barrel, and she and I among other kids used to raid those barrels—cut off the spoiled parts and sell them to restaurants. There was a baker shop which sold two loafs of stale bread for a nickle. They would do that to help the poor children. They could always get filled up at least on bread. Mama Lucy and me had to do it lots of times. Many kids suffered from hunger. Their father could have done some honest work for a change. *No,* they would not do that. It would be too much like right. *(Archive)*

Those words and others far more bitter are balanced by the dozens of pages in which he expresses gratitude to a little-known family that he came to consider his salvation, about whom he wrote, "If it wasn't for the nice Jewish people, we would have starved many times. I will love the Jewish people all of my life." In an article he wrote for *True* in 1947, Armstrong told of his first job, selling coal from a wagon "for a young white boy whose folks had several wagons that paraded all over the city. . . . They were the Karnoffsky [sic] family." Their son Morris "liked the dickens outa me," he wrote, describing how they hustled coal to the prostitutes in Storyville. The "Karnoffskys" don't appear in his book on New Orleans. Yet in his last years, Armstrong wrote at length of a Karmofsky family, tracing their progress in the black section of New Orleans, the prejudice they faced, and the great wealth they ultimately achieved by buying property all over the South. He remained in contact with them for much of his life and it may be that after the *True* article, they asked him not to write of their déclassé start in and around the red-light district. Armstrong's 1969 memoir refutes at least two widely accepted details of his biography—that his first job was selling newspapers and that he obtained his first cornet in the Colored Waif's Home. He started working at the age of seven:

The Karmofskys lived on the corner of Girod and Franklin Streets, one black away from the Girod Street Cemetery in the colored section. . . . Things were getting pretty rough for Mayann, me, and Mama Lucy, especially without a father. But we managed beautifully with the Karmofskys in my corner, and Mayann had her little hustle in the white folks yard. Mama Lou didn't work. The Karmofsky family came to America from somewhere in Russia long before I was born. They came to New Orleans as poor as Job's turkey. They settled in a neighborhood which was nothing but a gang of rundown houses with the privies out in the backyard. . . . They had a pretty good size yard, so they started a little business in no time at all. That's where I came in. With little money that they had, they bought two small horses, two small wagons, harness for the horses. I alternated with the two sons. One went out in the street, buying old rags, bones, iron, bottles, any kind of old junk. Go back to the house with the big yard, untie the wagon, pile up the old rags in one place, the bottles, bones, and the rest of the junk, all in separate places.

Soon there would be big piles of everything. There was enough room for piles of stone coal which the older son, Morris, sold in the streets also. Especially in the red-light district, mostly in the evenings way into the night. He sold it five cents a waterbucket to lots of the sporting women standing in the doorways. Alex would go out early in the mornings on his junk wagon—stay out all day, me right alongside of him. Then I would help Morris at night. The first job that I ever had, so I was very glad of it. . . . I began to feel like I had a future and "It's a Wonderful World" after all. (*Archive*)

At night, Mrs. Karmofsky would insist that Louis have dinner with them ("I still eat their food, matzos, my wife Lucille keeps them in her breadbox"). Later, Mrs. Karmofsky taught him to sing "Russian Lullaby"—"so soft and sweet, then bid each other good night. They were always warm and kind to me . . . something a kid could use at seven and just starting out in the world. . . . When I reached the age of eleven I began to realize that it was the Jewish family who instilled in me singing from the heart." By that time Mayann had moved her family to Perdido Street, next door to where Uncle Ike, now a widower, and his two youngest sons had also moved. They lived in one room; Louis and Mama Lucy (who was assigned to sweep up) slept on a pallet on

A page from the memoir Armstrong wrote between hospital stays in 1969. (*facing page*)

When I would be on the Junk wagon with
Alex Karnofsky (ONE OF THEIR SONS) I had a little Tin Horn, the
Kind—the People in Celebrates with,—I would blow this
this long Tin horn without the Top on it, Just
hold My fingers Close together, Blow it, As
a Call for old Rags—Bones—Bottles or Anything WITHOUT THE TOP
that the x KIDS people had to sell. The Kids
would bring bottles and receive pennies
from Alex. The Kids loved the sounds, of my TIN HORN,
The Karnofskys lived on the Corner of Girod
and Franklin streets. One Block Away from
the Girod Street Cemetary. we use to
Call it the Girod's Grave yard. IN THE COLORED SECTION

We kids used to Clean the Graves on FOR THE
Decoration Days. For the families of the Dead.
used to Make a Nice little Taste. (Tips)
I had a lot of Lucky Moments with the Karnofsky.
After blowing the tin horn so long—I wondered
how would I do blowing a real horn, a Cornet was
what I had in Mind. Sure enough, I saw a
little Cornet in a pawn shop window—Five dollars—
My luck was Just right—with the Karnofsky
Loan me on my Salary—I saved 50¢ a week and
bought the horn. All dirty—but was soon pretty to me.

Bunk Johnson inscribed this old picture to "my greatest friend, Prince" Louis Armstrong in the late 1930s.

the floor, while Mayann and "stepfather" Tom Lee, who the kids liked, had the bed. "We had a great understanding, especially about sex time between Mayann and Tom," he wrote, describing the grunts he and Mama Lucy pretended not to hear in the darkness. Mayann had them say prayers every night and blessings before every meal. He always insisted that he never got out of the habit of bedtime prayer.

Louis developed a vocal quartet with his friends and they would harmonize for hours at a time on the street. According to the *True* article, they would scrape tins and blow harmonicas to draw a crowd. One boy performed an early form of breakdancing—standing on his head on a bean can, spinning around while the rest cried encouragement. Louis's first instrument was a tin horn that he had started playing on the Karmofsky rag wagon: "One day I took the wooden top right off the horn, and surprisingly I held my two fingers close together where the wooden mouthpiece used to be, and I could play a tune of some kind. Oh, the kids really enjoyed that." He was eleven and convinced he had "music in my soul."

> After blowing the tin horn so long I wondered how I would do blowing a real horn. A cornet was what I had in mind. Sure enough I saw a little cornet in a pawn shop window—five dollars. My luck was just right. With the Karmofskys loaning me on my salary, I saved fifty cents a week and bought the horn. All dirty—but was soon pretty to me. After blowing into it a while I realized that I could play "Home Sweet Home"—then here come the blues. From then I was a mess and tootin' away. I kept that horn for a long time, I played it all through the days of the honky tonks. People thought that my first horn was given to me at the Colored Waif's Home for Boys (the orphanage). But it wasn't. (*Archive*)

This account confirms the generally disputed testimonies of Bunk Johnson, who (see William Russell's chapter in *Jazzmen*) insisted that Louis started playing in 1911, and of Sidney Bechet, who (in *Treat It Gentle*) also said he saw Louis with a cornet before he entered the Waif's Home.

In 1912, Louis had his sea change. He dropped out of school and quit working for the Karmofsky family. ("I became a little large for the job. Anyway they came into larger businesses.") He had long since become

Little Louis in the Waif's Home
Brass Band, c. 1914.

infatuated with the great musicians who played outside the tonks to draw a crowd, especially Joe Oliver, who he idolized. Although his quartet was getting so good that established musicians, including Bechet, stopped by to hear him sing, he was undoubtedly frustrated in his desire to master the cornet. He begged for pointers and was usually sloughed off. He started getting into trouble. As all the world knows, things came to a head in the early hours of January 1, 1913, when he was out celebrating New Year's with friends. On a dare, he borrowed his stepfather's .38 revolver and fired six blanks into the air. He was collared for disturbing the peace and, after spending a night in jail, was remanded to the Colored Waif's Home for Boys. Under the direction of the sainted Captain Joseph Jones, a former cavalry officer and a legend among southern educators, the home was organized along military lines. Jones drilled the boys with wooden rifles and instilled in them a sense of personal value. Other instructors offered vocational training in carpentry, gardening, and music.

Although records of the Waif's Home, which became part of the Milne Municipal Boys Home and as such survived until 1956, were

The Waif's Home had become the Boys Home when Armstrong returned with his orchestra in 1931.

apparently destroyed, Capt. Jones recalled at the end of his life that Armstrong was in custody at least twice. According to Joseph L. Peyton, the clerk of court for Orleans Parish Juvenile Court since 1940—and the successor in that job to his father, who had it from 1908—Louis was in and out of the Waif's Home during his early teenage years. Peyton says that Louis's chief crime was stealing newspapers from the white boys, who sold them on streetcars. That was a "white-only" job, he says, and whenever Louis was seen leaving a streetcar with papers under his arm, he was arrested and returned to the Waif's Home. Before long, Capt. Jones took him under his wing and got through to him. So did Peter Davis, who taught music and formed an orchestra.

Davis was wary of Louis at first, but after a six-month probation period permitted him to play tambourine, then alto horn, bugle, and finally cornet. He was proud of playing "Taps," and worked constantly at developing his embouchure. He cut grooves in the mouthpiece so it would hold to his mouth, and practiced every chance. Realizing he had an exceptional talent on his hands, Davis would occasionally take Louis home with him on his day off and allow him to play duets and sing hymns with his niece, Ida, a pianist. Louis responded to the discipline of the home—in later years he spoke of it warmly and made several low-key charitable visits; indeed, he was somewhat reluctant to leave when, in June 1914, he was put in care of his father. Not surprisingly, he didn't take to looking after Willie's "other" family and soon returned to Mayann and Mama Lucy.

F O U R

Louis seems to have had no time for repose as a child, and he never asked for any as an adult. At seventeen, he played parades with astonishing energy, earning the respect of older musicians as well as his contemporaries, who showered him with affectionate nicknames. "Even in my young days I accumulated several," he recalled in 1969. "Given by your little pals and people who like you . . . they all liked me and my cornet playing. Boy every time I looked around, somebody in some band had laid a new name on me. The Dippermouth is still around whenever I go to New Orleans and run into some of the old timers. Brings back real pleasant memories of the good old days. Here's some nicknames that very few fans I doubt ever heard of, such as Boat Note, Hammock Face, Rhythm Jaws." (Archive) He learned every theater and tonk in town as he felt his way through the underground that was black New Orleans.

To earn money, he took a grueling job driving a coal wagon and kept at it until the armistice in November 1918. The day he heard of the peace, he "immediately dropped that shovel, slowly put on my jacket—looked at Lady [his mule], and said, 'So long, my dear, I don't think I'll ever see you again. . . .' I haven't seen them since." (My) Weeks later he married Daisy Parker, a prostitute who tried to hustle him at the Brick House, a cabaret in Gretna catering to longshoreman and, in Armstrong's words, "one of the toughest joints I ever played in." Writing in 1954, he recalled, "we were both young and giddy. Daisy was a brown-skinned girl and I was in love with her. She was a little skinny but she was cute. She was older than me and more experienced in the rough ways of the New Orleans tenderloin district." She was also insanely jealous and quick to bring out the razor she always carried. They soon separated, though the marriage lasted four years.

Fate Marable's Band on the S.S.
Capitol, c. 1920. Left to right:
Henry Kimball, Boyd Atkins,
Marable (at piano), Johnny St. Cyr,
David Jones, Norman Mason,
Armstrong, George Brashear, Baby
Dodds.

Fate Marable's Band on the S.S. *Sydney*, c. 1919. Left to right: Baby Dodds, Bill Ridgeley, Joe Howard, Armstrong, Marable, David Jones, Captain Streckfus, owner of the line (in hat), Johnny Dodds, Johnny St. Cyr, Pops Foster.

Before the year was out, Louis was living with Mayann while working at Tom Anderson's, "playing all sorts arrangements from the easiest to the hardest and from the sweetest to the hottest. T'was called jazz back there in those days. I was also doubling with the Tuxedo Brass Band." Things picked up now. He had a reputation for playing blues and an ingratiating manner, and he was never too tired to work. In 1916, Captain Joseph Streckfus experimented by putting black musicians on one of his steamers, the *S. S. Sydney*. At first jazz was kept to the upper deck, while a sweet band played on the lower, but it became so popular that he fired the fox-trotters. Fate Marable, a pianist who had played on riverboats since 1907 and was renowned for the way he manipulated the calliope that announced the ship's arrival in port, was put in charge of the band. One night he heard Louis sitting in with Kid Ory's band at Co-operative Hall and decided he had to have him on the boat.

Finally quit the band at Tom Anderson's to go on the boat— excursion boat called the *Steamer Sydney.* I joined Fate Marable's band. That's when—during our intermissions—he would help me out with my reading music. And me being a very apt young man I learned a whole lots of reading music real quick. Fate Marable was a good bandleader—and very strict on us when it came to playing the music right. He is absolutely responsible for a lot of youngsters' successes. (*Goffin*)

When people talk about jazz traveling up the river they are paying tribute to Marable, whether they know it or not. When the boat docked at various stopovers on the Mississippi, the robust piping of the calliope brought thousands of people to the river's edge to hear a music rarely played outside of New Orleans. The musicians who worked with Marable would play significant roles in jazz for decades to come, among them Baby Dodds, Johnny Dodds, Johnny St. Cyr, Pops Foster, Wellman Braud, Honore Dutrey, Red Allen, and David Jones, who also coached Louis with his reading. Among the young white musicians who heard Marable's men were Bix Beiderbecke and Jesse Stacy. Jack Teagarden first heard Armstrong on the dock in New Orleans: "Suddenly, across the muddy waters of the Mississippi, came faint but bell-clear sounds of a high-pitched cornet . . . that cornet was filling the night with the hottest, the sweetest and purest jazz I'd ever heard."

Louis played excursions with Marable through the summer of 1921, but he also played the New Orleans cabarets in those years. The best band in the opinion of many was the one Joe Oliver and Kid Ory led together. In early 1918 Oliver, like many musicians before him, moved to Chicago; several months later, Ory asked Louis to take his place. That offer crystallized his position as the most esteemed of the young players. He boasted a resplendent tone and an irresistible ebullience even then. He was considered prodigious and he knew it. Most of the players, he wrote in 1969, "were fading out—some of them were still pretty good, but nothing like when they were in their heydays. Maybe it was because most of them worked too hard doing other hard jobs such as longshoreman on the docks all day, unloading ships, and lots of other hard labor which kept them too tired to even look at their instruments let alone play it, which makes them rusty."

In 1921, the young Fletcher Henderson, who was touring the South as Ethel Waters's pianist, heard Louis and tried to lure him to New York, where he intended to organize an orchestra. Louis begged off, saying he didn't want to leave his band. But a year later, when his

Sidney Bechet in New Orleans, 1944.

Don Murray, Bix Beiderbecke, Howdy Quicksell, 1926. Bix is said to have first heard Armstrong when the Streckfus Steamer docked in Davenport, Iowa, in 1919.

Armstrong visiting New Orleans
with his movie camera, late 1930s.

mentor and idol King Oliver wired him to come to Chicago, Louis left with alacrity. On the afternoon of August 8, four days after his twenty-first birthday, he played a funeral with the Tuxedo Jazz Band, packed a small bag, including a trout sandwich his mother had fixed, and caught the evening train.

F I V E

The Lincoln Gardens Cafe on Chicago's South Side was a large balconied ballroom with a revolving cut-glass ball that refracted the light. It became famous in 1922, when King Oliver brought in his Creole Jazz Band. He is said to have earned his sobriquet by cutting Freddie Keppard one night in Storyville, but it didn't stick until he made his reputation up north. At thirty-seven, he was a stern taskmaster but a rather genteel man, loyal to his home boys (as Louis was), and ready—with twenty years of playing behind him—for the big time. The band he presented on opening night, June 17, was made up of men from New Orleans: trombonist Honore Dutrey, clarinetist Johnny Dodds, bassist and banjoist Bill Johnson, drummer Baby Dodds, plus pianist Bertha Gonsoulin from California. By the time he sent for Louis, he had replaced the pianist with another woman, Memphis-born Lil Hardin. Louis said later (see Appendix) that the band sounded so good the night he arrived, he didn't think he could play with it. But when he opened formally the next night, he knew he was home:

> The first number went down so well we had to take [an] encore, that was the moment Joe Oliver and I developed a little system whereby we didn't have to write down the duet breaks. I was so wrapped up in him and lived his music that I could take second to his lead in a split second. (My.)

Oliver and his wife found him a place to live and taught him the ways of Chicago. Within weeks, Louis got hold of a typewriter and was writing his old friends. The earliest surviving letter (in the Jazz Archive at Tulane University) was written September 1, 1922, to the veteran brassman Isadore Barbarin, whose son, drummer Paul Barbarin, was a contemporary, friend, and bandmate of Louis's.

Louis and King Oliver in Chicago, c. 1923. (facing page)

Mr. Barbarin.

Dear Friend.

Yours of this afternoon has been received. And I take great pleasure in letting you know that I was glad to hear from you. I'm well as usual and also doing fine as usual. Hoping you and family are well. Pops I just had started to wondering what was the matter with you. You takin' so long to answer: Well I know just how it is when a fellow is playing with a red hot brass band and they have all the work he don't have time to be bothered with writing no letters.

Well I understand that Pops. I heard all about you all having all those funerals down there. I'm sorry that I ain't down there to make some of them with you all. The boys give me H . . . all the time because [I'm] forever talking about the Brass Band and how I used to like to make those parades. They say I don't see how a man can be crazy about those hard parades. I told them that they don't go hard with you when you are playing with a good band. Joe Oliver is here in my room now and he sends you his best regards. Also all the boys. I heard the Celestin lost his sister. Well that's too bad. I feel sorry for the poor fellow. I will tell Paul what you said when I see him again. The next time you meet Nenest ask him what is the matter with him he don't answer my letter. Ask him [if] he needs any writing paper-stamps to let me know at once and I'll send him some at once . . Ha . . Ha . . Well old pal I tell you the news some other time. I have to go to work now. Good knight.,

All from Louis Armstrong. 459 East 31 St. Chicago, Ill.

First stop after New Orleans: King Oliver's Creole Jazz Band, 1923. Left to right: Honore Dutrey, Baby Dodds, Armstrong (holding a slide trumpet he never actually played), Oliver, Lil Hardin, Bill Johnson, Johnny Dodds. (*facing page, top*)

A late edition of King Oliver's Creole Jazz Band, 1924. Left to right: Charlie Jackson, Snags Jones, Buster Bailey, Oliver, Zue Robertson, Lil Hardin, Armstrong, Rudy Jackson. (*facing page, bottom*)

I choose to believe that the closer is a pun rather than a spelling error, of which the letter has several. In any case, the use of "Pops" indicates Armstrong's talent for coining slang. Baby Dodds later said that he'd never heard such phrases as "you cats" and "look out there Pops" in New Orleans until Armstrong started using them on the bandstand. Among the words that Louis is believed to have coined or popularized in his early years are several that became part of the language: *chops, jive, scat, gutbucket, mellow* and *solid* (as terms of approbation), and *Pops, Face,* and *Daddy* (as forms of address). He's even been credited with the hoariest of all bandleader puns, "not too fast, not too slow, just half-fast," perhaps because he had the brass to use it on network radio and television.

The Armstrong discography begins with the recordings of King Oliver's Creole Jazz Band—thirty-seven performances (many other takes were made but destroyed) waxed between April and December 1923. The most enduring tale of those sessions tells how Armstrong had to play twenty feet behind the rest of the band, because his huge sound overwhelmed the ensemble and recording equipment. True or not, Armstrong made an impression—despite his role as second cornet to Oliver's lead and the absence of solo space. The polyphonic New Orleans style, which Oliver honed to perfection, was not designed to parade the skills of virtuoso soloists. Two years later, Armstrong would ignite the revolution that established jazz as a soloist's art. With Oliver, however, he had to prove himself a team player. Despite restraints, the young man, who Oliver introduced as his adopted son, made an astonishing debut on records. One needn't have a trained ear to be taken aback by his virtually "straight" readings of the trio themes on "Froggy Moore" and especially "Chimes Blues." His declamatory tone and rhythmic dash are unmistakable. His best work with Oliver came at subsequent sessions—his breaks on "Tears," which prefigure his mature style; his full chorus and coda on the sublime "Riverside Blues"; the thrusting counterpoint between the two cornets on "Mabel's Dream"; and the celebrated double-cornet breaks on "Snake Rag," "Buddy's Habits," "Where Did You Stay Last Night," and two incomparable examples of collective propulsion, "Chattanooga Stomp" and "I Ain't Gonna Tell Nobody."

Louis was also getting a feel for show business, mustering the self-confidence that would eventually allow him to conquer the stage in Chicago and New York. One source of inspiration was his favorite entertainer, Bill Robinson, the subject of an enlightening homage:

Bill "Bojangles" Robinson was Louis's favorite entertainer, 1935.

He was the sharpest Negro man that I personally [have] ever seen in my life onstage, since the first time that I ever laid eyes on him at the Erlanger Theater in Chicago in 1922. I had just come up from New Orleans. . . . I had Bill Johnson, who had been on the RKO Circuit, take me to the matinee show one day so I could see this man whom I had heard and read about in my early days in N.O. Bojangles came up to every expectation and opinion that I had of him before I saw him in person. I am sitting in my seat in the theater, very anxious to see this man, and sure enough the great one appeared. As he came out of the

wing onstage, the first thing that hit him was the flashlight. Sharp—Lord knows that man was so sharp he was bleeding (our expression when we mention someone that's well dressed)— Anyway he had on a sharp light tan gabardine summer suit, brown derby, and the usual thick-soul shoes in which he tapped.

It was a long time before Bojangles could open his mouth. That's how popular he was and well-liked by all who understood his greatness as a dancer and a showman. He waited after the thunderous applause had finished, and looked up into the booth and said to the man who controlled the lights—Bill said to him, "Give me a light, My color." And all the lights all over the house went out. And me sitting there when this happened, with the whole audience just roaring with laughter. When I realized it, I was laughing so loud, until Bill Johnson was on the verge of taking me out of there. I hadn't heard anything like that before or witnessed it either. Then Bojangles went into his act. His every move was a beautiful picture. I am sitting in my seat in ecstasy and delight, even in a trance. He imitated a trombone with his walking cane to his mouth, blowing out of the side of his mouth making the buzzing sound of a trombone, which I enjoyed. He told a lot of funny jokes, which everybody enjoyed immensely. Then he went into his dance and finished by skating off of the stage with a silent sound and tempo. *Wow* what an artist. I was sold on him ever since. (*Archive*)

In February 1924, Armstrong married Lil Hardin, who voiced impatience with Louis's second-banana loyalty to King Oliver. For his part, he was infatuated with the idea of winning the hand of so sophisticated a woman—educated, older, and desired by everyone in the band:

From the first night on the bandstand I noticed that all of the boys in Joe's band had been very busy trying to make a play for Lil, who was the Belle of the Windy City of Chicago at that time. Well, as for me, I was wrapped up in music and did not pay any attention at first to the fact that Lil was stuck on me. But who was I to think that a big high-powered chick like Lillian Hardin who came to Chicago from Memphis, Tenn.—the year of 1917—right out of Fisk University—Valedictorian of her

Louis and Lil in Chicago, 1924. (*facing page*)

Freddie Keppard, 1920s.

classes—Who me?—I thought to myself. I just couldn't conceive the idea—that's all. (*Goffin*)

The other band members grumbled with jealousy—one of them called Armstrong "a country sonbitch" for courting her—but Louis and Lil confided in each other about their bad first marriages, and when Mayann visited Chicago and gave her approval, they filed their respective divorces and married. With Lil on his arm, he began acting the sport, taking her to the Dreamland Cafe and tipping May Alix and Ollie Powers to sing for them. One musician they went to hear was an old rival of King Oliver's, Freddie Keppard, and Armstrong was not impressed. Armstrong's later criticism of Keppard is ironic in light of attacks with which he would later be plagued:

> Freddie Keppard slipped out of the scene into oblivion. A heavy drinker. His ego when he was a young man and [the] clowning that he did must have been rather amusing for laughs, to get the recognition he achieved. But he sure did not play the cornet seriously at any time. Just clowned all the way. Good for those idiot fans, who did not care whether he played correct. . . . The first time I heard Freddie Keppard at an after hours joint was on the Southside of Chicago, he did not move me at all. He played a lot of almost high drunken notes. (*Archive*)

In 1969 he also had harsh words for the woman pianist who had tried to convince him that Keppard had a better tone than Oliver. He was upset because "she did not know jazz [but] had the nerve to accept the title as a piano player, and at the same time sitting in bands with the most famous jazz men in the world! How she got that job—that I can't figure out until this day. . . . Read music, yes—as an improviser—hmm—terrible. . . . This chick admits all she was interested in was the paydays, more money than she's ever made. Am sure she hasn't made near that much salary since the band broke up. Because music is much more modern nowadays and she was corny then. Guess who?" It's hard *not* to guess he was referring to Lil Hardin, though they maintained a cordial relationship until his death. Musically, his assessment of Lil isn't too surprising; but his candor indicates his lasting loyalty to Oliver and his ambivalence about leaving him at Lil's insistence. She convinced him to accept an offer from Fletcher Henderson, and he headed for New York.

The spell Armstrong cast on the best musicians in New York can hardly be overestimated. Only one other soloist in jazz history, Charlie Parker, in the 1940s, would ever cast so wide a net over every breed of musician. Like Parker, Armstrong was perceived as a rube, an ignorant country boy with a funny manner. A widely told story found him ignoring a *pp* marking during rehearsal. Henderson stops the band and asks him if he knows what *pp* (*pianissimo*—very softly) means. "Yes sir," Louis announces. "Pound plenty!" Musicians didn't laugh long—they were too busy overhauling their styles to match the rube's heady rhythms, blues sensibility, and incomparable sense of proportion.

Every great improviser is a great editor. It's easy to run scales up and down the horn; but picking out the notes that mean something is hard. Interpreting a phrase in a way that makes it personal is the mark of a master. Louis's ability to project feeling and his innate sense of musical logic were modern in ways that made everyone else sound fussy and antiquated. He taught New York to swing. Danny Barker, the New Orleans-born guitarist who later toured with Armstrong's big band, has suggested that Armstrong's greatest achievement was to jettison the jaunty second-line two-beat rhythm of New Orleans in favor of the evenly distributed four-four beat that is the basis of swing. Indeed, the swing era has been characterized as orchestrated Armstrong.

When Louis joined Henderson, the orchestra specialized in commercial pieces—fox-trots and waltzes—for the dancers at the Roseland Ballroom, as well as self-consciously crafted jazz numbers. Henderson's ingenious arranger, Don Redman, and such instrumentalists as saxophonist Coleman Hawkins and clarinetist Buster Bailey (whom Louis had known in Chicago and recommended to Henderson) were well-schooled virtuosi who listened closely to the records coming out of Chicago. But the orchestra's early spin-offs, though deferential, lacked the tang of authenticity. Armstrong's spellbinding improvisations served as antidotes to the baroque doodling, plodding time, and overwritten arrangements of the day. They are the sparkplugs that start the ensemble throbbing on "Go Long Mule," "Copenhagen," and—notwithstanding his difficulties with a plunger mute (a technique made famous by Oliver but rejected by Armstrong)—"Shanghai Shuffle." Louis's stirring chorus on "One of These Days" and his theme statement on "Everybody Loves

My Baby" are savory moments in otherwise leaden performances. The pioneering Don Redman admitted, "I changed my style of arranging after I heard Louis Armstrong." Who could resist his passion and robust attack? Yet not even Henderson was prepared to let the complete Armstrong come through. Although the brief scat break at the close of "Everybody Loves My Baby" marks Louis's recorded debut as a singer, he was not allowed to sing onstage, let alone on other Henderson records.

Not the least refreshing aspect of the sojourn with Fletcher was the chance to travel. After six months at the Roseland, the band toured New England. "We were the first colored big band to hit the road," Armstrong wrote Goffin. "We went all through the New England states. We spent our first summer up in Lawrence, Mass." On days off, he and Buster Bailey would go swimming—"one of my famous hobbies," he noted, "outside of typing." Still, he never forgot Henderson's refusal to let him sing. In a privately recorded discussion in 1960 (which shows, as his public writings often do not, how confident he was of his talent and potential commercial value), he told Fred Rabell, "Fletcher didn't dig me like Joe Oliver. He had a million-dollar talent in his band and he never thought enough to let me sing or nothing. He'd go hire a singer that lived up in Harlem that night for a recording next day who didn't even know the song. And I'd say, 'Let me sing.' But no, all he had was the trumpet in mind, and that's why he missed the boat." That's one reason he left Henderson after fourteen months, having made nearly forty records with him. He was also feeling pressure from Lil to come home to Chicago. She was getting jealous, and with good reason. Louis was in great demand in and out of the studios. His recording activities in New York were by no means confined to the Henderson band.

An exceptional series of records by the Clarence Williams Blue Five combined the breezy entertainment of vaudeville (vocals by Eva Taylor and Virginia Liston) with the sweeping exuberance of a lean New Orleans-style cabaret band. They paired Louis with the only man who, for a very short while, seemed his equal as an improviser in those transitional years, soprano saxophonist and clarinetist Sidney Bechet. The highlights include Armstrong's impeccable lead and slashing breaks on "Cake Walking Babies from Home" and his note-bending and call-and-response with the reeds on "Papa De-Da-Da." Above all there is his explosive chorus on the Blue Five version of "Everybody Loves My

Baby," in which he uses a plunger mute in homage to Oliver, ripping and snorting against the beat, accenting against expectations (for example, the fourth beat of the tenth measure), raising the roof during the stoptime release, and growling his way into the last eight bars. The record was a huge success and the talk of Harlem. Some of the lyrics from those sessions also attracted attention: "Pickin' on Your Baby," a mild protest piece about a pickaninny rose, offers sly contrast with the Fanny Brice hit "Second Hand Rose" (1921), and "I'm a Little Blackbird" archly advocates miscegenation.

The stopper was still on, though: The full radiance of Louis's music and personality was simmering, waiting for release. But his reputation spread among musicians and producers, and he never had to ask for work. His three numbers with Ma Rainey and Her Georgian Jazz Band (actually a pickup ensemble from the Henderson Orchestra) demonstrate the sensitivity, economy, and forthrightness that made his obbligati so highly valued. His most successful collaboration was with the Empress, Bessie Smith. He said of their nine sides together, "She'd always have the words and tune in her head, and we'd just run it down once. Then she'd sing a few lines, and I'd play something to fill it in, and some nice beautiful notes behind her. Everything I did with her, I *like*." Other sessions with singers in New York and Chicago were less consistently

New York jazz learned to swing when Louis Armstrong joined the Fletcher Henderson Orchestra, 1924. Left to right: Howard Scott, Coleman Hawkins, Armstrong, Charles Dixon, Henderson, Kaiser Marshall, Buster Bailey, Elmer Chambers, Charlie Green, Bob Escudero, Don Redman.

good but constitute a relatively little known cache of important early Louis. The variety of material is impressive—fast blues, slow blues, vaudeville novelties, basic pop. The singers were usually billed as blues divas, but many weren't, and only a few sustain interest in their own right—notably Bertha Hill, Sippie Wallace, Hociel Thomas, and Clara Smith. Yet Louis, brimming with energy, rarely let the singer or the material get him down.

One amusing session starred Lillie Delk Christian, a justly obscure cabaret singer whose vibrato quivered as fast and furious as Alvin and the Chipmunks'. The best of the eight sides she cut in 1928 with Armstrong's Hot Four is "Too Busy": She trudges through the sappy tune without the remotest suggestion of swing, but after an instrumental interlude, Armstrong sneaks up on her with some impromptu scat that swings so hard you can almost hear Lillie's stomach rising. Bertha "Chippie" Hill, on the other hand, was a genuine blues singer, and Armstrong obviously enjoyed working with her. The material is excellent and his cogent fills on "Lonesome Weary Blues" and "Low Land Blues" rival his work with Bessie Smith. The Sippie Wallace sessions benefit from the presence of her teenage brother, pianist Hersal Thomas, whose backup on "Special Delivery Blues" anticipates Thelonious Monk's "Blue Monk." Margaret Johnson's "Changeable Daddy," Eva Taylor's "You Can't Shush Katie," and Hociel Thomas's "Sunshine Baby" are among the other worthy sides from Armstrong's apprenticeship as a sideman.

S I X

Lil had a place for him in her band at the Dreamland Cafe (at seventy-five dollars a week) when Louis returned to Chicago. Fletcher had thrown him a lavish going-away party, assuring him a spot in the band if ever he wished to return (despite Louis's getting drunk at the party and throwing up on Henderson's tux). For a while Armstrong figured he would return, since Lil's band seemed such a comedown after "Fletcher and his fine band," but he soon realized he was building a reputation in Chicago worth nurturing.

I had become so popular at the Dreamland [that] Erskine Tate from the Vendome Theater came to hire me to join his Symphony Orchestra. I like to have fainted. Erskine Tate had a 20 piece orch playing at a moving picture house called the Vendome Theater located at 31st and State Streets in Chicago. In those days they had silent films instead of the talkies. His Orchestra would furnish the music for all the scenes in the films. And when the picture would break the Orchestra'd play overtures etc., and then they'd finish with a red hot number—then blackout—then the picture would start over again. . . . So when Erskine Tate came for me [I'd been trying] to get the experience of playing classic and symphony music, etc. Well, here's your chance, I said, ask Lil. She said, "Boy, if you don't get out of this house and go on down there to Erskine Tate's rehearsal, I'll skin you alive." I said, slowly, "Well, all right, I'll go." I went down there and the opening night was sensational. I remember the first "swing tune" we played, called "Spanish Shawl." I wasn't in Tate's Orch 2-weeks before I was making records with them for the Vocalion Recording Company. I became quite a figure at the Vendome. Especially with the gals. (*Goffin*)

Alpha, Louis, and friend among the stars, early 1930s.

One of the gals was a nineteen-year-old named Alpha Smith, for whom he eventually divorced Lil. He had become a figure with the guys, too, especially young black musicians. When the lights went down for the musical interludes, the audience could see his trumpet poking above the pit; his solos got tremendous ovations. Tate would arrange for Armstrong to have a different specialty number every week. Doc Cheatham, who switched from saxophone to cornet after seeing Armstrong at the Vendome, recalls that as soon as the "spotlight hit Louis for his feature, man, the people were screaming so much you couldn't hear what he was playing half the time." On several occasions, Armstrong asked Cheatham to sub for him. The first time the spot hit Cheatham, the audience went wild—until everyone realized it wasn't Louis. "You could just measure the diminishing of the screams, right down to nothing, and I'm up there playing like a fool." While at the Vendome, Armstrong started playing trumpet as well as cornet, possibly at Tate's suggestion, though he continued to use both instruments through 1927. It's impossible to distinguish between the two on old records, but the trumpet is said to have a more brilliant tone, due in part to the design of the tubing, which gives it a longer, sleeker look.

On November 12, 1925, Armstrong made his first recordings as a leader. The session was the beginning of a monumental series that would last through 1928 and produce sixty-five performances for Okeh Records. Had he stopped performing at the end of 1928, Armstrong would never have become an international celebrity, an ambassador of jazz and goodwill, a media star, a folk hero, and more. But he would still be regarded as the single most creative and innovative force in jazz history. Notwithstanding a handful of trite numbers and the intrusion of some vaudeville hokum, the Okeh recordings are no more dated—which is to say, diminished in the power to enlighten and astonish—than Bach cantatas. With Armstrong, jazz was in the hands of a virtuoso instrumentalist whose vision transcended the limitations of what was construed as pop music. Armstrong's genius surmounted everything, from poor material and uninspired associates to the constraints of recording technology and the winds of fashion. Here was unexampled expressive power in a new, authentically American mode. Even the nature of his virtuosity was sui generis: This was not a man who could interpret the Haydn trumpet concerto, but an artist who produced a tone of insuperable brilliance and improvised musical statements that are as logical and emotionally satisfying as any written score.

To say that Armstrong and his music were not appreciated as such by the academy or the white public is to belabor the obvious. In the 1920s, jazz was excoriated from the pulpit, blamed by women's groups for the increase in rape, belittled by intellectuals and musicologists, scorned as whorehouse music, and worse. This was a music innovated by blacks without the benefit of a conservatory imprimatur. As such, it affronted the generation of New England humanists who were self-consciously attempting to do for American music what Whitman had done for American poetry—give it a voice. When the man who embodied that voice made himself known (in sweet guttural tones), they saw to their dismay a smiling Negro with a trumpet and repaired to their ivory-covered dens, hoping he would go away. Devoted black urban audiences, augmented by a handful of whites, kept the music alive in a difficult period. Armstrong had no nationwide following as of 1926, but records on which he appeared were selling in large numbers. Among the bestselling "race" records of 1925 and 1926—all featuring Armstrong—were Bessie Smith's "St. Louis Blues," Clarence Williams's "Everybody Loves My Baby" and "Cake Walking Babies," Fletcher Henderson's "Sugar Foot Stomp," and his own recordings of "Heebie Jeebies," "Muskrat Ramble," and "Cornet Chop Suey."

Like King Oliver's Creole Jazz Band, Armstrong's Hot Five consisted of Orleanians—Johnny Dodds, Kid Ory, Johnny St. Cyr—plus Lil. Unlike Oliver's band, the Hot Five and its successors (the Hot Seven and the Savoy Ballroom Five) existed only to make records. Armstrong continued to appear with stage orchestras. The primary difference between the Oliver and Armstrong records (the Clarence Williams sessions can be seen as transitional here) is the changeover from a group effort, where polyphony dominates, to a music for soloists. Modest embellishment gives way to daring improvisation, two- and four-bar breaks are expanded into solos of a full chorus or more, and the multiple refrains of ragtime composition are winnowed down to the cyclical choruses of popular songs and the blues. Armstrong was lucky to be recording for Okeh, which employed the best sound techs in the business. But he was nervous that first day, and the Hot Five got off to an orderly but conservative start, recording three numbers: in "My Heart," Armstrong's solo pivots on a lick that prefigures by five years the pop song "Them There Eyes"; "Yes I'm in the Barrel" opens with an evocative riff before moving into tempo; and "Gut Bucket Blues" boasts a compelling Armstrong solo plus his genial verbal introductions of the musicians. It was a warm-up session.

At a far more productive second date the following February, the Hot Five came into its own with a double-sided hit in "Heebie Jeebies" and "Muskrat Ramble." The first is famous for the impetuous vocal that put scat singing on the map and fostered countless imitations. Armstrong always insisted that the sheet music slipped from the stand and he started scatting to save the take. His unforgettable vocal is the high point of an otherwise uninspired performance, and it's hard to believe he didn't know exactly what he was doing. That chorus did more than introduce a language of nonsense syllables that jazz singers could use when a song's lyric proved too constricting; it embodied a joyous, vernacular, and convincing attitude that complemented the spontaneous nature of the new music. Young singers didn't merely ape the idea—they wanted Armstrong's gravelly voice as well. It would be another four years before singers realized how versatile his voice was, but from the moment Louis's "novelty" vocal hit the streets, other musicians were, in Earl Hines's recollection, sticking their heads out the window trying to catch colds to sound like Louis. The flip side, "Muskrat Ramble," became an immediate jazz standard (so enduringly popular that a rock 'n' roll version ensued in the early sixties). Another piece, "Oriental Strut," incorporated 1920s exotica, an "Oh, By Jingo!"-inspired vamp, and stoptime—a

Armstrong established more pop tunes than any other musician. "Sleepytime" was his theme song, and few other musicians played it. "St. Louis Blues," by contrast, was the most frequently recorded jazz classic in the decades before World War II. "Sugar Foot Stomp" was based on Oliver's "Dippermouth Blues."

Armstrong, St. Cyr, Dodds, Ory, Lil, 1926.

To Sonny

common gambit in which the soloist improvises freely while one or more members of the band seem to stop the flow of time with a unison stomping on certain beats. The accents might fall on the first beat of alternate measures, for example, or on the first three beats of every measure.

The breakthrough performance of the session was the beaming "Cornet Chop Suey." Here the soloist is paramount, and the other horns less a partnership in the front line than a backup, trying to keep up. Excepting a piano solo, Armstrong is the whole show, from the martial introduction through an exciting sixteen-bar passage of stoptime breaks to a chorus of elegantly phrased eighth-note figures with melodic ideas that were widely imitated for years. Louis later said he wrote "Cornet Chop Suey" sitting on a staircase during a break on a jaunt around Chicago. The masterpiece by the original Hot Five personnel was made twenty months later, by which time Louis was a studio veteran. The tantalizing melody of "Struttin' with Some Barbecue" is built on a major seventh in a way that prefigures "Samba de Orpheus," the Brazilian hit of forty years later. Although the performance is carefully arranged with an introduction, varied backups for the three soloists (Dodds and Ory split a chorus), and unison figures, the performance is a showcase for the entertainer as artist, flaunting his brilliance with mercurial rips, dazzling triplets, a glissando that seems to swallow its own tail. The twelve-bar intro precedes a traditional theme statement, but Armstrong's improvisation stops tradition in its tracks: Accompanied by banjo accents on the offbeats, he arcs over the ensemble, defying gravity and bar lines.

Like Paganini, Armstrong embodies the musician as sprite. Yet his presentation is underscored by a canny ingenuousness that is without precedent or equal. Like a prodigious child showing off for the grown-ups, Armstrong invites us to participate in the celebration of his gift. Whether the invitation is made explicit in spoken remarks that puncture any trace of solemnity about the artist's role or is conveyed through the sheer bravura of his instrumental technique, a democratization of artist and audience takes place. He looks us right in the eye, evoking the promise of a common clay, as if to say, "Now dig this," before blowing us away with a mastery that is awesome but never intimidating. The generosity of his impulse as an artist/entertainer made the Hot Five and Seven possible and guaranteed his later triumphs as an ambassador of the musical world he created.

His disarming street-smart liberality came to the fore at the December

1927 session, when the Hot Five recorded three sides with a guest musician, guitarist Lonnie Johnson, who would enjoy a second career in the 1950s as a blues singer. In the 1920s, he was much admired by jazz musicians for his jaunty counterpoint to Baby Cox's vocal on Ellington's "The Mooche," his triplets on the initial recordings of the Chocolate Dandies, his duets with Eddie Lang, a white guitarist who adopted a pseudonym (Blind Willie Dunn) for the occasion, and his appearance with the Hot Five. Johnson plays a pivotal role in Armstrong's "I'm Not Rough," shadowing the three-chorus trumpet solo with trills, providing the sole accompaniment for the vocal, and bearing down in the final passages with fourth-beat accents. His startling solo is made up entirely of evenly articulated triplets, foreshadowing the rhythms of rock 'n' roll. He seems to spur Armstrong to a new level of abandon—one that nearly upsets the band's balance on the less successful "Savoy Blues."

Alpha feeding Louis peanuts in London, 1934.

The best of the Armstrong-Johnson records is the ingenious "Hotter Than That," based on a strain of "Tiger Rag." After the introduction, Louis romps through the theme, bursting into a two-bar break at bar fifteen, the melodic content of which appeared in many guises during the next decade (the Ink Spots sing it on "Java Jive"). What should have been Armstrong's second break (at bar thirty-one) functions instead as a relay point—Johnny Dodds begins his chorus by bagging that break. In the same fashion, Armstrong picks up from Dodds to begin an improbably complex scat chorus, highlighted with devious cross-rhythms. His finest vocal to date, it was a stunning example of a musician superimposing one rhythm over another, and its implications ran deep. (Compare Miles Davis's similar gambit in the first four bars of his second chorus of "No Blues" on At Carnegie Hall.) Then he vocally exchanges two-bar phrases with Johnson's guitar, anticipating the duet for voice and clarinet in the 1928 "West End Blues." After a trombone solo, Armstrong's trumpet explodes with a break and improvisation capped with twelve high-Cs spaced over seven bars. "Hotter Than That" is three minutes of daunting surprises.

Armstrong's energy level seems all the more remarkable if you take into account that in 1926, he was working day and night. He played four shows at the Vendome, finishing at eleven, then went over to the Sunset Cafe, where he was featured in the big band led by Carroll Dickerson. Switching from Lil's band at the Dreamland to the Sunset was necessary, since he was now spending much of his time and money on Alpha. It was notable for other reasons. The Sunset was owned by Joe Glaser, a mob-connected promoter whose eventual partnership with Armstrong would make one an international star and the other an internationally powerful booking czar. In the 1920s, Glaser wasn't interested in personal management, but Louis was doing well on his own.

> Wow was I making nice money so I had a good chance to buy Alpha some nice things with my extra money Lil didn't know about. . . . I used to love to take her out on Sunday and we would drive out to Blue Island. Bill Bottoms (Joe Louis's ex-dietician) was the owner of the roadhouse out there, and Alpha, me, Tubby Hall, who was the drummer in Carroll Dickerson's band at the time, and his girl—the four of us would drive out in my brand new Ford car with the yellow wire wheels. (*Goffin*)

Alpha turned out to be interested primarily in "furs and diamonds"— "a no good bitch," in Armstrong's final estimation. The Sunset, however, turned out to be a godsend. Early in 1927, Glaser fired Dickerson, who had a drinking problem, and turned the band over to Louis. He was now fronting his first band at a major club, surrounded by some of the best players in Chicago, including pianist Earl Hines. For a while the Okeh recording setup remained the same, though he made some changes for a few sessions in May, replacing Ory with John Thomas, and adding Pete Briggs, who played tuba in the Sunset band, and drummer Baby Dodds, his old friend from the riverboats. The Hot Seven, as the new group was called, recorded eleven titles, demonstrating a substantially richer texture and a more provocative and assured Armstrong. The irresistible "Potato Head Blues," its valorous theme evoking the brass band roots of New Orleans jazz, is the band's seminal performance. A highly charged Johnny Dodds solo and a banjo break herald Armstrong, who struts through his stoptime chorus with a certitude that borders on arrogance. It's a rousing celebration of self, underscored by searing emotion. His syncopations are dazzling; his lead work in the final chorus is musical ecstasy. One of the record's admirers was Tallulah Bankhead, who insisted on playing it onstage for the three years she starred on Broadway in *Private Lives*. "It is one of the greatest things in life, in case anyone who is uninitiated to the true jazz wants to dig a great example of Louis," she wrote, "and while it may seem incongruous to

Jelly Roll Morton and His Red Hot Peppers. Left to right: Omer Simeon, Andrew Hilaire, John Lindsey, Morton, Johnny St. Cyr, Kid Ory, George Mitchell, 1926.

put such a record in a Noel Coward drawing room comedy, I just had to have a snatch of Satch to alleviate the tedium of playing the same part for so long."

The boldness of Armstrong's and Dodds's solos dominate "Wild Man Blues," for which Armstrong shared composer credit with Jelly Roll Morton, though he attributed the melody to Morton. "S.O.L. Blues" and "Gully Low Blues" are two versions of the same piece (the former was suppressed until 1940, because of its lyric and shit-out-of-luck acronym), each noted for Armstrong's fierce descending arpeggios. "Weary Blues" begins with a fiery solo by Dodds and a punchy one by Thomas and peaks with a flamboyant Armstrong takeoff that lands him in unexpectedly high terrain. Baby Dodds's cymbal-whacking ignites the finale of "Willie the Weeper"; "Twelfth Street Rag" succeeds in modernizing a piece that seemed naïvely raggy even in 1927; "Melancholy" has a lovely melody, reminiscent of "I Ain't Got Nobody," and a variation by the trumpeter that is lovelier still.

A significant indication of Louis's preeminence in 1927, at least among jazz and trumpet enthusiasts, was the publication of two books by the Melrose Bros. Music Company in Chicago: *Louis Armstrong's 50 Hot Choruses for Cornet* and *Louis Armstrong's 125 Jazz Breaks for Cornet.* The Foreword in both volumes accurately boasted, "Hundreds of jazz cornetists, who, by the way, are an important feature in all jazz orchestras, have adopted the Armstrong style of playing. . . . His ability is enthusiastically endorsed by all the great and near great." The books are of great value. As the Foreword explains, "The solos in this book depart in principle of production from any solos on the market. They are genuine inspirations obtained, not by the old method of the artist writing down his solos one note at a time, but from actual recordings. Special phonograph recording apparatus was employed to make them. They are red hot inspirations extracted from red hot jazz recordings." In other words, the solos were created exclusively for publication. Incredibly, the Edison cylinders on which Armstrong recorded them were destroyed, so all we have are the published transcriptions. (Bent Persson, a Swedish trumpeter and bandleader, has recorded four record albums that employ all the transcribed solos and breaks in the context of simulated Hot Five and Hot Seven performances.) Still, they constitute a significant part of Armstrong's output in the 1920s, displaying his facility at improvising variations on dozens of tunes that he never otherwise recorded or, most likely, played—including Morton compositions, New Orleans pieces, and pop songs.

S E V E N

For a short while, Armstrong found himself hustling for work again. He had quit the Vendome in April 1927, and in July the Sunset Cafe went dark. After a few unsuccessful gigs, he teamed up with Earl Hines and Zutty Singleton to hustle jobs.

> Earl, Zutty, and I stayed out of work so long until it was impossible for me to get my car out of the shop, even after it was fixed. Things [had] gotten so tough with us until fifteen cents looked like fifteen dollars. But we did not lose our spirit, and we all kept that ol' clean shirt on everyday, and ol' Earl Hines kept the big fresh cigar in his mouth everyday. Zutty and I both admired that. We were still riding in this "Pneumonia

Special." That's the name we gave this hauling car. You'd be surprised to know how happy we were. (*Goffin*)

The three men even rented a dance hall on the West Side, called the Usonia, and drew pretty good crowds until a drunk came in one night and shot the place up. At the same time the Savoy Ballroom opened nearby and "was doing all the business in town." After the dance hall went bust, Louis was in hock as well as out of work. Fortunately for him, the Savoy fired the original house bands, led by Charles Elgar and Clarence Black—"two good bands," Armstrong recalled, that "would cut any band that came to the Savoy for one night"—and hired his old boss, Carroll Dickerson.

In Europe, 1934.

> Carroll had all the old timers rejoin him. Of course, Earl Hines couldn't make it, on account he had just given Jimmie Noone his word to play in his little four piece combination down at the Apex nightclub on 35th St. So Carroll hired Jean Anderson on piano. . . . But just the same with Jean, Zutty, Fred Robinson, Homer Hobson, Jimmy Strong, [Bert] Curry, Crawford Wethington, Peter Briggs, Mancy "Peck" Cara, Louis Armstrong, and Carroll Dickerson himself, if I have to say it myself, we made up one of the damnedest bands there were. . . . (*Goffin*)

Louis was not yet twenty-seven in July 1928, but he considered himself one of the "old-timers" on the Chicago music scene and was especially pleased when Dickerson's men went into the Savoy and cut the "young boys" in "Clarence Black's band down to a low gravy." Adding insult to injury, they also whipped Black's men in a basketball game. "We'd just finished recording, etc. So it all turned out just fine—then we became the favorite band of the house also." (*Goffin*)

Louis was justly buoyed by those recordings. After six months away from the studio, he had returned with Hines and several members of the Dickerson band. At five sessions recorded between June 26 (the spunky date with Lillie Delk Christian) and July 5 (the entire Dickerson band), he surpassed everything he'd already done. The group was still called the Hot Five, though it was a sextet, and if Jimmy Strong, Fred Robinson, and Mancy Cara weren't as accomplished as Dodds, Ory, and St. Cyr, they *were* members of his working band and willing to take his unorthodox instructions. Singleton, on the other hand, was an excellent drummer, and Hines, of course, was a revelation—the first pianist to play skittery linear figures, reflecting Louis's influence (it was said of Hines that he played "trumpet-style" piano, though his attack was orchestral). Hines's unerring sense of time enabled him to track Armstrong through his most daring conceits.

One of the new Hot Five's records came to symbolize more than any other the ascendancy of a classic American music. The most celebrated and analyzed of Armstrong recordings, "West End Blues" opens with a clarion call to arms—a blazing virtuoso trumpet cadenza that, in Gunther Schuller's words, "served notice that jazz had the potential to compete with the highest order of previously known expression." Its keening momentum, which defies notation, remains undimmed and peerless. How can one explain the large number of violinists who can play Bach's D-minor Chaconne when no trumpeter, in or out of jazz, has convincingly replicated Armstrong's nine-measure intro? Working with a strangely banal King Oliver blues, Armstrong refashioned the twelve-bar theme into a sensationally varied performance. Each chorus differs from its neighbors: a sober trombone solo squired by woodblocks; a simple but enchanting duet by clarinet and voice; a dreamy piano solo; and finally, Armstrong's splendent trumpet, holding one perfect note for four measures, then caroming into a pattern of falling arpeggios. The trite clop-cymbal sign-off sounds like an addled expression of amazement.

The recordings of 1928 are widely regarded as Armstrong's peak. The Pittsburgh-born Hines inspired him more than anyone since Oliver, and their collaborations became the foundation for a music utterly independent of the conventions of New Orleans. The greatness of "West End Blues" is undeniable, but it is not an isolated crowning achievement. Armstrong made other records as good that year, and at other junctures in his career. "Muggles" is the foundation for tens of thousands of jazz records that are successions of solos, though few can match its drama. What it lacks in organizational esprit is compensated by a climactic solo in which Armstrong turns a flagging blues into a brisk twenty-four-bar rhythm fantasy plus an emotional twelve-bar blues. His runway is a four-bar break that has as much in common with the preceding solos as a jet has with Wright aircraft. In the next five bars, he bounces between two pitches (A and C) and in the following seven employs only the C and its octave—an imperious example of "less is more." Then he skids into halftime with a four-bar transition, gliding into a closing chorus that is built almost entirely on the expressive power of seventh chords.

"Weather Bird" is the only Armstrong-Hines duet and remains the standard for off-the-cuff encounters. Extreme liberties are taken with the material (a three-strain rag by King Oliver) and the meter as the two masters jab and feint in a freely swinging, often witty scuffle that ultimately has them exchanging solitary measures. The competitive edge between the two friends elicits smiles after numerous hearings, but what makes the record more impressive is the unfaltering emotional content. There is beauty in the madness. They go at each other again in an episode of the less compelling "Skip the Gutter." Hines contributes a fanciful backup to Armstrong's vocal on "St. James Infirmary," and plays celeste on the oracular "Basin Street Blues"—a dramatic vignette in which the trumpet emerges *pp* from the hushed ensemble, attains full bloom, and then disappears in favor of a scat vocal that goes deeper than the song's words ever could.

Don Redman, a colleague from the Henderson band, appears on several selections as instrumentalist and composer. His famous "Save It Pretty Mama" offers superb Hines and an Armstrong-style Redman sax

Louis Armstrong and His Stompers at the Sunset Cafe. Left to right: Earl Hines, Pete Briggs, Honore Dutrey, Armstrong, Bill Wilson, Tubby Hall, Arthur "Rip" Bassett, Boyd Atkins, Joe Walker, Al Washington, Willard Hamley, Chicago, 1927.

LOUIS ARMSTRONG

Direction
JOE GLASER, Inc.
R K O Building Rockefeller Center
New York, N.Y.

solo. "Heah Me Talkin' to Ya?" has supple work by all three, though
Armstrong is surprisingly tranquil. Alex Hill's imaginative arrangement
of "Beau Koo Jack" features Armstrong's whiplash trumpet breaks. "Tight
Like That" is the masterpiece of their work together, engendering one
of Louis's most expansive and scrupulous improvisations. The prelude,
incorporating risqué vaudeville nonsense, kicks into Armstrong's smoky
rendering of the theme and Hines's variations on it. At his return, the
trumpeter begins the first of three architectonic choruses with a solemn
scene-setting motif (E natural to B natural), played five times. His two
subsequent choruses also turn on sturdy motifs (including a naughty
ditty from World War I), each opening at a higher interval, so that all
three build cumulatively in range and fervor. The inspiration may be
sexual, but the music erects a cathedral of the spirit.

"Tight Like That" manages to be cagey and direct, spare and effusive,
vaulting and crude, high and low. In this three-minute spectacle, the
entertainer and the artist are inseparable, and bound for trouble among
the puritans. What manner of artist spices his performance with rude
jokes about pleasures of the flesh? What sort of entertainer can so
forthrightly convey the acute sadness of the human comedy? Setting up
the final payoff, Armstrong interpolates an adolescent jingle ("Oh, the
girls in France . . .") and then makes of that very phrase the stuff of
great passion. Still, in 1928 Armstrong the entertainer was invariably
at the disposal of Armstrong the artist. What would happen if the
ebullience behind the artistry were to find shape in sheer personality,
unleashed and unfettered?

The ARTIST As ENTERTAINER

O N E

His brethren could not readily forgive this power of pleasing which, strictly speaking, is a gift. . . . Make no mistake: this is a delightful kind of fame, the secret envy of many of those great purists, who can only warm their hands at the somewhat pallid flame of the approbation of the elect.

—*Claude Debussy*

ebussy, writing as Monsieur Croche, was paying homage to a far less innovative musician than Armstrong, Jules Massenet. He admitted that a gift for pleasing "young milliners" was hardly indispensable to art and acknowledged the inhibiting effect of Massenet's fertility. Yet Massenet "was the most truly loved of all contemporary musicians," not because his operas condescended to the public, but because they spoke directly to it—a fact not lost on those who envied his unstoppable success. "To endeavor to overthrow those whom they imitate is the first principle of wisdom with certain artists," Debussy continued, noting that the true artist struggles less with his colleagues than with himself. Like Massenet, Armstrong troubled a core group of his admirers by remaining true to himself rather than to them. He took jazz away from purists, who, it must be said, took an exceedingly long time to claim it but no time at all to promulgate rigid definitions as to its substance, and gave it to the young milliners and anyone else who wanted it.

Armstrong shrugged off the idea that jazz was the private domain of blacks (he was an early supporter of white musicians and led, with Joe Glaser's managerial support, a mixed band, even when it cost him work) or Americans. Urged by the commentator on a 1960 TV show to confirm the common observation that European jazzmen copied Americans, he snapped, "We don't look at it that way. . . . How do we know who copied what?" He understood, as many didn't, that the strength of jazz lay in its international appeal and that chauvinistic hauteur implied constraints that were bad for business and for his musical message. By 1960 he was quick to insist that he was an "ambassador" of music only and had nothing to do with politics. Yet his insistence on the universality of jazz was indisputably political, and he put it over with a litany of indisputable maxims. "A note's a note in any language." "Jazz will give

The King and his subjects at a jam session at the Paramount Theater, 1938. Left to right: Tommy Dorsey, Bud Freeman, Pops Foster, Armstrong, Eddie Condon, Henry "Red" Allen, George Wettling. (*facing page*)

Always ready for an interview, England c. 1959.

Johnny Collins
presents
The International Star
Louis Armstrong
World's Greatest Trumpet

Gibson
CHICAGO

you beautiful ideas, make you feel good." "As long as it sounds good, we don't care who wrote it." "The best band in the world is the clowns' band in the circus. You gotta be a good musician to hit a bad note at the right time." "I like trumpet players who play what they feel. If they want a high note, get it over with." "Styles don't faze me." "People love me and my music, and you know I love them. The minute I walk on the bandstand, they know they're going to get something good. I see to that."

Publicity, 1931.

Sometimes he responded to interviewers who tried to feed him their own prejudices with the patience of a schoolmarm; sometimes he acquiesced and switched to a lighter subject. At his best, he parried them with wit, as in a 1960 radio interview with British journalists in Kenya. He was questioned about his vices. "I do all the things that you do." About the Noël Coward-like beauty of his song "Someday." "Can't you name somebody a little lesser than Noël?" About rock 'n' roll. "Oh, that's our church music." About modern jazz. "They make a thousand notes to get around the one." About his appeal to the young. "Yes, I'm young myself." About his hectic schedule. "I never felt yet that I didn't want to get on that stand." About his popularity in Africa. "Always have been Africans all over New Orleans." About an East African song in his repertory. "We like everything we play." About how high he could go. "Well, I can get up to p." About the duke of Windsor's statement "I'd rather hear Louis Armstrong play 'Tiger Rag' than wander into Westminster Abbey and find the lost chord." "I agree with that."

Those jazz purists who had long since decided Armstrong's place in an arcane schema of the true and false jazz were not amused. In 1946, B. H. Haggin, the bullheaded but sensible music critic for *The Nation*, devoted a column to what he called the "falsifying schematization" of jazz, specifically as played by Armstrong. A correspondent had written to argue that any critic who failed to distinguish between Armstrong's music of 1925 and his "obviously different music" of 1928 was promoting "hopeless confusion," to which Haggin responded, "The same thing is gained by calling a Hot Five and a Savoy Ballroom Five both jazz as is gained by calling a work of Mozart and a work of Beethoven both symphony; and confusion is created by giving them two names." By then, Armstrong was very likely the most famous musician in the world and was frequently cited with Charlie Chaplin as the most famous of Americans.

The Armstrong-Hines recordings of 1928 had marked the end of that phase in Armstrong's career when he could confine himself to the province of jazz per se. No longer would a coterie of rapt fans have him to themselves. By 1929, business at the Savoy in Chicago was slow and payments were late. Tommy Rockwell of Okeh Records wired Armstrong to return to New York, offering him work and management. Armstrong showed the wire to Carroll Dickerson, Zutty Singleton, and the others, and they all thought the band was too good to break up. They were living together in a Chicago flat, preparing their own meals, playing poker and blackjack, shooting craps, and being "good sports about it." As Armstrong later wrote Goffin, "I was one guy who always stuck with a bunch of fellows, especially if I liked them." When Rockwell sent a second wire, Armstrong called a meeting of the band.

> I told them, well fellows, you all know how well I love you all, and you boys love me too. What say if we have our cars fixed up and Mr. Rockwell has just sent me enough money and I can give each man in the band $20 to eat off of and help buy gas, and we'll all go to New York together? They all jumped up into the air with joy and said that's great. . . . We were popular all through the towns we passed through—Toledo, Ohio, Cleveland, Detroit, Buffalo. We went 40 miles out of our way to see Niagara Falls, etc., and everyone was so glad to see us. They all had been hearing our broadcasts from the Savoy Ballroom in Chicago the whole time we were there. . . . Zutty and I were riding in my car. In fact Zutty did pretty near all the driving. I did most of the sleeping . . . and when Zutty arrived in New York, the minute we were crossing 42nd and Broadway my radiator cap blew off and steam was going every place—and were we embarrassed. The cops came over and saw we had Chicago license on our car, and asked us, "Hey there, have you boys any shotguns in that car?" We gladly said, "No suh boss." He smiled and went away. . . . We all finally arrived in Harlem, everybody suffering with the shorts, meaning we were all broke. So I immediately went downtown to Mr. Rockwell's office. He certainly was glad to see me. He said, "Louie" I've just arranged to put you in the *Great Day* show. I said, Oh fine Mr. Rockwell, but, er, wer—I brought my band with me and you'll have to book us someplace. Mr. Rockwell hit the ceiling saying, "Band?

I did not send for your band, I sent for you only." I said (very calmly), Just the same Mr. Rockwell, we're here now, I just couldn't leave my boys that's all. I know you can book us someplace. Another thing, we all need money so you'll have to let me have about _____ dollars to keep up eating, room rent, and our laundry until we go to work. After all, they must hold their heads up, and stay sharp because they're all sharp cats and can play their asses off. Finally Mr. Rockwell gave in and gave me all the money I wanted and inside of two weeks we had a job in Connie's Inn in Harlem, at 131st + 7th Ave. That club and the Cotton Club were the hottest clubs in Harlem at that time—and Harlem was really jumping. All the white people would think it was a real treat to spend a night up in Harlem. *(Goffin)*

The incident with the cops and the showdown with Rockwell indicate Armstrong's willingness to play the game when called for and to stand his ground when necessary. His intransigence was as much respected among musicians as his loyalty. One reason he was eventually able to effect what he considered an ideal business partnership and marriage is that he found equally strong and loyal people, in Joe Glaser and Lucille Wilson, who knew where he drew the line, and respected it. As it turned out, he was lucky to have the band, since he wasn't given a part in *Great Day*, which was a flop anyway. The floor show at Connie's, however, had a score by Fats Waller that attracted enough notice to warrant a shot at Broadway, where it ran 219 performances as *Hot Chocolates*. One of the highlights was Armstrong's rendition of "Ain't Misbehavin'," performed at first from the pit and later onstage. After the show, he'd race back to Connie's Inn in Harlem—"My band really used to play the hell out of Connie's show"—where he'd bring the house down with his backing of Louise Cook's erotic shakedance and lead off the dance set with "Indian Cradle Song." One night the leading white musicians came uptown to Connie's and threw a party for Louis. Bandleader Ben Pollack presented him with a gold watch inscribed, "Good luck always to Louis Armstrong from The Musicians on Broadway."

Of course Louis had had the attention of white jazz players since the time he arrived in Chicago, and as soon as he returned to New York, Eddie Condon convinced Rockwell to let him produce an integrated

The loutish manager Johnny Collins never appreciated what he had in Louis Armstrong, 1931. *(page 108, top)*

Louis conquers Europe, 1933. *(page 108, bottom)*

The heir to Oliver's throne in Chicago, 1931. *(page 109, top)*

Looking sharp. Louis in the early 1930s. *(page 109, bottom)*

Louis ARMSTRONG

Limbering up, 1930s.

record date. At 8 A.M. the next morning, Louis was in a recording studio for the first time since "Tight Like That," three months earlier, fronting a mixed band including the marvelous trombonist Jack Teagarden. They recorded a blues jam, "Knockin' a Jug," which Armstrong dominated as effortlessly as he had "Muggles." That same afternoon he fronted Luis Russell's nine-piece band, with Condon and Lonnie Johnson sitting in, and recorded two landmark sides. "Mahogany Hall Stomp," named after Lulu White's Storyville establishment, captures the New Orleans spirit and offers a vivid glimpse of Armstrong the structuralist: The first of his three muted choruses consists of short electric, rhythmically displaced phrases; the second is one full-moon note held for ten measures; and the last is a five-note riff played six times. The solo, so simple and so effective, became a standard part of the piece whenever he played it. The other number put Armstrong on a new course: "I Can't Give You Anything But Love" was his first pop song in the company of an ensemble (Armstrong's admiration for Guy Lombardo's buttery reeds is much in evidence) that did little more than parade the chords as a scrim, leaving him free to distort, kid, and ultimately alchemize the material. Again, his improvisation became a classic in its own right—Ethel Waters sang it verbatim on her recording of the song.

A new Louis Armstrong seemed to be taking over from the old. To some degree, the newness was an illusion. Armstrong had been playing with big bands throughout his years in Chicago. With Erskine Tate's "symphony" he had enjoyed a taste of stardom and a repertory that ranged from movie accompaniments to pop songs to operatic showstoppers. But now he was out of the pit and on the stage. Now he was sharing the domain of Bert Williams and Bill Robinson. He was looking the audience in the eye when he sang, dramatizing the song, making it come alive as a vehicle for the fun and games of his incomparable extemporizations. His utterly original way of putting over a song—of selling it, of keeping the audience enchanted with it—was as instinctive and ingenious as any other aspect of his achievement. He figured out how to make his music part of a larger presentation, the Louis Armstrong Show. Like Bojangles, he offered a unique and prodigious talent; like him, too, he presented that talent as one aspect of a giant, all-encompassing personality that could absorb all the light in the room and shine it right back at the audience. "The minute I walk on the bandstand, they know they're going to get something good. *I see to that.*"

Louis Armstrong never aspired to be a studied virtuoso, who walks to center stage, bows, plays God's music, bows again, and leaves. He demanded a reaction whether he played for dancers or listeners. He thrived on the roar of the crowd, and like a great preacher or blues singer, he knew how to elicit the whoops and cries and moans of pleasure. In 1933, he was filmed in Denmark in a stunningly effective presentation that parodies the "correct" performer. "Good evening, ladies and gentlemen," he says, bowing. "I'm Mr. Armstrong." The glint in his eye is mischievous and dauntless: This guy is *in charge.* He counts off the tempo and transforms "Dinah," a cheap ditty, into a miraculous rhapsody in which his every physical movement—the facial mugging, the savvy footwork, and angle of his trumpet—complements the galvanizing irreverence of his music. "There are no bad songs," he once told an interviewer, much as Van Gogh might have said there are no bad colors. Armstrong was no longer one of the boys in the band: He was a musician, singer, bandleader, comic, dancer, actor. That unique radiance heard in "Potato Head Blues" now coursed through the man himself.

The Bobby Jones of jazz, 1930s.

During the performance of "Dinah," he extends a phrase in the song's release with a descending scat arpeggio, delivered with a funny bug-eyed expression that is exactly right for the musical content of the phrase. This is known as mugging, a comic art that Armstrong perfected with a skill equal to Jack Benny's deadpan or Oliver Hardy's slow burn or Cary Grant's second take. Armstrong's mugging is so much a part of his vocal performances that it is impossible for anyone who has seen him to listen to his records without imagining his facial contortions. Even when he delivered himself of a ballad, he had an array of expressions— half smiles, a trembling of the lips, a widening of the eyes, a scrunching of the nose—that fit the notes and underscored the lyric. Mugging was a kind of body English done with the face; it was a way of acting out the music. No one else ever did it as well, and soon no one else did it at all. He was constantly under attack for mugging: The barbs were ludicrous (he demeaned his art by clowning) and patronizing (he was playing the role of an Uncle Tom). During his initial visit to England, in 1932, he was described as "barbaric" by one intellectual, who admired his music but didn't think lay persons were ready for the shock of seeing him in the flesh. Indeed, he was pelted with tomatoes at one concert. In his astute account of that tour, Chris Goddard observed that Armstrong "shattered all those restricting elements which European musical attitudes

had grafted on to jazz in order to ensure its status as 'Art.' " Of course the sensibilities of the masses were largely won over by then, at least in the United States, though intellectuals on both sides of the Atlantic would continue to stew.

T W O

Paris, 1934.

The recording Armstrong made of "Ain't Misbehavin' " at his second session in the summer of 1929 was a hit that confirmed his burgeoning popularity as well as the use of pop songs as standard source material for jazz interpretation. Along with his other records in that period, it helped set the stage for the popular acceptance of jazz that would follow six years later, after Benny Goodman's triumphant tour of 1935. For the next seventeen years, Armstrong would be heard almost exclusively with big bands. His voice mellowed in the thirties, proving to be far more lithe and pleasing than anyone expected. It matured into a handsome tenor, full of feeling and humor, offering irresistible contrast to the ever increasing brilliance of his instrumental technique. But to many it conveyed an abstruse language of grunts and moans. Even as late as 1936, in his introduction to Armstrong's book *Swing That Music*, Rudy Vallee—whose voice was considered normal—felt obliged to defend the musicality of Armstrong's vocals: "They often seem to be the result of a chaotic, disorganized mind struggling to express itself, but those who know anything about modern music recognize his perfect command of time spacing, of rhythm, harmony, and pitch and his flawless understanding of the effects he is striving to achieve."

Armstrong's recording of Waller's "Black and Blue," abetted by a sympathetic trombone and reeds that swoon in commiseration, was invoked by Ralph Ellison in the prologue of *Invisible Man*, to send his hero into a sanctified reverie. Dan Morgenstern has pointed out that the song was originally conceived as the lament of a dark-skinned woman who loses her man to a lighter rival: Not until Louis removed the verse and sang it with "such dignity and passion" did it become "the 'protest' song which from then on it was considered to always have been." Armstrong's two versions of "When You're Smiling," one with a vocal and one without, show the influence of B. A. Rolfe, a classical trumpet player who prompted him to phrase an octave above the orchestra. Both versions close with rapturous high-note choruses, pure distillations of

Armstrong endorses Selmer trumpets. 1930s, (*facing page*)

Armstrong fronting the Luis Russell band on the night in New Orleans when the white announcer refused to announce him. Left to right: George James, Charles Alexander, Lester Boone, Al Washington, Armstrong, Tubby Hall (drums), Mike McKendrick (banjo), Zilner Randolph, John Lindsey (bass), Preston Jackson. (*overleaf*)

"Memories of You": Lionel Hampton and Armstrong, Culver City, 1930.

melody, from which a listener would be hard put to imagine the physical drama that accompanied such music in concert. Fortunately, we have Irving Kolodin's eyewitness account of 1933:

> He announces "When You're Smiling" and this time he has a new act. He backs off, downstage left, leans half-way over like a quartermiler, begins to count, (swaying as he does) "one, two, three" . . . he has already started racing toward the rear where the orchestra is ranged, and he hits four, executes a slide and a pirouette; winds up facing the audience and blowing the first note as the orchestra swings into the tune. It's mad, it's meaningless, it's hokum of the first order, but the effect is electrifying. No shabby pretenses about this boy! He knows what his audience will take to their hearts, and how he gives it to them. His trumpet virtuosity is endless—triplets, chromatic accented eerie counterpoints that turn the tune inside out, wild sorties into the giddy stratosphere where his tone sounds like a dozen flutes in unison, all executed with impeccable style and finish, exploits that make his contemporaries sound like so many Salvation Army cornetists. Alternately singing choruses and daubing with the handkerchief at throat, face, forehead (he perspires like a dying gladiator) the while a diamond bracelet twinkles from his wrist, he finally gets off the stage to rest.

In 1930, Armstrong made his first trip to California, where he was booked into Frank Sebastian's Cotton Club in Culver City. By that time Tommy Rockwell had been promoting him as a single, which meant a final break with Carroll Dickerson and the men from Chicago. Armstrong later complained that the breakup was fueled when members of the band started arriving late for the engagement at Connie's Inn. For one reason or another, management fired him. But he must have realized, too, that he could no longer shoulder the responsibility for keeping an orchestra working, and he acquiesced when Rockwell convinced him to front other bands. The band Leon Elkins led at Sebastian's Cotton Club included trombonist Lawrence Brown, later a major figure in the Ellington orchestra, and drummer Lionel Hampton, who, Armstrong recalled, played "some little bells which he kept besides his drums, and he was swinging the hell out of them too." About two months into the seven-month gig, a better band was brought in, directed by Les Hite. Artistically, it was another fertile season. He made his first movie, playing incidental music in an obscure feature film called *Ex-Flame,* which no longer seems to exist. Through radio, he quickly became a favorite of the Hollywood community, which soon packed the club. He made astonishing records.

His first record in California was his last as a "sideman," and a ringer in his discography: Country singer Jimmie Rodgers's "Blue Yodel No. 9," to which he added aggressive obbligato. The sessions with Elkins produced the razzle-dazzle "I'm a Ding Dong Daddy," in which Louis scats enthusiastically ("I done forgot the words," he explains mid-break) and plays a piping climax that coined the phrase Dizzy Gillespie later reset as "Salt Peanuts." The Hite sessions closed with a grandstanding rival in "Shine," which Armstrong made into a tour de force of self-avowal despite a lyric that embodies racial condescension. In his posthumously published comments on "Shine," Otis Ferguson credited it with "a point and rage and loveliness that have nothing to do with the original intention or the auspices under which it was carried out."

Louis made his first great Los Angeles records with the Les Hite band, 1930. Lionel Hampton kneels in the middle.

After a thousand hearings, he noted, "it is still true and good, moving a person to sadness, pride, etc."

Between those monuments of virtuoso transfiguration, he recorded some of his most enduring ballad performances. "I'm Confessin' " suggests that his immense influence on Bing Crosby was reciprocated. (Armstrong could be a sly parodist. As John Chilton has pointed out, a touch of Al Jolson is heard in "My Sweet," recorded earlier in 1930.) "Body and Soul," which Louis introduced to the jazz repertory, and "If I Could Be with You" are completely refurbished: The soupy saxes and static rhythms spur Armstrong to ever more outlandish conceits. "Sweethearts on Parade" is more remarkable, since the song is trash—his vocal inflections, including sighs and grunts that trail away from the actual words like shadows, are as expressive as his keening trumpet invention, complete with extrovert breaks that quote "High Society" and reveille. (Lucille Armstrong told me he used to say, "Don't listen to the tune I'm playing, listen to the notes I'm playing.") For "Memories of You," Armstrong pulled a vibraphone from a corner of the studio and persuaded Hampton to record his first solo on the instrument.

Still, the trip to California ended in calamity. Every day Louis drove for thirty minutes or so from his room in Los Angeles to the club in Culver City. After work and during intermission, he would occasionally repair to his car to get high on pot. One night he was sharing a joint with Vic Berton, a white drummer who recorded with Red Nichols and others, and the cops busted them. They spent the night in jail and the next morning were sentenced to six months and a thousand dollars each. Rockwell sent a shady character named Johnny Collins out to California to fix the case; the sentences were suspended, though Armstrong and Berton had to stay in the jail hospital weekday nights for a while. Armstrong never forgot the lesson and publicly declared he would never smoke again. His protestations were considered hilarious in jazz circles, because Armstrong was a lifelong connoisseur of marijuana. I interviewed more than a dozen musicians who said Armstrong introduced them to it. Most of them shook their heads with laughter at how much he loved rolling cigar-size joints after leaving the bandstand. It wasn't just a recreational substance to him but a nostrum on the order of his favorite physic, Swiss Kriss. He swore by it and proselytized for it—even wrote a letter to Eisenhower asking him to make it legal.

At a time when indiscriminate use of physically addictive drugs is ravaging the country, marijuana is once again vilified as part of the

Irony compounds itself: When this picture was taken, Louis was married to his second wife, Lil; it's inscribed to his third wife, Alpha; the boat bears the name of his fourth wife, Lucille. c. 1931. (*facing page, top left*)

Louis and Alpha Smith, early 1930s. (*facing page, top right*)

Louis and Alpha in England, 1934. (*facing page, bottom left*)

Louis took Alpha with him to Europe in 1934. They later married. (*facing page, bottom right*)

scourge. I don't want to imply anything heroic in Armstrong's appetite for it, but it was an important part of his life, and some find a direct link between it and his live-and-let-live temperament. He started smoking soon after he arrived in Chicago and used one of his nicknames for it as the title of an early masterpiece, "Muggles." Usually, he called it gage. He was in all other respects relatively health conscious. He drank in moderation (never before a gig) and smoked Camels, but watched his diet, never used hard drugs, never popped pills. Each day was planned around the job, and he kept himself in shape for it. After, though, in

Down South, 1940.

his usually mobbed dressing room or on the bus, he would use pot to unwind. In the sixties, an interviewer asked him how he felt about the likelihood that marijuana would be made legal. He said, "That won't help the poor cats they put in jail."

Other troubles brewed in California. Lil came out to see him, and he discovered she was having an affair with a man she said was her masseur. Alpha followed shortly after, and Louis was now determined to get a divorce. Worse, Collins convinced him that he had cut a deal with Rockwell and was now his manager. En route to New York, Armstrong was booked by Collins in a club in Chicago called the Showboat. The band, which included Zilner Randolph, Charlie Alexander, Preston Jackson, Tubby Hall, Lester Boone, and John Lindsey, was one of his favorites: "Now there's a band that really deserved a whole lot of credit that they didn't get. They made some of my finest recordings with me." Several well-known bandleaders came down to honor "Louie Armstrong—all white folks call me Louie." Everything seemed to be going fine, until he realized he was caught in the middle of a managerial war with mob overtones.

The prodigal son returns to the Waif's Home: Captain Joseph Jones and Louis Armstrong, 1931. (*facing page*)

Nothing made Armstrong prouder than having his own ball team. Unfortunately, the Secret 9 were afraid to tarnish their beloved uniforms. Joe Lindsey and Sherman Cooke stand to Louis's left. 1931. (*overleaf*)

Funny thing how I did not know that Johnny Collins and Rockwell were having [a] feud over my contract. Why and for what I've never found out till this day. All I know is whoever were the gang in New York sent gangsters to Chicago where I was working and tried their damndest to frighten me into quitting the job and come to New York to open up back at Connie's Inn again. And I felt that as dirty as Connie fired me and my band, I did not want any parts of those people ever again. I am just that way. If you kick my ass once you can bet I won't go back if I can help it so you can kick it again. And Connie's Inn was going down by degrees, and at that time I was the rage of the nation. But nay nay, never no Connie's Inn. One night the gangsters started a fight in the Showboat in Chicago, right in front of where I was standing playing my trumpet. I usually stood playing with my eyes closed [leaning against a post] down on the dance floor. I mean they were really fighting worse than a bunch of spades. One of the gangsters took a chair and hit a woman over the head with it and the chair crumpled up all in a lot of little pieces. Some of the pieces hit my horn but even *that* could not make me leave the bandstand, you know? The

ARMSTR
BASE
OF Ne

NG'S SECRET "9"
BALL TEAM
N ORLEANS, LA.
1931

PARTY IN HONOR OF
DUKE ELLINGTON AND LOUIS ARMSTRONG
AT TONY'S TAVERN - 52 W - 31ST STREET
FEB. 14, 1935 - CHICAGO, ILL.

Captain must go down with the ship. Then, too, things like that never frighten me. I've seen too much of that bullshit during my days of playing music. Ain't but one incident at the Showboat that kind of got me, and it happened one night as we were just playing and the people were all dancing and having a ball. Our dressing room was also located on the same side of the bandstand. A pretty large one at that. I usually blow my trumpet with both of my eyes closed and as I was blowing, I felt someone touching me very quietly, speaking in a whisper. It was a big burly-looking gangster saying, "Somebody wants you in the dressing room." I said, "Sure, I'll go in as soon as I finish this dance set." And I didn't pay any attention to it. So after the set was over, I ran real lickety split to my dressing room to see who it was. I rushed to the door thinking it was one of the cats, and there, bless my lamb, who I did see was a white guy with a beard on his face thicker than one of those boys from the House of David. So he spoke first—"Hello" (kind of sarcastically). I still ain't hep to the jive. I said, "Hello" (very pleasantly). He said, "Do you know who I am?" I said, "Why, er, no, no I don't." In fact it really didn't matter as long as he talked about music. I just knew he and I were going to really run our mouths a while musically. Then this guy said, "I am Frankie Foster." At first I still didn't pay any attention—to that extent anyway. Then it dawned on me what he said and I turned in cold sweats. . . . By this time he had his big pistol, pulling it out as he said, "My name is Frankie Foster," and he said he was sent over to my place to see that I catch the first train out to New York. I still try to make it appear that he ain't frightening me. I said, "New York? Why that's news to me. Mr. Collins didn't tell me anything about it." Frankie Foster said, "Oh yes, you're going to New York at Connie's Inn, and you're leaving tomorrow morning." Then he flashed his big ol' pistol and aimed it straight at me. With my eyes as big as saucers and frightened too, I said, "Well, maybe I *am* going to New York." Ooh God. Then Frankie Foster said, "Ok. The telephone receiver is down waiting for you to come and say you'll be there. Now you and me are going to the telephone booth and you'll talk." By this time anything he ordered of me was alright, because it is no trouble for a gangster to pull the trigger, especially when they have you cornered and you disobey them. Soooo we went to the phone with a gun in my side and sure enough someone said hello, a familiar voice too. Yes sir, I know that voice if I hear it a hundred years from now. The first words he said to me was, "When are [you] gonna open here?" I turned and looked direct into Frankie Foster's face and said, "Tomorrow. A.M." (*Goffin*)

In 1934, Armstrong kept his promise of 1931 to return to New Orleans to play exclusively at a black dance hall.

Armstrong never revealed whose voice he heard on the phone; it may have been Rockwell or Connie Immerman or their gangland sponsor, Owney Madden, who had a distinctive voice and was alive and well long after Armstrong wrote Goffin. In any case, Louis had humored the thugs, but he had no intention of going to New York. Collins managed to sneak him out to Louisville on the eve of the Kentucky Derby, where—even on the run—he managed to make history by leading the first black band ever to play the Roof Garden of the Kentucky Hotel. From there, the band toured the Midwest and the South, including Armstrong's first return to New Orleans, where he played Suburban Gardens—a white nightclub in Jefferson Parish—for three months, visited the Waif's Home, and presided over a baseball team named after him. The boys were so proud of the uniforms, emblazoned with the name *Armstrong,* and so nervous about tarnishing them, that their playing suffered—much to the horror of the team's sponsor. The visit itself was tarnished on the night he opened at Suburban Gardens, when a radio announcer said, "I haven't the heart to announce the nigger on the radio." With the quick-wittedness that made him legendary, Armstrong asked the band for a chord, calmly took the microphone in hand, and did his own introductions. Similarly, when his appearance before a black audience was cancelled without reason, he made sure the black community got word of his promise to make a secret trip to New Orleans to play only for blacks—a vow he kept in 1935, when he slipped into town to play a black dance hall called the Golden Dragon, and was gone before the press ever knew about it.

In the fall of 1931, the band passed through Chicago again, to record. Although Armstrong avoided playing New York and Chicago for most of the next four years, his discography does not indicate much of a disruption in his career because the records he made that year were, as he said, among his best. "Sleepytime Down South" would soon become his theme song. "(I'll Be Glad When You're Dead) You Rascal You" also became an Armstrong trademark, especially after it was reprised the following year in a Betty Boop cartoon in which his disembodied head wails it at a fleeing white figure. Armstrong said that at a 1932 concert in England, he dedicated it to George V with the words, "This one's for you, Rex." It's a motley group we hear on those Chicago sessions, a comedown from the spit-and-polish band on the West Coast, but Louis is a blithe spirit, whether he's crooning "When Your Lover Has Gone" or scaling peak after peak on "Chinatown," the latter a vaudeville tune that—like so much other unlikely material—would become a jazz standard after Louis showed everyone how to make it work. His glissando-break on "Lazy River," following a whirlwind double-time vocal, is so precipitous that skeptical musicians accused him of using a slide trumpet.

His variations on "Between the Devil and the Deep Blue Sea" are neat and modern, as economical as the earlier "Mahogany Hall Stomp": He shapes the first sixteen bars with winding, asymmetrical phrases; uses two sustained high notes for the release; parades a riff to finish the chorus. "Blue Again," with its impeccable phrasing and weighted momentum, is the record Gil Evans said inspired him to become a musician. "I Surrender, Dear," which Rudy Vallee called his "recorded masterpiece," is one of the grandest examples of his vocal art, a glossary of expressive tricks. (You can project Louis Prima's whole career from this performance.) Perhaps the definitive vocal from these sessions is "All of Me," yet another jazz standard introduced by Armstrong— according to Whitburn's statistics, it would have been number 1 in February 1932. It's a sublime demonstration of a style that gives the illusion of self-accompaniment. His interpolations, wordless or not (he gets the same mileage from "mmmf" as he does from "oh baby"), extend and answer the vocal line encompassed by the lyrics proper.

When he returned to New York, Armstrong was hit with a lawsuit by Rockwell and Immerman. He countersued, and when an offer came to tour England for the first time, he and Collins jumped at it. Though Armstrong wasn't universally adored on that first venture abroad, the trip was as much a revelation to him as it was to English jazz musicians. Surely he saw his potential for conquering the international arena. Yet his career remained blighted for another two years as his legal predicament obscured his increasing mastery of the stage. Prohibition had come to an end and, with it, some of the control the gangsters exercised over the lives of musicians who worked their gin mills. Still, they continued to turn up the pressure. Louis returned to New York to briefly appear

Marian Anderson sits next to Louis at a gathering in Stockholm in the early 1930s.

in another Connie Immerman show, *Hot Chocolates of 1932*, and cut a new series of records for Victor, his first label affiliation since Okeh.

The backup bands, though often stiff and encumbered by poor arrangements, included some of the young lions who, having built on Armstrong's foundation, would help to bring the swing era into flower: drummers Chick Webb and Sid Catlett, tenor saxophonist Budd Johnson, pianist Teddy Wilson, and, ironically, an altoist named Louis Jordan, who would challenge Armstrong's preeminence among blacks twenty years later as the leading light of rhythm and blues. The records are uneven, and Louis sometimes seems to strain to compensate for the material. Yet even by the standards he'd already set, and despite his troubled private life and the fitfulness of the band, "I Gotta Right to Sing the Blues" suggested a new peak in his ability to transform a pop song into a far deeper experience. Of course, Harold Arlen's song had a life of its own: No one but Armstrong could have made "That's My Home" or "He's a Son of the South" a compelling experience. A new version of "Basin Street Blues," though it lacked the mystery of the original, dazzled with its offhanded bravura, and the incomparable "Laughin' Louie" confirmed the unpredictability and taste for paradox of a man who was down but a long way from out.

He was soon touring again, returning to Europe the following summer for a long stay—first London, then Scandinavia (a crowd of ten thousand greeted him at the railway station in Denmark), Holland, Belgium, Paris (where he spent a long vacation), Italy, and Switzerland. Early in the tour he broke with Collins, whose heavy drinking, incompetence, and rudeness to the artist he was bleeding had become intolerable. Armstrong remained a wanderer, though. Except for a single session in Paris (which produced the two-part "Sunny Side of the Street," an instrumental ode to pot called "Song of the Vipers," and the pyrotechnics of "Super Tiger Rag"), two and a half years would pass before he made another record.

T H R E E

Louis Armstrong's professional and private lives were at ebb tide when he returned to the United States in 1935. His lip had become infected in Paris and a doctor told him not to play for six months. Collins was suing him for breach of contract. Lil was pressing for divorce, and Alpha, for marriage. He returned to Chicago and renewed his friendship with Joe Glaser, the tough-talking erstwhile manager of the old Sunset Cafe, who was also down on his luck. They formed a partnership that became the most important professional relationship in both of their lives. They didn't socialize much, but they talked on the phone incessantly, and a kind of love developed between them.

Armstrong's devotion to Glaser galled many of his admirers, who were put off by Glaser's crude manners and strong-arm business tactics. He was apparently connected to the mob, at least in his early years, and was rumored to have been involved in a murder. He made himself a millionaire through Armstrong, but then he made Armstrong a millionaire too. The most frequent criticism of him is that he worked Armstrong and his band too hard, though it's difficult to imagine Louis *not* wanting to work. Even when he was dying, he made notes to himself about returning to the road. It's certainly true, however, that as late as the "Hello Dolly" years, Armstrong was playing zigzag one-nighters, traveling in a bus that had no heat (the stylish pianist Billy Kyle is said to have died from pneumonia because of one of those tours). Sallie Young, Trummy Young's widow, recalls that since Louis never complained, the younger musicians didn't feel they had the right to, either. On the other hand, Glaser was probably the only man who could have extricated Armstrong from his managerial war and pushed him to the unprecedented prominence he would soon enjoy. Glaser was notorious for signing potential Armstrong rivals and putting a freeze on their careers. Louis always came first. Jack Bradley recalls that the one time he made a disparaging remark about Glaser in Louis's presence, he was brought to tears by Armstrong's nonstop barrage of curses. He later explained to Bradley, "First there's music, then there's Mr. Glaser, then Lucille."

There is much speculation about how much of Armstrong's earnings Glaser took. Lucille said it was 50 percent, but pointed out that Louis wanted for nothing. Glaser provided the ideal kind of management for him, leaving him free to concentrate on music. He didn't have to worry about taxes, bank accounts, checkbooks, contracts, the hiring or firing of musicians, or anything else but playing. In collusion with Lucille, Glaser once prepared to surprise Louis with an estate on Long Island, but he refused to move from Corona. He said he liked the neighborhood and the people. He insisted on having two wads of paper money in his pocket every night after the show. One was his, and the other was to dole out to people who lined up for handouts. At an engagement in Los Angeles, an old connection from the Cotton Club days told him

Arrival in Hawaii—"Aloha, Louie Armstrong," 1952.

he was working as a driver but his car was in the shop and he couldn't pay the bill. Armstrong bought him a limousine. Glaser hit the roof, but he paid for it. It has been argued that Armstrong's insistence on calling him Mr. Glaser when a third party was present indicated some sort of servility. No one says that of Duke Snider, who throughout his autobiography refers to Mr. Rickey. Armstrong was proud of his association with Glaser. When the two disagreed and Louis was adamant, Glaser backed off. A running argument between them concerned pot. According to Jack Bradley, "Glaser would scream and Louis would say, 'Fuck you.'"

Glaser may have reminded Armstrong of the no-nonsense bosses he had known and admired in his honky-tonk days, not to mention the Karmofsky family. Pianist Barbara Carroll, whose husband, Burt Block, worked for Glaser for fifteen years, describes him as "very opinionated, very quick to anger, very amusing, though he didn't know he was amusing, and very generous in certain ways. He had tremendous affection for Louis and did whatever he thought would further his career, and from Louis's point of view, what could have been better? He took care of whatever made Louis happy, he was there for him." Something of an

Joe Glaser accompanied Louis and
Trummy Young to Hawaii, 1952.

Times Square, New York, 1938.
(overleaf)

eccentric, he kept salamis hanging on the walls of his apartment, drying out, and if he liked you he'd give you one. He was famously crude: He'd order a bowl of peanuts in a posh club and flick the shells on the floor. He employed few men, but his Associated Booking Corp. handled everyone, including Duke Ellington, Dinah Washington, and Billie Holiday. "He was very concerned about Billie," Carroll recalls, "but Louis was his baby." The publicity books he prepared for Louis were fifty-page "manuals" that advise how and in what size typeface he should be billed. The 1949 edition suggests: "Louis 'Satchmo' Armstrong, world's highest paid colored musician, trumpet player extraordinary and now acclaimed as the international 'Trumpet King of Swing.' "

In a letter to attorney William Hassan, in 1961, Glaser boasts—in a record-breaking run-on—of having brought Louis to Chicago from New Orleans, "when King Oliver was working for me in one of my places and told me to bring up this sensational young trumpet player who he said was even better than King Oliver and of course history shows that Louis Armstrong did prove to be greater and attained greater stardom than King Oliver within a few years." Glaser had little to do with Armstrong's career before 1935, but—according to Armstrong's ac-

Bing and Louis in Hollywood, c. 1936. (*above*)

Louis Armstrong fronts the Luis Russell Orchestra, 1936. Left to right; front row: Gus Aiken, Louis Bacon, Shelton Hemphill, Russell, Greely Walton, Moon Johnson, Charlie Holmes, Bingie Madison. Rear, left to right: Nathanial Story, Jimmy Archey, Paul Barbarin (drums), Lee Blair, Pops Foster. (*preceding overleaf*)

On the set of a film Soundie (a music video for jukeboxes), with drummer Sid Catlett, guitarist Lawrence Lucie, bassist John Simmons, and entertainer Velma Middleton, 1941. (*facing page, top*)

On the set of *New Orleans*, with Zutty Singleton, Red Callendar, bass; Charlie Beal, piano; Bud Scott, Kid Ory (leaning against piano), Barney Bigard, clarinet, 1946. (*facing page, bottom*)

count—he did put his name in lights for the first time, at the Sunset in 1926. "He watched over Louis like the treasure he was," Duke Ellington wrote. There can be no doubt that however ambivalent anyone else was, Armstrong had very strong feelings about Glaser. On March 31, 1969, lying in bed in Beth Israel Medical Center, Armstrong interrupted a rewrite of his account of the Karmofsky family to write the dedication page of his autobiography:

> I dedicate this book
> to my manager and pal
> Mr. Joe Glaser
> The best friend
> That I've ever had,
> May the Lord Bless him
> Watch over him always
> His boy and disciple who loved him
> dearly. Louis
>   Satchmo
>   Armstrong

Glaser died five weeks later, on June 4. On July 29, in a letter to blues singer Little Brother Montgomery, Armstrong wrote, "I was a sick ass, yea. My manager + my God Joe Glaser was sick at the same time and it was a toss-up between us who would cut out first. Man it broke my heart that it was him. I love that man, which the world already knows. I prayed, as sick as I was, that he would make it. God bless his soul. He was the greatest for me + all the spades that he handled."

From the time they shook hands in 1935 (Armstrong told friends that there was never a written agreement with Glaser), Louis's star soared. That fall he signed a contract with Jack Kapp's Decca Records that lasted seven years—until the recording ban of 1942—and produced some of his best and certainly his most diverse work. After the ban, Armstrong emerged as one of the industry's few free agents, recording for RCA, Decca, Columbia, and anyone else who could afford Glaser's asking price. In 1936, he was featured in a major Paramount film, *Pennies from Heaven*, opposite Bing Crosby. In 1937, he appeared in two more movies (there would be twenty-eight others during the next thirty-two years), and became the first black performer with a network radio series, sponsored by Fleischmann's Yeast. During the next ten years he became a fixture of the entertainment world. He played the best theaters, dance

With Dorothy Dandridge, 1947.

Trummy, Louis, Billy Kyle, Peanuts Hucko in *The Beat Generation*, 1959.

From *Pennies from Heaven*, 1936. The masked drummer is Lionel Hampton. (*facing page, top*)

With Billy Kyle and Trummy Young in *High Society*, 1956. (*facing page, bottom*)

halls, and nightclubs; kibitzed with Crosby on radio; recorded a series of unique and inimitable trumpet concertos. Still, he pushed himself, trying to impress other musicians, playing outrageous strings of high notes that would result in a bloodied lip and bring cheers from the crowd and accusations of vulgarity from the critics. He was mesmerized by the spotlight but never unnerved by it. Jean Bach recalls the night at the Apollo when he was emcee and was supposed to introduce a white adagio team, whose name he could never remember. "So he was announcing the band members, the various acts, and now it came time to announce the adagio number and he said, 'And now folks,' and you can see he's troubled and stalling and he's thinking what the hell are their names, 'cause he knew all the other acts personally. Finally he looks out in desperation and says, '*The two ofays!*' "

Jack Kapp's recording philosophy was to hurl every kind of song at his artists and then hurl the artists at each other. In short order, Armstrong recorded Hawaiian songs, jazz originals, pop tunes, country and western, novelties, spirituals, the Elder Eatmore monologues, as well as encounters with Ella Fitzgerald (the exquisite "You Won't Be Satisfied"), the Mills Brothers, Billie Holiday, Bing Crosby, Gary Crosby, and the Lynn Murray Choir. Often the material was beneath him, but it didn't much matter. Nearly every session produced at least one gem. Never had his voice sounded quite so appealing as on such records as "Thanks a Million," "Ev'ntide," "You Are My Lucky Star," "I'm Putting All My Eggs in One Basket," and "I Double Dare You," among many others. His trumpet playing entered a phase of fat-toned solos forever arching upward and brought a new generation of players under his spell. Asked what a musician needed on the road, Bunny Berigan quipped, "A toothbrush and a picture of Louis Armstrong."

Armstrong could now make a melody his own simply by virtue of his phrasing. His solos could no longer be evaluated in terms of the distance he placed between the original material and his variations. He had learned how to stare the material down and—through an alchemical combination of rhythmic finesse, unflagging radiance of tone, and perfect taste—turn trite ditties into powerhouse statements. Armstrong the entertainer was recalling King Oliver's dictum to play the melody; Armstrong the artist was seeing that the melody was somehow made worthy of him. Thus a minor effort by Hoagy Carmichael, "Jubilee," became a euphoric march, an extravagant display of brassy richness, in which Louis wails like a second-line king against the strutting trombones

Lucille in her dancing days,
Harlem, 1930s.

in the last chorus. "Skeleton in the Closet," the novelty number from *Pennies from Heaven,* starts with Louis narrating a ghost story (reminding us how winning an actor he was), then suddenly swinging the lyric, and finally transferring it to the trumpet with a soaring two-bar lick that would crop up nearly twenty years later in his "Hello Dolly" solo. With original material, he could be empyrean from the first note: In "Swing That Music" and the swing arrangements of his "Struttin' with Some Barbecue" and Jelly Roll Morton's "Wolverine Blues," his solos journey from inspired exposition through mild embellishment and rhythmic displacement to punching high-note climaxes.

There were other triumphs. In 1938, Armstrong recorded the first jazz version of a spiritual, "When the Saints Go Marching In." The piece, which Edward Boatner had collected and published twenty-two years earlier, had been recorded once by a gospel group but was not widely known. Danny Barker remembers how Mama Lucy criticized her brother for tarting up a piece from the church. When Barker told Armstrong what she had said, he got angry and remarked that she didn't see anything wrong with playing bingo in the church. At one of several 1940 sessions floated by Sid Catlett's drumming, Armstrong chanted three numbers that may constitute the first examples of rap music; the best of them, an original called "You've Got Me Voodoo'd," has such memorable rhymes as *potion/emotion, Venus/between us,* and *Circe/mercy.* Armstrong's wit surfaced in other ways. With the success of "Saints," Kapp had him record several spirituals backed by a white choir. On "Going to Shout All over God's Heaven," Louis made known his impatience with writers and choirmasters who put "colored" pronunciations in the mouths of black performers. Armstrong's New Orleans accent was strangely Brooklynese: He said *woik* and *hoit.* He never said *daid, gwine, see-gar,* or *hebbin.* On "Going to Shout" the white choir intones, "hebbin, hebbin"; Armstrong growls right back at them, "heaven, heaven."

The impressive band that backs Armstrong on the best of his Decca recordings was organized by the Panamanian pianist Luis Russell. In 1919, at seventeen, Russell won a lottery and used his winnings to move to New Orleans. Years later he worked with King Oliver, and ultimately formed his first important band by raiding Oliver of several disgruntled musicians. Russell made a number of excellent records, honing a unique style that combined the buoyant second-line pulse of New Orleans with arrangements and soloists that embodied the best in swing. It was

Glaser's brainstorm to sign the Russell band as a touring unit for Louis. Uneven arrangements (by Chappie Willet and Joe Garland) and lack of rehearsal time (the band would often arrive at the studio dog tired from a road tour) combined to keep the pressure on Louis; he had to make the records lively. But the band had a lot going for it, not least a vital rhythm section (Pops Foster on bass and either Sid Catlett or Paul Barbarin on drums) and several fine soloists, including trombonist J. C. Higginbotham, altoist Charlie Holmes, and clarinetists Bingie Madison and Albert Nicholas. Ironically, the greatest figure in the Russell band became odd man out when Louis fronted it; under the circumstances, there was little for Henry Red Allen, a superbly idiosyncratic trumpet player from Algiers, Louisiana, to do. Writing in the hospital in June 1970, Armstrong expressed warm feelings for Russell ("that good New Orleans piano, very tasty and swingy"), Allen, Higginbotham, and the others. "There were several boys from my hometown, N.O., so you can imagine how well I felt at home with them . . . I was very proud and happy to have played in the band every night." He was especially pleased in 1938, when Glaser booked him and the band alongside the Bill Bojangles Robinson Revue at the Cotton Club in downtown New York—not least because it gave him the opportunity to meet a curvy dark-skinned chorine with liquid eyes and a ready smile.

It seemed to me that Lucille was the ideal girl for me. In fact our lives were practically the same. Good common sense—great observers (not for any particular reason), but were not particular about showy people etc. What we didn't have we did without. . . . I paid strict attention to her when she was working in the chorus at the Cotton Club. Beside the salary that she was making at the club there wasn't too much. (Nothing like the girls made that were working for Ziegfeld and his Follies.) With her salary she had to help to take care of her family, which consisted of her mother, her two brothers, Jackie + Sonny, and a sister Janet. . . . For extra money, Lucille had to sell cookies to the members of the cast, which took in everybody, including Bill Robinson and me. Every night before the 1st show Lucille would be a very busy young girl trying to get dressed and put on her 1st show, and get rid of the cookies, which she would bring down from Harlem. . . . One night when Lucille came into my dressing room to deliver my box of cookies, I asked, "Honey?

Lucille Wilson was known as Brown Sugar when she danced in the Cotton Club chorus line, late 1930s. (*page 142*)

Cabin in the Sky, 1943. (*page 143*)

Roses are Red
Violets are Blue
Lucilles are 'Pink
I saw them on the
Clother Line
CLOTHES LINE
'UMP 'UMP 'UMP
I *Love* 'yooooo'
Your Hubby
'Pops.

1945

Louis and Lucille, 1942. (*above*)

This marriage will last. Lucille cuts the cake as the Rev. and Mrs. Mance and Lucille's mother look on. October 12, 1942. (*preceding overleaf*)

How many boxes do you bring down here every night?" And when she told me, I said to her, "When you come down here with your bundle of cookies, from now on just bring them all in here (meaning my dressing room). I'll take all of them." She did, which took a big load off her mind. I put them aside and when we'd finish work at the club, me and my good man Friday, Bob Smiley, would take them uptown in Harlem and the next day we'd take them over to the school and divide them up among the school kids. They loved them. I did too.

One night when Lucille came into my dressing [room] to deliver her cookies, I just couldn't hold back the deep feeling and the warmth that I had accumulated for her ever since I first laid eyes on her in the front line on the Cotton Club floor . . . swinging in that front line every night, looking beautifuller 'n' beautifuller every night direct in front of me, standing there directing the band and blowing my solos on my trumpet whenever it was time for me to blow 'n' wail. All of those beautiful notes along with Lucille's perfect dancing. Me diggin' those cute little buns of hers. Hmmm. That's when I automatically said to her, "Look, Brown Sugar" (the name that we show folks and musicians gave her during her early days right out the dancing school into show business; I always thought that it was a cute name). I said to Lucille, "You must have at least an inkling." Huh. Lucille raised her big fine eyes at me as if to say, "My, my, where did he get that word." Of course she didn't say it but I could tell by the tone of her eyes that she was wondering like hell. Pretty smart chick to be so young and around us old timers, too. She's *too much*. And to me, she's everything. I said, "Lucille, I might as well tell you right now, I have eyes for you, and have been having them for a long time. And if any of these cats in the show shooting at you, I want to be in the running." Lucille looked at me and just laughed. But before we both knew it, we were taking in the shows (movies) between our shows. Riding uptown in Harlem every night after our last show. That's when I had that big long rust-colored Packard car that Mr. Glaser had bought for me, and boy was it sharp. It was the hottest car in town, and the talk of the town. Bob Smiley, my right hand man, a tall goodlooking six foot brownskin cat, used to drive this fine long Packard while Lucille + I would sit in the backseat and she looking just like a li'l ol' doll and me sharp as a wedding (you know what) and happier than 2 peas in a pot (pod to you). *(Archive)*

It remained for Armstrong to divorce Alpha and convince Lucille of the benefits of Swiss Kriss (he noted they were both losing their figures from the excess of Italian food they consumed after their shows). On October 12, 1942, they married.

F O U R

In the spring of 1943, Lucille bought a house in Corona, Queens, a black suburban community about twenty minutes outside of Manhattan. Louis was traveling at the time and expressed vigorous opposition to the idea. America's most famous musician had never owned a home. For more than twenty years, he had lived in hotels and flats, often boarding with black families on the road, living much of his life on buses and trains. Perhaps the fixity of a house frightened him, or the responsibility that went along with it. When he arrived at Penn Station, he took a cab to Harlem to hang out for a few hours before calling home. He asked Lucille to wait outside, told her if he didn't like what he saw, he'd leave. When his cab pulled up, he tipped the driver twenty dollars and asked him to wait. He got out, looked around, saw that Lucille wasn't outside and finally rang the bell. Lucille opened the door: "Welcome home, honey." "This is our home?" "Yes." He walked around, climbed the stairs to the second floor, where the master bedroom and his office were, went up to the attic, then down to the basement, and out to the yard. She had fixed up every room and prepared an elaborate meal. Louis was speechless. He ran out to the cab and invited the driver in for dinner. The three of them ate and drank for three or four hours.

Armstrong came to love the house, though he didn't spend much time in it until the late sixties. The decor reflected Lucille's interests—he was crushed on returning after a long tour to find she had taken down the centerfolds he'd pasted up in his office. In later years, though, it was a valued retreat for him. The first-floor bathroom was the shrine of a man who had grown up near an outhouse. The walls and ceiling were covered with mirrors and the fixtures ornamented with gold. The sunny kitchen and breakfast nook looked out on the yard. Lucille had

Louis and his Packard, 1935.

With Sid Catlett in a publicity shot, 1949. *(page 148, top)*

The band spells relief "Tire Inspection," c. 1936. *(page 148, bottom)*

Arriving at the Turin airport with Lucille. Louis applies his lip salve, 1949. *(page 149, top)*

Drummer Sid Catlett rocks Armstrong's big band, c. 1940. *(page 149, bottom)*

an enormous dressing room adjacent to the bedroom, and down the hall Louis had a small rectangular office that became his refuge. He spent hours typing at his desk, listening to music, chatting with visitors. Louis had never owned most of his records. With the introduction of tape, he became obsessed with collecting all his performances and transferring them to reels of tape: It would be a permanent archive of his work, he thought. Sometimes he'd play an opera or one of his old records and improvise along with it, taping the result. He designed elaborate boxes for the tapes, pasting up montages of photographs and magazine typeface.

On his return from the hospital in 1969, he compiled a catalogue of his reel-to-reel tape collection that runs to 175 pages. The taped material includes most of his own records; a recorded message he made for his friend, attorney Bill Hassan; privately recorded concert performances; a Fleischmann's Yeast broadcast; his radio and TV interviews; a Tallulah Bankhead recitation; talks with Lucille; unaccompanied "rehearsals"; records by Edith Piaf, Johnny Ray, Roy Eldridge, Bix Beiderbecke, Duke Ellington, Harry James, Joe Bushkin, Thelonious Monk, Art Tatum, Fats Waller, and numerous others, some introduced with Armstrong's comments; home duets with Bobby Hackett; a birthday party with comments from neighbors; a bull session with Redd Foxx; risqué jokes recorded backstage at the Chicago Theater; "chops sessions" with Velma Middleton; Jelly Roll Morton's Library of Congress recordings with Armstrong's added narration; a conversation with Robert Merrill; his readings of letters and holiday greetings from fans; many TV broadcasts; excerpts from operas, including some that he sang or played along with; radio broadcasts of Crosby, Jolson, Cantor, and others; Bea Lillie; Jackie Moms Mabley; Israeli, Arabic, and Italian folk songs; Martin Luther King's funeral service; Mary Lou Williams's Mass; a show on the New York Mets; various New Orleans bands; hotel-room chatter; a 1963 concert by Pete Seeger; Jimmy Owens leading the Radio Orchestra of Holland; thirty-seven demos from his *Country and Western* album; a talk on pot with Max Jones; the cast album of *Applause*, and on and on. Unfortunately, Armstrong usually recorded both sides of the tape at slow speed; worse, the tapes have been closeted in the sweltering basement of the house for so long that they may no longer be salvageable.

In later years, Lucille would try to convince him to move. With Glaser's help, she located a property with a mansion and swimming pool, and drove him out to look it over. He couldn't see the point. He liked living near Shea Stadium, though he let it be known that he was

Louis doted on the neighborhood kids at his home in Corona, Queens, c. 1949. (*above*)

Pops goes to work. Corona, Queens, c. 1963. (*facing page*)

By the mid-1950s, Louis never traveled anywhere without his hi-fi rack, including a reel-to-reel tape recorder.

Making a home recording, c. 1947.

Louis visits Milt Gabler (to his left) at his Commodore Music Shop in the late 1940s. Gabler produced him at Decca from 1944 on. (*facing page*)

dismayed at not being invited to sing the national anthem at a Mets game. He liked the people in the neighborhood. When he and Lucille had a brick facade built on the house, he asked neighbors if they'd like the same—since it wouldn't be right for his house to look too high and mighty—and had the brickwork extended down the length of the block. He loved the kids who sat with him on the stoop or came in to watch westerns on television. "We've both seen three generations grow up on our block," he wrote in 1970. "White + black, and those kids, when they grew up and got married, their children still come around to our house and visit their friends Louis and Lucille. That's how close they feel towards us . . . when I would return home, all of those kids in my block would be standing there right in front of my door, waiting to help me unload my luggage and take it into the house." When he was a teenager in New Orleans, Louis had adopted the retarded son of a cousin and supported him all his life, but he had no children of his own.

Surely the security Lucille provided him with helped shelter him from the storms of the 1940s. First, there was the squabble over bebop. The ultimate comments were made not in magazines, but on records. Armstrong recorded an outlandish parody called "The Boppenpoof Song," which was withdrawn by Decca after two weeks because copyright owners of "The Whiffenpoof Song" found it tasteless; and Dizzy Gillespie, who would later call Armstrong's place in music "unimpeachable," recorded an imitation of his "I'm Confessin'" that even his target thought was pretty funny. By the late 1940s, Armstrong was more troubled by the popularity of rhythm and blues, which seemed to drain away his audiences, especially in black communities, where he had long been king. Before that, he'd been forced to confront the fact that big bands were no longer economically feasible. Glaser tried to get him to break up the band, but Armstrong held out stubbornly for a while, until the quality of the orchestra itself began to diminish. In 1944, when the band's music director was Teddy McRae and Dexter Gordon had a chair, the morale was disastrously low. Producer Milt Gabler, formerly of Commodore Records, had come to Decca and was assigned to supervise the band's first session after the two-year recording ban (a strike called by the American Federation of Musicians): None of the three sides was considered good enough to release.

In 1947 everything turned around again. Armstrong had just completed filming an atrocious movie called *New Orleans*, which seemed to suggest that the story of jazz was nothing more than the passing of a native

music from black primitives who inhabited Storyville to the white ruling class. (Billie Holiday, playing a maid, got to introduce the song "Do You Know What It Means to Miss New Orleans," though the dialogue called for her to tell her mistress that it was just a blues she made up while dusting.) As ludicrous as it was, it focused a lot of positive attention on jazz, especially on Armstrong—possibly because it represented a backwater against the new music coming to life after World War II. In any case, the time seemed propitious for Armstrong to scale his music down to the size of a New Orleans ensemble. The first test came in February 1947, when Armstrong appeared with a band led by the gifted New Orleans-born clarinetist Edmond Hall at Carnegie Hall. Three months later, on May 17, he led his own all-star band for two shows, at eight and midnight, at Town Hall. It was the kind of triumph that can determine the direction of an artist's career.

F   I   V   E

Leonard Bernstein once suggested that the reason philistines think jazz a "low-class" music (he was writing in 1955) is that "historically *players* of music seem to lack the dignity of *composers* of music." He argued, however, that "the player of jazz is himself the real composer, which gives him a creative, and therefore *more* dignified status." Although the philistines are still among us, Bernstein's argument seems no more pressing in the 1980s than a discussion on whether separate-but-equal is a sensible approach to race. That fight has been won, even if the victory is not yet reflected in appropriate government subsidies for its most emblematic musical art. Still, Armstrong's life raises a tangential question: How does the creative genius who is a player-composer sustain a career after the initial burst of creativity? If he follows the examples of great performers of classical music, the answer is to carry one's art into associated realms—teaching, musical activism, writing. Armstrong, however, lived only to perform and developed an entertainment style that allowed him to perform before huge, clamorous audiences all his life. The wonder is not that he made himself a compelling entertainer, but that despite the toll of countless one-nighters, he sustained a vigorous and, yes, dignified level of artistry.

One of the highlights of his 1947 Town Hall concert was a version of Hoagy Carmichael's "Rockin' Chair." He first recorded it in 1929 as

With Billie Holiday in *New Orleans*, 1946. (*preceding page*)

Cozy Cole, Jack Teagarden, Louis, Arvell Shaw, Barney Bigard, Earl Hines, 1949. (*facing page, top*)

The historic Town Hall concert that confirmed Armstrong's return to a small ensemble. Left to right: Jack Teagarden, Dick Cary, Armstrong, Bobby Hackett, Peanuts Hucko, Bob Haggart, Sid Catlett, 1947. (*facing page, bottom*)

a duet with Carmichael, and it became a fixture in his repertory—but the 1947 version is definitive. Essentially, it consists of two duets: a brief instrumental episode in which his trumpet is heard against Bobby Hackett's, and the comic vocal. Hackett, an incomparably lyrical player who idolized Armstrong but had none of his might, plays a series of figures that spur Armstrong's theme statement; the two seem almost to be playing different instruments—or, put another way, if Hackett's sound is fifty watts, Armstrong's is a hundred and fifty. The bulk of the performance is a vocal duet by Armstrong and Jack Teagarden that illustrates a similar contrast. They take turns singing the melody and providing comic responses, though Armstrong gets all the laughs. At one point, Teagarden is about to sing a response and Armstrong rolls over him with a scat break. The audience cracks up, not just because it's funny, but because it imparts a musical frisson. It may be vaudeville, but it's vaudeville on a very high level.

Town Hall showed Armstrong the way to go. Soon he was on the road with a sextet, Louis Armstrong and the All Stars. For several years, it really was a band of stars, with Teagarden, Trummy Young, or Tyree Glenn on trombone, Barney Bigard or Edmond Hall on clarinet, Earl Hines or Billy Kyle on piano, Sid Catlett or Cozy Cole on drums, and Milt Hinton or the young Arvell Shaw on bass. It was the highest-paid jazz combo in the world, and through a series of concert albums—*At Symphony Hall, At Pasadena, At the Crescendo*—it revitalized mainstream jazz with a style unlike any other. At a time when most small jazz groups played bop, cool jazz, or Dixieland, the All Stars furnished an alternative that was, in Ellington's phrase, beyond category. Only the instrumentation suggested New Orleans traditionalism. The extraordinary level of musicianship, the swing rhythms, the diversity of repertory, and the live-and-let-live ambience of a band that allowed each player to do as he liked during his solo feature, not to mention the comedy routines with singer-dancer Velma Middleton, all suggested a genre beyond genres.

As Louis's popularity continued to grow, Glaser did all he could to manufacture a new identity for him: Louis Armstrong, ambassador of goodwill. That role was solidified in 1956, when he went to West Africa. In Accra, he was greeted by more than one hundred thousand people, an unprecedented turnout for which Armstrong had a ready explanation: "After all, my ancestors came from here and I still have African blood in me." At a concert in Ghana, he sang "Black and Blue"

Louis's mail could find him without an address—or his name.

Jack Teagarden was a charter member of the All Stars, 1948. (*facing page*)

Tens of thousands greeted Armstrong at every stop during his tour of Africa. Edmond Hall and Trummy Young are directly behind him, 1956.

Satchmo the Great, 1957.

Edmond Hall, Trummy Young, and Louis are joined by several local trumpeters in Africa, 1956. (*facing page, top*)

At another stop, Lucille was asked to dance, 1956. (*facing page, bottom*)

and brought tears to the eyes of Kwame Nkrumah, a moment captured in the film of the tour, *Satchmo the Great.* In the meantime, he produced a string of hit records at home: "A Kiss to Build a Dream On," which he introduced in the movie *The Strip;* "Mack the Knife," which helped spur the Kurt Weill revival; "Blueberry Hill," a 1949 record recycled in 1956 in the wake of Fats Domino's success. He was the token black performer on dozens of TV shows, often appearing with Bing Crosby and Frank Sinatra—his duet with Sinatra on "Birth of the Blues" (*The Edsel Show*) was a standout. He was a much honored man. That's why all hell broke loose when he spoke out on civil rights.

The year 1957, perhaps the longest in Armstrong's life, had an ominous start. In February, he played a concert in Knoxville, Tennessee, before a segregated audience of eight thousand whites and one thousand blacks. A stick of dynamite was hurled at the auditorium from a passing car. The unruffled Armstrong told the audience, "That's all right, folks, it's just the phone," averting a panic. The bombing was blamed on the White Citizens Council, which had protested the use of the building for concerts attended by both races. Asked if the incident would affect his southern tour, Armstrong told a reporter, "Man, I'll play anywhere they'll listen."

A different kind of controversy hit the papers in July, when he arrived to play the Newport Jazz Festival and was told a birthday tribute had been planned and he was expected to appear in every segment of a long show, without rehearsal. Exhausted when he got off the bus at 5 P.M., he was appalled when told what was expected of him at 8. "We haven't rehearsed," he argued, "and I'm not going to go out there and make a fool of myself." He exploded when a festival official had the temerity to tell him that since Ella Fitzgerald was on the show, Velma Middleton couldn't appear. "I'm playing with my band and my singer and none of this other shit." Glaser tried to mollify him, but to no avail. At one point, beleaguered by photographers and hangers-on, he walked into the musicians' room wearing nothing but a rag on his head and told everyone to get the hell out of his dressing room. He played his set his way, Ella sang "Happy Birthday," and that was that. But the press was scathing. Recalling that night, Lucille said, "He kept his own counsel and nobody could turn him around."

On September 19, Armstrong was playing Grand Forks, North Dakota, when Governor Faubus of Arkansas barred black children from entering a school. Armstrong was planning a widely noted tour of Russia for the

State Department at the time. He told a reporter that night that he would cancel the tour, because "the way they are treating my people in the South, the government can go to hell." He said Eisenhower was "two-faced," had "no guts," and was allowing Faubus—an "uneducated plowboy"—to run the country. When the reporter showed Armstrong his notes from the interview, he signed the paper and wrote, "solid." "It's getting almost so bad," he said, "a colored man hasn't got any country." As to the Russian trip: "I'll do it on my own. The people over there ask me what's wrong with my country, what am I supposed to say?"

Frenchy Tallerie would get embroiled in a real fight between Armstrong and the press in 1957. Here he looks on as Louis spars with Jimmy Bivins, 1949.

A furor ensued, including a call from the State Department asking him to reconsider the trip (Benny Goodman ended up making it). The next day while Armstrong was asleep, his road manager, Pierre Tallerie, told reporters Louis "was sorry he spouted off." When Armstrong woke up, he fired Tallerie and told the press, "He's speaking for himself. My people—the Negroes—are not looking for anything—we just want a square shake. But when I see on television and read about a crowd in Arkansas spitting on a little colored girl—I think I have a right to get sore . . . do you dig me when I still say I have a right to blow my top over injustice?" The attacks were immediate, vicious, and lasted more than a year. Lucille recalled, "Of course he was hurt, but a lot of the people who led in the attacks, like Adam Clayton Powell and Sammy Davis, Jr., later got on the bandwagon when it was safe." Interviewed on TV, Davis said Armstrong did not speak for the Negro people, called him "a great credit to his race," and finally conceded that he agreed with his meaning but not "his choice of words."

After Eisenhower sent troops into Arkansas and explained why on television, Armstrong said, "Things are looking better than before," and sent a wire to the White House: "If you decide to walk into the schools with the little colored kids, take me along, Daddy. God bless you." But he put more fuel on the fire in October, when he remarked that he'd rather play in the Soviet Union than in Arkansas, because Faubus "might hear a couple of notes—and he don't deserve that." He was, in fact, scheduled to perform at Arkansas University, an engagement that was cancelled by vote of the student body. Glaser responded, "Who cares?" In January 1958, Jim Bishop, a columnist for the *New York Journal-American*, called for a boycott of Armstrong's concerts. "He is scheduled to star on an upcoming TV show," the author of *The Day Christ Died* wrote. "For one, I will not look." He concluded, "I checked

Backstage, 1950s. (*facing page*)

An irresistible front line: Trummy, Pops, Bigard, c. 1960.

the newspaper files to see what Louis Armstrong had done for the people of his race. I haven't found anything and now I ask the musician himself: 'What have you done for your people, except hurt them?'" The following May, Armstrong was set to appear on *The Steve Allen Show* along with Van Cliburn. Allen hoped they would play a duet. Cliburn's manager refused, fearing for his client's image, but when the show was over the two men played "Melancholy Baby."

On the assumption that all the fuss would interest the FBI, I requested Armstrong's file under the Freedom of Information Act, and was surprised to discover that the G-men had started tracking him in 1948, when his name appeared in the address book of someone they considered suspect. In 1950, an informer told the FBI that Armstrong was dissatisfied "with the situation" at the Flamingo Hotel, but was assuaged with "a bottle of scotch and a couple of reefers." He came to their attention again in 1951, when his name appeared on the letterhead of the Negro Actors Guild of America, Inc. The file heated up in 1956, when Louis was invited to participate in a "Congress of Scholars of the Negro World" in Paris, sponsored "by the leftist 'Présence Africaine,' " and was solicited by George Murphy to play at the Inaugural Ball. The file for 1957 records the Knoxville bombing, Armstrong's press conferences, the cancelled concert in Arkansas, as well as an anonymous letter stating, "Louis 'Satcho' [sic] Armstrong is a communist, why does State Dept. give him a passport?"; a signed letter asserting that he is "a patriotic American"; clippings regarding his 1960 tour of Eastern Europe and Africa, including notification that "a Communist Propaganda Booklet Attacking US Racial Policy" was distributed in Lomé, Togoland, "at approximately the dates on which Louis Armstrong performed in Lomé"; a comment from the director himself on an admiring letter about Armstrong, indicating "that Armstrong's life is a good argument against the theory that Negroes are inferior;" a 1965 document issued by the White House that says Jack Valenti requested a name check on Armstrong; and a 1963 three-page teletype to the Dallas office concerning Jack Ruby's unsuccessful attempt to do business with Joseph Glaser.

Curiously, they had no information on the accusation made by Egyptian authorities in 1959 that Armstrong was the leader of an Israeli espionage network (to which Louis replied, "Why don't you tell these people who are spreading all this stuff to come around and I'll tell them a few good traveling salesmen jokes"); or about the 1964 cancellation of an Armstrong concert by the University of Alabama, and the refusal that same year by South Africa to allow Armstrong to perform there with a mixed band; or about his remarks in Copenhagen in 1965 after he read of the riots in Selma ("They would beat Jesus if he was black and marched"); or his refusal to appear on the Oscar telecast in 1968, after the assassination of Martin Luther King, Jr., an action in which he was joined by Sidney Poitier, Diahann Carroll, and Sammy Davis, Jr.

Billy Kyle, Trummy Young, Louis, and Lucille during a tour of South America, late 1950s.

The criticisms of 1957 took their toll, and the inexplicable accusations of Tomming cut deep. Lucille defended his decision not to march. "He gave money, but there was no point in marching and getting his mouth bashed in. He was an artist first. He talked politics with me and he was aware that every word he said had impact." When Larry King interviewed Armstrong in 1967 for *Harper's*, he said, "As time went on and I made a reputation I had it put in my contracts that I wouldn't *play* no place I couldn't *stay*. I was the first Negro in the business to crack them big white hotels—Oh yeah! I pioneered, Pops! Nobody much remembers that these days." Two years later, writing in his notebook, he elaborated on his resentment:

> I think that I have always done great things about uplifting my race, but wasn't appreciated. I am just a musician, and still remember the time, as an American citizen, I spoke up for my people during a big integration riot—Little Rock, remember? I wrote Eisenhower. My first comment, or compliment, whatever you would call it, came from a Negro boy from my hometown New Orleans. The first words that he said to me after reading what I had said in the papers concerning the Little Rock deal— he said as we sitting down at a table to have a drink. He looked straight at me and said, "Nigger, you better stop talking about those white people like you did." Hmmm. I was trying to stop those unnecessary head whippings at the time—that's all. (*Archive*)

If Armstrong had an insatiable appetite for applause, he was imbued with the kind of pride that allowed him to choose his honors with more discrimination than is generally realized. In 1949, when his fame was fanned by the success of the All Stars, he was invited to be king of the Zulus at the New Orleans Mardi Gras. He jumped at the chance and reveled in the ceremony. The press and some musicians attacked him

Left to right: Woody Herman, Bobby Hackett, and Barney Bigard listen while Willis Conover interviews Armstrong for the *Voice of America*, 1955. (*page 166, top*)

Edward R. Murrow and Louis at a screening, 1956. (*page 166, bottom*)

Louis (center) didn't like to see entertainers wear burnt cork, but appearing as king of the Zulus was an honor he relished. Mardi Gras, 1949. (*page 167, top*)

Tommy Dorsey and his wife, Pat Dane, stop by to hear Louis at the Rag Doll, Chicago, c. 1945. (*page 167, bottom*)

The All Stars brought Armstrong a great deal of attention, including this 1947 magazine cover. *(facing page)*

Armstrong appeared in nearly three dozen movies, including *Jam Session* (1944), *When the Boys Meet the Girls* (1965), *Satchmo the Great* (1957), and *The Strip* (1951). Several African nations issued stamps in his honor, including (from top to bottom) the republics of Gabon, Nigeria (second and fifth stamps), Rwanda, and Mali. His records were issued by many companies in the 78 rpm era, including (left, top to bottom) Columbia (a reissue of Okeh's "Cornet Chop Suey"), Decca ("Me and Brother Bill" and "What Is This Thing Called Love"), (bottom, right), Okeh ("West End Blues"), and (right, top to bottom) Bluebird ("High Society") and British Recording Society (an English reissue of "Keyhole Blues"). The album jackets in the upper right are from comprehensive editions issued in Europe. The Columbias *(And His Hot Five, And His Hot Seven)* are part of a selective four-volume series issued in 1954 and still in print. *Ambassador Satch,* recorded during a European tour of 1955, suggests Armstrong's new role as ambassador of goodwill. For some reason, sculptors, doll makers, *(overleaf, caption continued on page 177)*

for participating in what they considered a barbaric ritual, because the king must wear blackface. Yet for Armstrong, the invitation was the equivalent of getting an honorary degree from one's alma mater. Twenty years later, in a year when the White House earned reams of positive publicity for honoring Duke Ellington on his seventieth birthday, the office of Nixon's "cultural adviser," Leonard Garment, called Jack Bradley and said, "The White House is interested in Louis this coming year, can you intercede?" Armstrong's reply: "Fuck that shit. Why didn't they do it before? The only reason he would want me to play there now is to make some niggers happy." Republicans, like elephants, never forget. The week Armstrong died, Rep. Charles Rangel, a Democrat from New York, recommended him for a Medal of Honor. According to Rangel's office, "It wasn't even reported out of committee."

S I X

Louis Armstrong's fame during the fifties and sixties has long obscured his musical achievement in those years. The All Stars concerts fell into a routine, though as Lucille was quick to point out, "He always opened with 'Indiana' and closed with his theme, 'Sleepytime Down South,' but the rest of the program he would change to suit the audience. His mind worked so fast. He could hear gnats walking on cotton." When a new player came into the band, Armstrong let him find his way through the music in his own way. His instructions to Cozy Cole were, "We don't have time to say a lot of things up there, just cock your ear and straight ahead." Arvell Shaw didn't realize he was doing okay until he'd played several gigs and Louis started turning around to him and smiling. Milt Hinton was amazed at how much pressure Armstrong put on himself to play something fresh every night. According to Cole, he "really played" about 80 percent of the time; his chops would be down the other 20. During the height of the All Stars' success, when "Hello Dolly" was riding the charts, a typical concert might go like this:

First a brief strain from "Sleepytime Down South," ending with Armstrong singing—arms outstretched, face crinkled with a grin— "Good evening, everybody." Then the inevitable "Indiana." After one of his signal tunes, perhaps "A Kiss to Build a Dream On," he'd say, "Now we're gonna take you down to my hometown, New Orleans," and

TWENTY CENTS

FEBRUARY 21, 1949

TIME

THE WEEKLY NEWSMAGAZINE

Artzybasheff

LOUIS ARMSTRONG
When you got to ask what it is, you never get to know.
(*Music*)

$6.50 A YEAR

(REG. U. S. PAT. OFF.)

VOL. LIII NO. 8

Louis Armstrong and His Orchestra—Trumpet King of Swing!

Jam Session
A COLUMBIA PICTURE

RÉPUBLIQUE GABONAISE
100f
POSTES LOUIS ARMSTRONG

POSTE AÉRIENNE
150f
LOUIS ARMSTRONG (1898-1971)
RÉPUBLIQUE DU NIGER

M-G-M presents "WHEN THE BOYS MEET THE GIRLS"

THE HOT FIVE
LOUIS ARMSTRONG

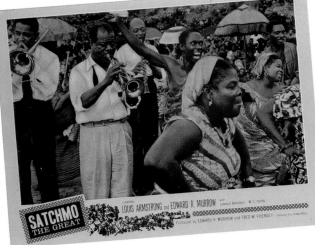

STARRING LOUIS ARMSTRONG and EDWARD R. MURROW with Leonard Bernstein • W. C. Handy

SATCHMO THE GREAT

Produced by EDWARD R. MURROW and FRED W. FRIENDLY

30c
RÉPUBLIQUE RWANDAISE

270f
LES GRANDS MUSICIENS NOIRS • LOUIS ARMSTRONG
RÉPUBLIQUE DU MALI

1973
TRIBUTE TO THE FATHER OF JAZZ
—
LOUIS ARMSTRONG
• AMERICAN COIN & STAMP CO., INC.
Silver Creations Ltd.

POSTE AÉRIENNE
100f
LOUIS ARMSTRONG (1900-1971)
RÉPUBLIQUE DU NIGER

M-G-M's Musical Melodrama of the Dancer and the Drummer!

THE STRIP

STARRING
MICKEY **ROONEY** • SALLY **FORREST**
WILLIAM **DEMAREST** • JAMES **CRAIG**
with KAY **BROWN**

Music! Music! Music!
LOUIS **ARMSTRONG** (Trumpet) "SATCHMO" AND HIS ORCHESTRA
FEATURING
JACK TEAGARDEN (Trombone)
EARL "FATHA" HINES (The Hot Pianist)
BARNEY BIGARD (Clarinet)
GUEST STARS
VIC **DAMONE** • MONICA **LEWIS**

Written By Allen Rivkin
JOE PASTERNAK

Jazz Journal
DECEMBER 1958 VOL II N°12   TWO SHILLINGS

LOUIS ARMSTRONG
MALE SINGER
JAZZ CRITICS POLL
DOWN BEAT
1965

V.S.O.P.
(Very Spécial Old Phonography)
ARMSTRONG

LOUIS ARMSTRONG
ESM
LIP-SALVE
MADE BY
FRANZ SCHÜRITZ
MANNHEIM
GERMANY

COLUMBIA
LP
CL 840
European Concert Recordings by
AMBASSADOR SATCH

British
Rhythm Society
KEYHOLE BLUES

CL 851
THE LOUIS ARMSTRONG STORY
LOUIS ARMSTRONG LP COLUMBIA
AND HIS HOT FIVE
VOLUME 1

COLUMBIA LP
LOUIS ARMSTRONG
AND HIS HOT SEVEN
VOLUME 2
CL 852

DECCA
WHAT IS THIS THING
CALLED SWING
LOUIS ARMSTRONG
And His Orchestra
2267 B

play "My Bucket's Got a Hole in It" or "Tiger Rag" or "Way Down Yonder in New Orleans." About this time a sideman would get a feature number, which he was free to choose. Billy Kyle might play "When I Grow Too Old to Dream." Armstrong would be back to lead the band through a rousing "good old good one," like "Perdido." "Hello Dolly" would be done with two or three encores—he would give his name differently each time: "Hello Dolly, this is Louis/Satchmo/Dippermouth"—and he never ran out of new trumpet variations. Now the clarinetist would get the spotlight—Eddie Shu might play "Memories of You"; in earlier days, Barney Bigard would do a flashy "Just You, Just Me." Louis would return for "Ole Miss," another exuberant instrumental. His woman singer's primary responsibility was to give Armstrong and the others a rest. In the sixties, Jewell Brown would get the stage to do two or three numbers, like "Lover, Come Back to Me" and "Can't Help Lovin' Dat Man." In the fifties, he toured and sometimes recorded with Velma Middleton, an undistinguished singer to whom Louis was stubbornly loyal. An overweight woman with a girlish voice and the unexpected ability to do splits, she could be a funny foil for him, and their risqué duets on such songs as "Baby, It's Cold Outside" often brought the house down. Armstrong might close the first set with "The Saints." During the second set, the other musicians would have their specialty numbers. The trombonist would additionally sing a duet or two with Armstrong: Teagarden, Trummy Young, and Tyree Glenn all developed routines with him on "Rockin' Chair" or "That's My Desire" or "Back O' Town Blues." Arvell Shaw's pet number was "How High the Moon," with interpolations of Charlie Parker's "Ornithology." In the early days of the All Stars, Sid Catlett's drum solo was "Mop Mop," which Louis called "our bebop number, the only one in our files." In later years, Danny Barcelona, a journeyman drummer hired as a favor to Trummy Young, would find space for a windy smash-'em-up. Along the way, Louis would sing hits of forty years, like "Blueberry Hill" or "Lazy River" or "La Vie en Rose" or "I'm Confessin' " or "Mack the Knife," as well as his lovely ballad "Someday," which he said came to him (words and music) in a dream during a road tour. You knew the end was near when trombone and clarinet crooned a tender chord and Armstrong sang, "Now the pale moon's shining' "—the first words of "Sleepytime."

Not surprisingly, young jazz enthusiasts and many critics no longer attended his performances or bought his records. He was considered old-

(continued from page 168) and artists have never been able to capture Louis Armstrong's familiar image, though they keep trying. Three examples shown (left to right): a 1986 limited-edition decanter—the head comes out and the body contains bourbon, while the base is a music box that plays "Hello Dolly"; a statue sold in New Orleans souvenir shops; a 1984 limited edition from the Effanbee Doll Company. Trophies include a 1965 *Down Beat* plaque and a posthumous medal issued by the American Coin and Stamp Co., 1973. He appeared on hundreds of magazine covers, including *Jazz Journal*, December 1958. Franz Schuritz began manufacturing lip salve, endorsed by Armstrong, in the mid-1950s. The bugle and cornet were given to the Louisiana State Museum by bandmaster Peter Davis, of the Colored Waif's Home, where Louis Armstrong played both instruments. *(pages 170-171)*

Louis and Lucille in their home, 1971, shortly before his death. *(pages 172-173)*

Armstrong in France, 1959. *(pages 174-175)*

"People love me and my music, and you know I love them." *(facing page)* fashioned by many. Jazz had forged new worlds, and even Armstrong's demeanor seemed suspect in a day when jazz musicians were doing everything they could to avoid the label of entertainer. The point was to be hip and cool, like Miles Davis. Anyone who remembers the ruckus caused by Miles when he played with his back to the audience can only marvel at the pleasure he learned to take in later years as he found his own way to flirt with the audience. Davis himself remained one of Armstrong's most steadfast admirers. Still, jazz musicians were demanding respect as artists, and Armstrong, who was paradoxically the most respected of all jazz musicians, seemed to undermine their cause. He had too much fun out there. It was embarrassing. Artists don't grin and mug and roll their eyes.

The English music journal *Melody Maker,* though a pioneering advocate of Armstrong's art, felt obliged in 1957 to publish the opinions of one Chris Nelms, who said that Armstrong couldn't really play, that his "bleatings" didn't swing, that he had done nothing for music except line his own pockets. He was incensed that a musician with "the public stature of Louis" would say, when asked onstage by his pianist for a key, "I don't know, man, but it starts on my first valve." They weren't amused in the courts of Münster, Germany, either. It seems Glaser sued for a tax abatement on the grounds that Louis was an artist. According to a newspaper account, German law stipulated, "If it moves, it's entertainment, if it doesn't move, it's art." If it's art, you only have to pay half the regular entertainment tax. A professor from the Münster University of Music testified that Armstrong was indisputably an artist, but witnesses described unlikely movements onstage ("the clarinetist performed cartwheels," one reported) and Armstrong was designated an entertainer.

Armstrong's artistry continued to shine forth on records. While Joe Glaser refused to let him sign an exclusive contract and pushed for hits that would get radio play, a few producers—notably, Milt Gabler at Decca, George Avakian at Columbia, and Norman Granz at Verve—created sympathetic environments that produced outstanding performances and made use of the thematic possibilities inherent in the new long-playing format. Among several splendid albums were tributes to W. C. Handy and Fats Waller. Avakian liked to experiment with tape and he got some memorable effects, notably a seamless splice between vocal and trumpet on an exalted version of Waller's "Blue Turning Gray Over You" and an overdubbed duet on Handy's "Make Me a Pallet on

Pops and Velma Middleton, backed by Kenny John and Barney Bigard, 1953. (*facing page, top*)

Rehearsal for the concert at the Metropolitan Opera House. Armstrong, Roy Eldridge, Coleman Hawkins, Barney Bigard, 1944. (*facing page, bottom*)

Louis's favorite comic foil was Velma Middleton, who sang and did splits, 1950s. (*below*)

the Floor." Granz produced him in the context of a large orchestra, arranged by Russ Garcia, for a program of sophisticated pop songs and a uniquely autumnal interpretation of *Porgy and Bess*, opposite Ella Fitzgerald. Two albums of duets by Armstrong and Fitzgerald, backed by the Oscar Peterson Quartet, were no less effective: They energized each other on swinging material like "I'm Putting All My Eggs in One Basket"; on ballads ("Tenderly" is an unforgettable example), Armstrong showed he could still tap deep wellsprings.

Perhaps the most satisfying recording project of all was the four-volume retrospective *Satchmo*, elaborately annotated and boxed, with Armstrong's own narration between numbers. "I said someday they're going to do the life of Louis Armstrong," Gabler recalled, "and they're going to have to go to Columbia for all the Okehs. I thought I better go back and record on good clean tape, so I used Bobby Haggart to do the Hot Fives and Sevens and Sy Oliver for the rest, copying the original arrangement. Louis got such a kick out of doing it." At first, Armstrong would come in and record three hours in the afternoon, then have to rush to play a gig that would end at 1 A.M. The musicians were tired and grousing. Gabler convinced Glaser to let him pay whatever he would have made from a nightclub gig in addition to the recording fee, so that the band could record at night and at full capacity. Sy Oliver wrote the trumpet parts in red ink on the lead sheets but wrote under them, "Go for yourself." Armstrong often did, and much of the playing is inspired—for example, "King of the Zulus," a dramatic improvement on the old Hot Five version.

For a while there *was* talk about a Hollywood biopic—in a letter to Goffin, Armstrong said he wanted Louise Beavers to play his mother—but nothing came of it. Still, he continued to make guest appearances in the terminally dumb pseudojazz flicks of the day. He astonished several people on the set of *The Glenn Miller Story* when James Stewart—who was studying trombone for the lead role—asked him if he had any advice for keeping his lips from getting sore. "Yeah, daddy, when you go home tonight, have your old lady sit on your face." Everyone fell out the next morning when Stewart arrived on the set, looked at Louis, and gave him a salute. Armstrong could apparently disarm anyone. Two stories of his visit to the Vatican quickly made the rounds in musicians' circles. In one, the Pope holds out his ring and Louis slides his palm under it in a "gimme five" gesture. In the other, Pope Paul VI asked him if he had children and Louis said, "No, daddy, but we're still wailing."

Early Ella. 1940s. *(facing page, top)*

Louis and Miles Davis, 1970. *(facing page, bottom)*

At the Vatican with Pope Paul IV, 1968. *(page 182, top)*

On the set of Anthony Manne's *The Glenn Miller Story*, with James Stewart, Trummy Young, Cozy Cole, Barney Bigard, Gene Krupa, Arvell Shaw, Marty Napoleon, 1954. *(page 182, bottom)*

Trummy Young (left), Tony Randall, Jimmy Durante (in hat), and Henry Fonda (right) feelin' the spirit, President Kennedy's Inaugural Ball, Waldorf-Astoria Hotel, New York City, 1960. *(page 183, top)*

Louis backstage at Smith College, December 1, 1963, with a fan, four-year-old John Hassan. This was the concert at which he played "God Bless America" in memoriam for President Kennedy. *(page 183, bottom)*

Jack Bradley took this photo in the dressing room at Tuxedo Park, N.Y., in 1960. "Print up thousands of 'em," Louis told him. But Bradley never allowed it to be published until now.

With Trummy Young, 1959. (*facing page, top*)

Like many pictures in his scrapbooks, Armstrong captioned this one of himself with Lucille and Velma Middleton, late 1950s. (*facing page, bottom*)

Backstage at a Louis Armstrong concert was always a time for high spirits and old friends, c. 1950. Louis embraces Lil Hardin, bottom left, while Lucille pretends to pummel him. (*overleaf*)

Armstrong's wit, his utter lack of pretentiousness, and his unpredictability were legendary. It was on the Tommy Dorsey show that the bandleader innocently asked him what tempo he preferred and heard, "Not too slow, not too fast, just half-fast." Erroll Garner liked to tell about the time he stuck his head in Louis's dressing room after a show and said, "What's new?" "Nothin' new," came back at him. "White folks still ahead." Bobby Hackett told writer Max Jones of the rehearsal that Armstrong halted when a young trumpet player hit an A natural instead of an A flat. The kid, arrogant and determined to show off, said, "Well, you know, Pop, things change, man. Nothin' ever stays the same." Armstrong walked up to him and said, "Man, I'll tell you one thing that'll never change." "What's that?" "You'll always be a spade. You can bet on that. That ain't gonna *change!*" One year he posed sitting on the toilet in a homemade ad for Swiss Kriss and sent it out as a Christmas card. Jack Bradley, who frequently photographed him backstage, once shot him from behind when he was naked and unaware. He brought a print to Louis a couple of days later and asked if he minded if he kept a copy for himself. "No, daddy," he said. "Print up a thousand, send 'em to everybody." With Lucille's connivance, Bradley once snuck up on him in a grotesque mask. Armstrong looked up and said, "Oh, hi Jack." When he removed the mask, Louis shrieked in horror. He could surprise his musicians, too. On December 1, 1963, nine days after the killing in Dallas, the All Stars played a concert at Smith College. At the end of the show, as the ensemble was about to go into "Sleepytime," Louis walked to the mike and, unaccompanied, played a dirgelike interpretation of "God Bless America." When he finished, he told the stunned audience, "That was for President Kennedy. Good night," and left the stage.

He never lost his sense of competition. Armstrong loved Trummy Young, the trombonist and singer who had starred with the Jimmie Lunceford Orchestra in the 1930s; Louis saved his career by buying him a new set of teeth and encouraging him when he'd fallen on hard times, and Trummy eventually became one of the most popular members of the All Stars. Yet one night Trummy upstaged him and Louis told him to lay back. The next night Armstrong took too much Swiss Kriss and needed to leave the stage—"Take over," he told Trummy. "But, Pops, you told me to lay back." Louis just glared at him and no more was said on the subject. He rarely lost his temper, but he could be fierce when he did. Danny Barker once said Louis could get so mad he'd suck all

186

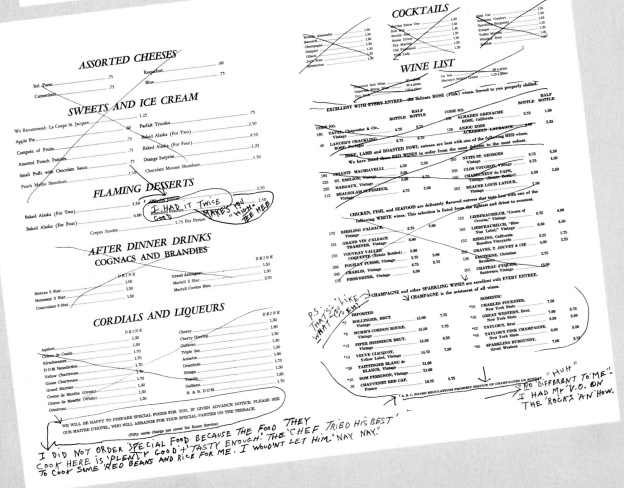

the air out of the room. Lucille said, "I think he invented cuss words, he had some I've never heard before. But his anger was always justified—he didn't hold things in." Bobby Hackett has told of the 1953 tour by Louis and Benny Goodman, which had an advance sale of over $1 million. Goodman told him it was his package and Armstrong would do as he was told. "You're nothin'," Armstrong told him, and proceeded to outplay him so badly that Goodman got sick. In Hackett's words, "Pops came close to killing him without touching him, just playing." Years later, when Jimmie Noone's name came up in an interview, Louis said, "Oh that's where Benny Goodman got his whole style."

By the early 1960s, Armstrong's career was in need of a boost. The Little Rock controversy had taken a lot out of him, and in 1959 he suffered a heart attack while playing in Spoleto. He often experienced shortness of breath and was instructed not to play the trumpet for periods of time. His latest records were uneven, and several suggested a willingness to embrace the neo-Dixieland revival. Gil Evans met him one night and was amazed that Armstrong knew and admired his collaboration with Miles Davis on *Porgy and Bess.* Armstrong was Evans's god, the man he considered most responsible for inspiring him to be a musician. When Armstrong suggested a collaboration—he jokingly added, "You're not gonna throw any of them funny chords at me, are you Pops?"—Evans followed up with a visit to Glaser's office. "Gil who?" Glaser wouldn't consider it, and Evans, who never brought it up again, always wondered if Armstrong thought he was the one who lost interest. Louis did make three remarkable records in 1961: Producer Bob Thiele managed to get him together with Duke Ellington for two trenchant albums in which, as usual, the superb musicianship proved mutually rejuvenating—the result is superbly played, modern, and beyond category; and Dave and Iola Brubeck wrote a Broadway-style musical called *The Real Ambassadors,* which, though dated in its topical references, spills over with Armstrong's majestic horn and magnetic voice. What he and Glaser coveted, however, was a record that could get radio play.

In 1963, David Merrick was set to bring a new musical to Broadway and he needed someone to record the title song. Louis was chosen and on December 3, the score's publisher took him to a studio to record "Hello Dolly" and another Broadway song, "A Lot of Livin' to Do," from *Bye Bye Birdie.* Armstrong shook his head in dismay when he read the lead sheet for "Dolly," according to Jack Bradley, who wrote about the session in a jazz magazine and predicted that given the right push,

He liked Swiss Kriss in part for the same reason he liked marijuana—both are natural herbs. When Louis sent this photo out as a Christmas card, a Hearst columnist launched an attack.

Armstrong prepared a series of diets and health charts—which he didn't rigorously follow.

He even annotated menus. (*facing page*)

"A Lot of Livin' to Do" just might get some airplay. The two sides were sold to Kapp Records, and eight weeks later "Hello Dolly" was on the *Billboard* charts, where it remained for twenty-two weeks, reaching the number 1 spot in May. If you remember 1964, you may cringe at the mention of "Hello Dolly," because it was ubiquitous. It's possible to hear something too much, and "Dolly" was on radio day and night, and Armstrong seemed to be on television almost as much. He made all the talk and variety shows, and even sang it a capella on *What's My Line?* Less than two and a half minutes long, "Hello Dolly" was a triumph for him, for his generation, for jazz. It was also a class record.

One of the classiest things about it was its independence from the egregious formulas of mainstream pop. True, strings were added for sweetening, but they are barely audible. The only real compromise with the standard approach and instrumentation of the All Stars was the addition of a banjo. The trite song, which has had virtually no life beyond Armstrong and the show itself, was an unswinging set piece on Broadway, pompous and logy. Armstrong had transformed dross into gold once again, and even got to play a full chorus of trumpet. The banjo was an ingenious touch. By the sixties, that ancient instrument, which dominated nineteenth-century popular music (whole minstrel troupes played them in unison) was little heard beyond Dixieland and bluegrass. The eight-bar banjo intro, oddly electric and percussive, worked like an alarm clock to introduce a performance unlike anything else on the Top Forty. The Dolly whom Armstrong so enthusiastically welcomed back was, as Frank Sinatra (who soon recorded a version he called "Hello Louis") and others realized, none other than himself— back on top where he belonged. Louis's rhythm section and the backing by Trummy Young and clarinetist Joe Darensbourg were right on the money, and his trumpet solo and burnished vocal were ringingly, inimitably Armstrongian. The whole performance was casually flawless.

Kapp rushed him back into the studio to cut ten more tunes so he could issue an album; predictably, there were attempts to imitate the formula—All Stars + banjo + hokey Broadway song = big bucks. Lacking the spontaneity of the original, they didn't work. Yet Armstrong's career was on a new course, and though his friends wished he would take it easy, he spent his sixty-third year, and the years that followed, on a bus, weaving from city to city and apparently relishing every gig. When the godawful movie of *Hello, Dolly!* was made, David Merrick gave Armstrong the royal treatment and star billing, even though he

With Duke Ellington on the set of Martin Ritt's *Paris Blues*, 1961.

Armstrong's two-minute appearance in Gene Kelly's elephantine movie *Hello, Dolly!* virtually stole the show from its star, Barbra Streisand, 1969. (*overleaf*)

was only in it for two and a half minutes. It was no secret that his record made the show a megahit, the longest-running Broadway musical up to that time. At screenings of the film, it was not unusual for audiences to applaud only during the climactic moment when the camera pans over to Armstrong and settles, at long last, on his mug—direct sunlight in an otherwise fluorescent movie.

Animal trainer, c. 1962.

S E V E N

Louis Armstrong's recorded works span nearly forty-eight years. In that time he employed about twelve hundred musicians in the service of more than a thousand songs, some of which he performed repeatedly in the presence of recording devices: "Sleepytime Down South" (his theme song) ninety-eight times; "When the Saints Go Marching In" fifty-eight times; "Basin Street Blues" fifty-three times; "Indiana" forty-seven times; "Muskrat Ramble" and "Struttin' with Some Barbecue" forty-three times; "Mack the Knife" forty-two times; "St. Louis Blues" forty times. Those figures are drawn from Hans Westerberg's Louis Armstrong discography, which was published in 1981—other performances have come to light since then. Even if one had the room to house all of Armstrong's recordings, legitimate and otherwise, one wouldn't necessarily want to listen to them all.

Yet notwithstanding the many meretricious, trite, foolish, formulaic, repetitive, tired records Armstrong was asked to make, the majority of his recorded performances are rewarding, often surprisingly so. In the late 1960s, for example, when he worked primarily as a singer, he was asked to interpret stage and film songs of the period, as well as country songs, Disney songs, and such "timely" drivel as "His Father Wore Long Hair," which has something to do with Jesus' father. Hip jazz fans did not buy those records, and they remain virtually unknown. I regret as much as anyone that Armstrong's last visits to the studio were supervised by cornballs, but there are gems—yes, gems—even in those sessions. At the "Long Hair" session, he also suffered the indignity of having to sing "We Shall Overcome" with a chorus of celebrities, as well as "Give Peace a Chance" and (talk about dated) "The Creator Has a Master Plan" with Leon Thomas. That was his penultimate and probably worst album ever (although the country album that followed is a fair rival). His voice was burned to a husk. Yet his readings of "My One and Only

With Lucille and the Sphinx, Egypt, 1962. (*preceding overleaf*)

"Still wailin'," c. 1959. (*facing page*)

Dizzy Gillespie, Jackie Gleason, Junior Mance (at piano), and Louis at rehearsal for Timex TV show, 1959.

With Lotte Lenya, 1955.

With Milton Berle, c. 1967.

A fan first of the Brooklyn Dodgers, then the Mets, Louis poses with pitcher Don Newcombe.

Spencer Tracy and Louis, c. 1945.

Louis and Harpo Marx, 1950.

Kay Starr and Louis each rode the charts in the 1950s.

Dave Brubeck and Armstrong at a session for "The Real Ambassadors," 1961.

Love," "Mood Indigo," and "What a Wonderful World" are poignant and treasurable, and his asides on the other tracks (e.g., "give me a little ol' peace, de-ah") remind us that he wasn't buying anybody's sentimental jive. You could lead Armstrong to the age of Aquarius, but you couldn't make him hallucinate.

Then there's "I Will Wait for You," the tear-jerking ballad from *The Umbrellas of Cherbourg.* Armstrong's is surely the only version in which the listener is made to understand why he's waiting and what he's got in mind for her when she gets there. His asides are happily lubricious, and one is bound to recall with pleasure that they come from the same man who created "Tight Like That" forty years earlier. For the same album, he was asked to salvage "Talk to the Animals," the song that almost brought Rex Harrison's career to a standstill. While the choir talks to the animals, Louis talks to them. When they mention crocodiles, he interpolates in about half a second, "scared of me as I am of them."

Disney Songs the Satchmo Way, recorded in 1968, contains Louis Armstrong's last great trumpet solos and is a masterpiece of its kind— in some ways the ultimate test of his alchemical powers. It's a record for children—with whistlers, a jolly choir, and arrangements that are square but never as cloying as they could be. Armstrong finds something of his own in every song. Through the kind of careful editing that characterized the Handy and Waller albums, his vocals and solos lead one to the other without a break, and they are spirited and inventive. One is not too surprised that he can find beauty in "When You Wish Upon a Star," though one may be startled at how effective his modalized reading of "Chim Chim Cher-ee" is, especially his two darkly beautiful sixteen-bar trumpet solos. The payoff, though, is the presumably intransigent material, like "Bibbidi-Bobbidi-Boo" (he attacks the non-sense syllables with contagious gusto), "Heigh Ho," "Whistle While You Work" and, most surprisingly, "The Ballad of Davy Crockett," which he interprets with a witty storyteller's parlando ("Oh, the buckskin buccaneer," he chortles as though he were having the time of his life), then lifts his trumpet to wail twenty-four bars in perfect hoedown rhythm. His performances here are the work of a great actor, and of an artist of incomparable naturalness and generosity.

He must have been in much discomfort during the Disney sessions. The purity of his sound on trumpet, especially, is all the more miraculous considering the state of his health. The arteries in his legs were clotted, which contributed to his heart problem, and he was habitually out of

On the radio with Tallulah Bankhead, Bob Hope, Jerry Lewis, c. 1950. (*preceding overleaf*)

With Lucille to his right, and Marty Napoleon to his left, Armstrong auditions Enrico, a young trumpeter, in England, 1968. (*facing page and above*)

Eight years after the Little Rock controversy, birthday greetings from the former President.

The only known photograph of Armstrong and Paul Whiteman, with Tyree Glenn (left) and concert promoter, St. John Terrell (right) at a July 4, 1966, birthday celebration in Lambertville, New Jersey.

Taking a break at a recording session, early 1960s.

breath. He suffered from ulcers and kidney problems. Still, he went from Disneyland to London, then back to Las Vegas, before submitting himself to hospital care in late 1968. In early 1969, he had to undergo a tracheotomy, and it was during his recuperation in Beth Israel that he learned of Joe Glaser's fatal stroke and insisted on seeing him, though he lay in a coma. When Armstrong was allowed home, he wrote furiously, digging into the deep past and paying tribute to the doctors and nurses who cared for him. He went back to London twice, recording the theme song to the James Bond movie *On Her Majesty's Secret Service* in 1969, and during the following year appeared on more than a dozen television shows in New York and Los Angeles. For *Esquire*'s December 1969 issue, he was one of several artists at or nearing seventy who were invited to offer advice to the next generation. "I feel that I did my interesting work as I have gotten into the older age bracket," he wrote. "Most of your great composers—musicians—are elderly people, way up there in age—they will live forever. There's no such thing as on the way out. As long as you are still doing something interesting and good. You are in business as long as you are breathing. Yeah."

Louis celebrated his official seventieth birthday at the Newport Jazz Festival in June. The Eureka Jazz Band, half a dozen trumpet stars, including Dizzy Gillespie and Bobby Hackett, and Mahalia Jackson were on hand to pay him homage. A furious downpour started shortly before he was scheduled to go on, and he walked out early so people wouldn't have to wait in the rain. It was customary during downpours for people to run back to the food kiosks for shelter or to hoist tarpaulins. On that evening, they stayed put, cheering in the rain, while Louis romped medley-fashion through several of his hits, assuring everyone from time to time that he wouldn't keep them long. Another party ensued in Hollywood. Two weeks before Newport, he had started to compose a letter to his fans. Reproduced here in its entirety, it begins "This is Louis Satchmo Armstrong speaking from his home in Corona":

Surrounded by members of the Eureka Brass Band and Bobby Hackett, Armstrong rehearses his seventieth-birthday concert at the Newport Jazz Festival, 1970. (*facing page*)

I've just gotten out of the Beth Israel Hospital. I've had a million things that happened to me, including the operation for tracheotomy. And I'm coming along just fine and I'm getting my strength back, even in my legs. I thought that it is real thrilling to send a message to my fans and friends from all over the world. Which I'd like to thank all of them from every nook and corner of the world, for their lovely get well cards and

In his den in Corona, Queens, 1971. (*above*)

Publicity photo, 1931. (*facing page*)

prayers which did wonders for me. I also want to thank my personal Doctor Gary Zucker—his staff of doctors, Mrs. Lucille Armstrong, Dr. Alexander Schiff, our company doctor, Ira Mangel, our road manager for many years for many years [sic], and still is. That is if I ever get back to work again. I am looking forward to it. I feel that I owe them, my public and fans, my services again. Which they are eagerly waiting for. I would also like all the nurses in intensive care [sic]—God bless them all. They worked so very hard along with my Dr. Zucker to save my life. And God knows that I was in real bad shape. I also would like to thank the private nurses on the 11th floor of the Beth Israel Hospital who served me around the clock. They were all so nice and kind. (*Archive*)

He insisted on taking an engagement at New York's Waldorf-Astoria early in 1971, followed by a couple of television guest shots. On February 26, in his home, he made his last record, an animated reading of "The Night Before Christmas," later distributed as a single by the Lorillard Company. He had another heart attack two weeks later and was put in intensive care until May 5, when he insisted on going home. On July 5, he asked Dr. Schiff to bring the band together for a rehearsal—he was ready to perform again. He passed away at five-thirty the next morning.

Appendix

n this document, presumably written in 1968, though it may have been later, Louis Armstrong copied out a letter from a childhood friend, interpolating his own comments. Their voices merge in a catalogue of names (and what names!) from their childhood days in New Orleans. I've attempted to distinguish Armstrong's observations from those of Larry Amadee, his correspondent, by printing the latter in italics; much guesswork was involved in that, especially since both men refer to Armstrong in the third person. I've maintained the style almost exactly, except for Armstrong's tendency to arbitrarily—or so it seems to me—capitalize and underline words. I've checked and corrected spellings of proper names where possible. One or two addresses of dance halls may be wrong, but Armstrong's memory is basically reliable. At the very end, Armstrong wrote "'s all," then crossed it out and wrote "more," adding the note about Fate Marable's opening theme. Of special interest are the new details of Armstrong's arrival in Chicago. Generally, his memory in 1968 bears out his recollections of 1954, in *Satchmo: My Life in New Orleans*.

NEW ORLEANS

Attempts to save the house in which Armstrong was born and the Colored Waif's Home were defeated in the mid-1960s. A brick from the Waif's Home.

A letter from Larry Amadee, a boy with whom I was raised up with in New Orleans, from the early days when we were both in the Colored Waif's Home for Boys, back of City Park Avenue. Real youngsters. He brought back some real and interesting memories of the good old days and the things that we both knew *all* about. And now his letter. From Chicago, Ill.—May 6th, 1968. As follows—

To the King of Trumpeters and the entire musical world. None other than Louis (Dipper) Gatemouth Armstrong. He's my boyhood pal, and definitely my lifelong friend and idol. Papa, I am feeling fairly good physically. Hoping you and your family are enjoying everything that life can offer.

I am indeed very sorry that I cannot make the trip to our good old home town (New Orleans). (Smile.)

Louis, I was down there for the Mardi gras a little over two weeks. I had a wonderful time during my stay. The celebration of 250 years Birth of Jazz was without a doubt the greatest of all events in the history of New Orleans. Out of all the trips that I have made in the past 50 years—the celebration of 250 years of Birth of Jazz was the greatest.

COLORED 1913   WAIFS' (JONES') NEW ORLEANS, LOUISIANA   HOME 1913

The Colored Waif's Home and its founder (inset), Captain Jones.

I have followed you all through your musical career—more than anybody else. You and I met in Professor Jones' Waif's Home for Bad Boys, the year of 1913. Remember?—Real youngsters. Back in those days, Buckeye Joe— King Oliver—was my favorite on cornet. We all named him Buckeye because he had a cataract on his eye and it seemed that he used to buck that eye when he would hit those fine high notes. And he could really hit them in those days.

(Bunk) Willie Johnson was No. "2" on my list. I didn't know very much about Buddy Bolden. Later in my teenage days I heard of him. I was told that he could blow the cornet so loud and strong until you could hear his cornet for miles and miles, and he went crazy from blowing so loud. That's the story that the old timers told me. Sorry that I did not hear him for myself and own judgement. But everybody said he was a character and blew a lot of horn. Bunk Johnson was a good cornet player with a beautiful tone. Bunk was a neighbor to my father + mother in the downtown section of New Orleans. That was when I was a kid. My father also knew such cornet players as Kid Rena, who also came up in the Orphanage Home of the Colored Waif Home for Boys with us, who also turned out to be a real good

Reunion at the Boys Home, with band instructor Peter Davis and Captain Jones.

cornet player. Hit high notes real good for a long time before he died. There's some more real good cornet players that I knew also—there were Red Brickay, Sidney Desvigne. Another good one. And Manuel Perez, (Satch played in his band) *he was a waltz and schottische king from Downtown in the 7th Ward, known as a (Stomp Down) Creole, meaning a full-blooded Creole. Better than black. He played cornet in the Onward Brass Band alongside King Oliver, whenever there were parades + funerals. And what a ragtime team they made. On Labor Day Parades with many brass bands—Joe Oliver and Manuel Perez would get all of the second liners, the raggedy guys who followed parades + funerals, especially when they played the tunes "Panama" and the "Saints."* The second liners would applaud and make the Onward Brass Band play an encore for them—which was unusual.

Speaking of more good cornetists in our young days, Andrew Kimball. He was a very good cornetist. He played with Professor John Robichaux at the St. Catherine Hall, just across the street from the Charity Hall on Tulane Avenue. He also played in Robichaux's Orchestra at the Lyric Theater at Iberville and Burgundy. Robichaux had the kind of Orchestra that could read music real well at first sight. Robichaux was a superb violinist and handled his Orchestra and those shows with the greatest of ease. And since the Lyric Theater was a strictly white theater for generations and they finally turned it over to the colored people, quite naturally they had to hire the best musicians. So that was it. Robichaux was THEE man. All of his musicians were well trained. But the youngsters filed in the theater to hear Kimble. He was just beautiful.

Now for more cornet players of destination in our teenage days in New Orleans, there was Buddy Petit, cornet, a good blues man. Especially for the honky tonks such as Savocca's, Spano's, Buddy Bottly's, etc., where all of the second rate pimps, whores, gamblers hung out all night. Buddy was definitely their choice. Especially when he blew those blues for them. He was also their choice at the Economy Hall. Whenever they gave a ball in the days of good old ragtime and jazz music, they hired him to play his cornet. Another good cornet player was Papa Celestin, although he blew his cornet from the side of his lips. He always delivered a real beautiful tone. Mellow and very pleasing to the ear. He was the leader of the Tuxedo Brass Band and they really were airtight.

I, Louis Armstrong, had the thrilling pleasure of playing second cornet with Celestin and his Brass Band. When my idol Joe King Oliver sent for me to join his Creole Jazz Band in 1922 in Chicago-Ill, to play second trumpet to him. I had just finished playing a funeral with Celestin and his Tuxedo Brass Band when I received the wire from Papa Joe (the name I always called him). And it was a hard decision for me to leave Tuxedo. My best break down in N.O. [was] with Celestin and at the same time I was playing on the Steamer Sydney—Excursion Boat with Fate Marable's Band. I loved both jobs and was pretty much satisfied. But I loved Joe King Oliver so much, and out of clear skies I find myself immediately after I had finished playing a funeral that day with Tuxedo going to the Illinois Central [Railroad] Station, that is inquiring about my ticket to Chicago. I made up my mind just that quick. Nothing could change it. Joe my idol had sent for me—wow. Fate Marable, Celestin, and the whole Tuxedo Brass Band came to the station with me that day. They said stay home, you are all set here, Joe Oliver's Band is scabbin' in Chicago. I told them these words: Joe Oliver is my idol. I have loved him all my life. He sent for me and whatever he's doing I want to do it with him. Just then I boarded the train with the fish sandwich (trout loaf) that Mayann, my dear mother, had fixed for me and I was on my way to be with the man I musically loved—King Oliver. I did not rest until I saw his smiling face. Although he missed me at the 12th Street Station because my train was late, and he had to go to work with the Creole Jazz Band at the Lincoln Gardens. The railroad where I arrived was at 12th Street + Michigan and the Lincoln Gardens was at 31st Street + Cottage Grove Ave., Chicago. Joe Oliver couldn't wait for the next train that I was to arrive on, so he tipped the porter to be on the lookout for me. The porter put me in a taxicab that would take me to the Gardens. When I got to the Gardens, King Oliver, Johnny Dodds, Honore Dutrey, Lil Hardin, Baby Dodds, Bill Johnson were swinging some tune and it sounded so great until I was almost in doubt whether I should go in the place and report to Papa Joe or just go on back to N.O. on the next train. In fact, from the music that I was hearing I did not think I was good enough to ever sit in the band. Somebody must have told Joe Oliver about my dumbness—standing out there and refusing to come in—so Papa Joe came outside and when he saw me, the first words that he said to me, "Come on IN HEAH, you little dumb sombitch, we've been waiting for your black ass all night. Ha ha." Then I was happy and at home just to hear his voice, and enjoyed every moment with him. Mrs. Stella Oliver, Joe Oliver's wife, was really swell to me. I ate all of my meals with Papa Joe. He liked the kinds of food that I loved and was raised on. We both were raised on soul food. Later about that.—

Now back to Larry Amadee and my choice or our choice of all the pioneers of Ragtime and Jazz Music through the years. In his letter to me, we agreed on everything that he said because it is right. So dig this. We also admired these cornet players. Lee Collins, Red Allen, Guy Kelly, Chris Kelly, Sam Morgan, Punch Miller. They *all* were good cornet players. Some more cornets—Freddie Keppard, Wooden Joe Nicholas (he was Albert Nicholas the great clarinet player's uncle). Maurice Durand was a very good cornetist, but was very much underrated. Larry Amadee sez, *I may be a layman but I am a damn good one.* How true. He took up boxing and training and he did wonders for Joe Louis with Blackburn, that is if you followed Joe Louis's career. Larry also told me *Louis, I am full of good music. I am an uncultivated critic. I know it when I hear it. I can't play it, I always could dance to it very good* (meaning good Jazz.) *Louis Armstrong is a Hall of Fame. Armstrong is a legend. King Oliver won my admiration during my boyhood days. His style hypnotized me. Funeral parades and furniture wagons. Advertisements. Our idol the late Joe King Oliver was in Savannah, Georgia. Stranded after many years illness, an old man. Louis Armstrong saw him there just before he died*

Louis and Bunk Johnson, 1945. (*facing page, top*)

On the stoop in Corona. Whenever he returned from a road tour, the kids would know, and they'd be waiting for him. c. 1968. (*facing page, bottom*)

Dizzy Gillespie (left) bears no "modern malice" at the man whose place in music he called "unimpeachable." c. 1960. (*page 218, top*)

With W.C. Handy and George Avakian at the famous 1954 record session. (*page 218, bottom*)

Three friends from New Orleans: Henry "Red" Allen, Armstrong, Zutty Singleton, c. 1961. (*page 219, top*)

Nightclubbing with Count Basie, c. 1940. (*page 219, bottom*)

218

The Astoria Hotel, Rampart and Gravier streets, 1961.

San Jacinto on Dumaine Street.

(when Louis [was] touching with Luis Russell's band) *and gave him a lot of money that he had collected on his one night stands, which was a great thrill to Louis Armstrong.* (He said.) *They buried King Oliver in New York and Louis Armstrong was right there at his funeral. He loved that man. He also wept.*

Amadee speaking—*Oliver had extra lungs close to perfection. When he was young. My first musical idol. Louis is the second idol. Joe and Louis are really incomparable, musically speaking. Among the old clarinet players the late Johnny Dodds, Joe Oliver's star clarinetist and one of the greatest of all times. The late Big Eye Louis Nelson was one of the greatest.* (In the early years.) *He refused to travel. Barney Bigard, a youngster from N.O., traveled with "Louie" for many years.* Louis Armstrong "sez" he thinks that Barney is the greatest clarinet player that he ever blowed with. Yes, he thinks Barney cut 'em all. Louis did not play any too much with Jimmie Noone, but admits that he is a real good man on the clarinet. He still thinks that Barney is the apple of his eye, clarinetwise. Tio-Picou-Sam Dutrey. Albert Nicholas is also a good clarinetist, said Louis—but I'll still take ol' Barnyard (our pet name for Barney).

Amadee mentions drummers and he's right. We see them eye to eye. Meelie Barnes, Albert Francis (whom I enjoyed working with at Tom Anderson's Restaurant in Paul Dominguez's Band, on Rampart near Canal Street. Early days.)

Some more good drummers whom I am very familiar with—Joe Watson, Pete Lacosso. Red Happy, in our minds the greatest drummer in the jazzland style. He was born great. He could sing, dance, be funny + play those drums better than anybody else. It was really a thrill to watch him work. He always had Something new up his sleeves that was real interesting, yea Red Happy Bolton. He and Black Benny were our choice, especially Louis Armstrong's, of all the all-time drummers in our teenage days in New Orleans. And God knows they were all great drummers. But Redhead Happy and Black Benny were the top characters. But good + great. Now there were other great drummers such—as Zutty Singleton, Paul (Tee Boy) Barbarin. Came up with us. Also played with Luis Russell. *Baby Dodds—*(On the boat with Fate Marable.) Snags, Joe Oliver's old ace. He was exceptionally good and kept Joe Oliver in stitches with laughter every night. He was snaggled toothed and no teeth in the front of his mouth at all. And when he takes a drum solo he looks straight at Joe Oliver and when he smiles at Joe with no teeth, Joe Oliver would crack up so bad, until we almost have to drag him off the bandstand. And we weren't much help, because we're all so tickled with laughing at Snags—we were all too weak to do anything. And it happened every time. Little Mack was a good drummer. Oh boy, he was known for his rhythm. The way he slapped those sticks on those drums was really something else. Joe Lindsey was a young fine drummer. He and I had a teenage band when we were very young. Joe Lindsey, being a nice looking youngster, got wrapped up with one of those big time sporting gals, giving him lots of money. And—well, you can figure out the rest of his life. He died with everything that you could think of. (All kinds of complications.) Chinees (his nickname) was another drummer from the old Economy Hall days. I enjoyed working with him also, but didn't see much of him. I was so busy being around Happy, Black Benny and Snags, did not see or play with the other fellers very much. Of course when I went to Chicago, I ran into another great drummer from New Orleans whom I thought was a real great drummer in Carroll Dickerson's Orchestra (which I played with for Joe Glaser at the Sunset), and that's none other than Tubby Fred Hall. (Minor Hall's brother. Both drummers of old in New Orleans. More about Tubby.) Now there was a drummer in my books who stood up with the best of them, and until this day of modern times. Of course, I must agree with Larry Amadee concerning Black Benny. Outside of being a great drummer and a good musician and our idol, he was a neat and handsome man with a well constructed body. Fearless. Would fight at the drop of the hat and *could* fight. (Story of the Fire Department— the Church + and the guy called Jesus.)

Economy Hall on Ursuline Street.

Here's the name of the Dance Hall sections during our young days— as follows—The Economy Hall (downtown across Canal Street), Co-Operators Hall (ditto), the Winter Garden (up from Canal Street), the Roof Garden (Rampart Street), the Sans Souci Hall (uptown), The Butcher Hill Hall (near the Protection Levee up in Charlton), Bradens Astoria Hotel dance hall (Rampart and Gravier), the Pythian Temple Roof Garden (located on Gravier and Saratoga Streets opposite the old Parish Prison), Pete Lala's Cabaret in Storyville (where Joe Oliver played for many years), Mrs. Cole's Willow Lawn (uptown), where Kid Ory's Band played for a long time. Later Joe Oliver joined them there. Ory + Oliver (or vice versa). The Fairgrounds Battlefield Hall, they also held horse races there. The Artesan Hall (all Creoles) in the 7th Ward, the Perseverance Hall (ditto), the Francs Amis Hall (Creole Section), the Independence Hall (ditto, Elmira Street near St. Claude St.), St. Mary's Hall (the same), Two Honky Tonks (3rd Ward), Savocca's

*S*hades and a Camel, c. 1948.

(Poydras and Saratoga), and Spano's (Poydras and Franklin Sts.), Pratts on Dryades + Perdido (later Howard Ave and Dryades St.), Henry Matranga's Honky Tonk (Franklin + Perdido Sts., 3rd Ward), where Armstrong came up, played at Matranga's.

Willie Jackson, singer + comedian, played the Lyric Theater, Iroquois Theater, and Tom Anderson before he came up north. Tom Anderson [was] No. "2", corner of Iberville and Basin St. in Storyville—Red Light District. Lulu White was the Queen of Storyville Red Light District. Louis Clark Wade and Morris Moore were the two big pimps bosses among the colored broads—and Paul Gross was a second rater in line. Butsey Fernandez was the big white pimp. Ludlum, Aaron Harris, Geo. Boe Hog, and Bob Keno were the leading colored gamblers that were well known. The boundary lines of Storyville—Basin Street to North Claiborne, Canal Street to St. Louis Street. Boxing Arenas—the Orleans Athletic Club, Tulane A.C., the Louisiana Auditorium, Pilsbury Garden A.C., Hypodrome A.C., Northside Club, National Baseball, Heineman Park, Tommy Burns Club. Two colored unknown clubs.

A large number of nicknamed characters that made history in the City of New Orleans, La. They fought each other because of hate, jealousy + rivalry. They would gang around different dance halls; there were real bullies in all the wards. In different neighborhoods—Uptown, Downtown, Front of Town, and Back of Town. Said Larry—*I know because I traveled around the city quite a bit in my boyhood days.*

I delivered groceries, drugs, shoes, I also worked on the ice cream wagons. Plus—I attended dances in different parts of the City of N.O. Louis started playing with the best older musicians during the times that I didn't run across him. So he got good real early. As a boy, I did not have much fear. I will arrive at my conclusion by beginning to name some of the well known characters. A good long story to my good friend and idol, Louis Armstrong. I do hope that this long historical story didn't bore you Gate/Satch.

The Memory of the Bullies and Trouble Makers. Black Benny, Jimmy Maker, Yellow Lugene, Dirty Dog, Red Devil, Cheeky Black, Long Head Willie Logan, Roughhouse Cameel.

Second Line Buddies. Nica Deemus, Rawhead, Black Sol, Black Lute, Hobo Crookit, Big Walter Bell, Cocaine Buddy, Ikey Smooth, Jakey Brown, Lips the Camel, Big Sore Dick, Foots Arrel, Nasty Slim.

The Females. Big Vi Green, Mary Meat Market, Funky Stella, Foote Mama, Crosseyed Louise, Mary Jack the Bear, Alberta, Steal Arm Johnny.

Notorious Group. Zeno Green—he wore those stack ties, nicknamed Stacktie Kid. He owned a little colored hotel at Rampart and Lafayette Sts. and worked at the Iroquois Theater as ticket taker, at Rampart and Perdido Streets. It was a small moving picture house we used to love to go and see Wm. S. Hart and Eddie Polo, etc. 10 cents admission. Raffle nights were on Tuesdays. If you had a lucky number on your ticket, you win a pound of delicious chocolates. Hmmm, but they were good. Redhead Happy played drums there. Kid Green was an ex-prize fighter, [and] won enough money to become owner of the Baton Rouge Hotel— Rampart and Lafayette Streets. Kid Green was also a dog trainer. Green had all of his white teeth pulled out and replaced with all gold teeth. Green bought a Boston bulldog and [had] all of his white teeth pulled and also replaced with gold teeth. Green taught his dog to smile only at white people on Canal Street, and growl and bark at colored people. That was because the white people would tip more money. Green had a gold chain and a blood red jacket on his dog. What a character. P.S. I knew Maurice Durand's mother, father and brothers. They all lived on Lizard Street, downtown in the 9th Ward.

Special attention Satchmo. Whenever you are on TV programs and wherever you may be in this country, if opportune time presents itself, please dedicate a number to me. My favorite song, "When the Saints Go Marchin' In." Give my regards to all. Sincerely yours in sports—
Larry Amadee
[address and phone number in Chicago]
We both were born on national holidays. Two of New Orleans' famous sons. Louis Armstrong, July 4, 1900, and Larry Amadee, Christmas December 25, 1898. Both men have the same initials—L.A. and L.A. 's all/more—
Fate Marable's Band on the Mississippi Excursion Steamboats. Our opening number was "In the Land of Beginning Again."

Discography

Albums are listed in rough chronological order within each section. Catalogue numbers denote LPs, though some compact discs are also included. The period of time covered by an album is given at the end of the entry, unless that information is part of the title. I've tried to limit repetitions and have focused on domestic albums that were in print during the past decade, though there are of necessity many exceptions. As all jazz lovers know, American record companies have failed to prepare definitive editions of Armstrong's major work. The long-playing record has been with us forty years and may soon be obsolete, but many of Armstrong's most acclaimed performances—most notably those controlled by Columbia and MCA—have never appeared on American LPs. His recordings with blues singers, for example, have been collated in France, England, Australia, Japan, and other nations, but never in the United States. Nor is there a satisfactory U.S. collection of his recordings with Fletcher Henderson. On those albums where Armstrong is heard on half or less than half the selections, I've specified the number.

THE APPRENTICE YEARS/SIDEMAN RECORDINGS
1923–1930

Louis Armstrong and King Oliver (Milestone M–47017). With King Oliver's Creole Jazz Band, Red Onion Jazz Babies. 1923–24.

King Oliver and His Creole Jazz Band 1923 (Smithsonian R001).

Louis Armstrong and Sidney Bechet in New York 1923–1925 (Smithsonian R026). With Clarence Williams's Blue Five, Red Onion Jazz Babies, Fletcher Henderson, Maggie Jones, Trixie Smith, Grant and Wilson, Perry Bradford's Jazz Phools.

Young Louis the Sideman (1924–1927) (MCA 1301). With Fletcher Henderson, Perry Bradford's Jazz Phools, Erskine Tate's Vendome Orchestra, Lil's Hot Shots, Jimmy Bertrand's Washboard Wizards, Johnny Dodds's Black Bottom Stompers.

Johnny Dodds, *The Spirit of New Orleans 1926–1927* (MCA 1328). Two selections.

Fletcher Henderson, *A Study in Frustration* (France, CBS 66423). Nine selections. 1924–25.

Fletcher Henderson, *Developing an American Orchestra 1923–1937* (Smithsonian R006). Five selections. 1924–25.

Fletcher Henderson, *The Pathé Sessions* (Australia, Swaggie 803). Seven selections. 1924–25.

Fletcher Henderson, *First Impressions* (MCA 1310). Two selections. 1924.

Louis Armstrong and Fletcher Henderson's Orchestra (England, VJM VLP-60). 1924–25.

Ma Rainey (Milestone M-47021). Three selections. 1924.

Bessie Smith, *The Empress* (Columbia G-30818). Six selections. 1925.

Bessie Smith, *Nobody's Blues But Mine* (Columbia G-31093). Three selections. 1925.

Rare Recordings of the Twenties, Vol. 1 (France, CBS 64218). With Maggie Jones, Nolan Walsh, Clara Smith, Sippie Wallace. 1924–27.

Rare Recordings of the Twenties, Vol. 2 (France, CBS 65379). With Clarence Williams's Blue Five, Hociel Thomas. 1924–25.

Rare Recordings of the Twenties, Vol. 3 (France, CBS 65380). With Lillie Delk Christian, Bertha "Chippie" Hill. 1926–28.

Rare Recordings of the Twenties, Vol. 4 (France, CBS 65421). With Blanche Calloway, Baby Mack, Hociel Thomas, Bertha "Chippie" Hill, Sippie Wallace, Victoria Spivey. 1925–29.

Jimmie Rodgers on Record: America's Blue Yodeler (Smithsonian R034). One selection. 1930.

Louis Armstrong Special (France, CBS 65251). With Carroll Dickerson, Seger Ellis, Louis Armstrong and His Orchestra. 1928–32.

THE ARMSTRONG ERA
1925–1932

Armstrong's Okeh recordings are the foundation of the jazz art. Incredibly, no complete edition exists. The *V.S.O.P.* series is the most comprehensive: It has all 128 titles by the Hot Five, Hot Seven, Savoy Ballroom Five, and the orchestras (Les Hite's and Zilner Randolph's) Armstrong fronted, but no alternate takes. An American edition announced by Columbia is apparently going to duplicate the *V.S.O.P.* programming, but the digital remastering on the first volume is disappointingly shrill. The remastering on the BBC "Jazz Classics in Digital Stereo" anthology is superb, and one can hope that engineer Robert Parker will eventually do all the Okehs; the necessity of relying on Europe for this level of craftsmanship is a disgrace that protectionism won't cure. The remaining Columbia and DRG albums are solid anthologies of Okeh selections (with alternate takes) and have been in print for many years, though the new Columbia series may knock them out. The Smithsonian collection duplicates Columbia's Armstrong-Hines volume and has many other selections as well. Except for two alternate takes, the Armstrong performances on the

two DRG albums are combined on a single compact disc (DRG CDXP 8450).

V.S.O.P. Vol. 1/2 (France, CBS 88001). 1925–27.

V.S.O.P. Vol. 3/4 (France, CBS 88002). 1927–28.

V.S.O.P. Vol. 5/6 (France, CBS 88003). 1928–30.

V.S.O.P. Vol. 7/8 (France, CBS 88004). 1930–32.

The Hot Fives, Volume 1 (Columbia CJ 44049). 1925–26.

Great Original Performances 1923–1931 (England, BBC REB 597).

Louis Armstrong and His Hot Five (Columbia CL 851). 1925–27.

Louis Armstrong and His Hot Seven (Columbia CL 852). 1927.

Louis Armstrong and Earl Hines (Columbia CL 853). 1928.

Louis Armstrong Favorites (Columbia CL 854). 1929–31.

Louis Armstrong and Earl Hines 1928 (Smithsonian R002). With Lillie Delk Christian, Carroll Dickerson.

Louis & the Big Bands 1928–30 (DRG Swing 8450).

Louis Armstrong, Jack Purvis, *Satchmo Style 1929–30* (DRG Swing 8451). Eight selections.

THE BIG BAND YEARS
1932–1945

The Decca recordings represent a radical change from the Okehs, but the best of them are every bit as radiant, and they contain much of Armstrong's finest singing and most exhilarating trumpet, as well as many treasurable novelties—including visits with other Decca artists. Unfortunately, MCA, which owns Decca, has been rather nonchalant about making them available here. A comprehensive edition was issued in Australia by Swaggie, called *The Louis Armstrong*

Orchestra 1935–41: A Chronological Study, and most of the material was released on a series of albums in France, some of which were briefly distributed in U.S. versions. For most American jazz enthusiasts, the Deccas remain a treasure not yet fully savored. I've included *Rare Items*—although it's been out of print for many years (most of the selections are on MCA 1312) and was electrically sabotaged for stereo—because its release was a revelation in the 1960s and for its classic liner notes by Dan Morgenstern. The six performances recorded in Paris in 1934, on Musicmouth, are also on Onyx, which has an alternate take of "St. Louis Blues," but not the other sessions from the European tour. The Bluebird reissue is exemplary.

Young Louis Armstrong 1932–1933 (Bluebird AXM2-5519).

European Tour 1933–1934 (France, Musicmouth 1900).

Tootin' through the Roof: Volume 2 (Onyx 213). Seven selections. 1934.

Back in New York (1935) (MCA 1304).

Rare Items (1935–1944) (Decca DL 79225).

Swing That Music 1936–1938 (MCA 1312).

Satchmo's Collector's Items 1936–1937 (MCA 1322).

Satchmo's Discoveries 1936–1938 (MCA 1326).

More Satchmo's Way (1938) (France, MCA 510.104).

Jeepers Creepers 1938–1939 (France, MCA 510.108).

Harlem Stomp 1939–1941 (France, MCA 510.113).

Heah Me Talkin' to Ya 1939–1941 (France, MCA 510.064).

Satchmo For Ever! 1935–1945 (MCA 1334).

**HIGH SOCIETY: LOUIS AND FRIENDS
1932–1961**

Louis in the 1930s (Collector's Classics 26). Jam session with Jack Teagarden, Bud Freeman, Fats Waller. Radio and film tracks. 1932–42.

New Discoveries (Pumpkin 109). With the Mills Brothers, Frank Sinatra, Benny Goodman, Duke Ellington, All Stars, others. Radio and TV broadcasts. 1937–61.

Louis with Guest Stars (MCA 1306). With Sidney Bechet, Billie Holiday, the Mills Brothers, Ella Fitzgerald. 1938–49.

Midnight at V-Disc (Pumpkin 103). With Jack Teagarden, Bobby Hackett, Lou McGarity, others. Four selections. 1944.

The First Esquire All-American Jazz Concert (Radiola 2MR-5051). With Roy Eldridge, Jack Teagarden, Coleman Hawkins, Art Tatum, others. Concert broadcast. 1944.

The Second Esquire All-American Jazz Concert (England, Saga E-6925). With Benny Goodman and Duke Ellington. Radio broadcast. One selection. 1945.

Havin' Fun (Sounds Rare SR 5009). With Bing Crosby, Joe Venuti, Jack Teagarden. Radio broadcasts. 1949–50.

More Fun (Sounds Rare SR 5010). With Bing Crosby, All Stars, studio orchestra. Radio broadcasts. 1951.

Ella and Louis (Compact disc: Verve 825 373-2). With Ella Fitzgerald and the Oscar Peterson Quartet. 1956.

Ella and Louis Again (Compact disc: Verve 825-374-2). With Ella Fitzgerald and the Oscar Peterson Quartet. 1957.

Porgy and Bess (Verve VE-2-2057). With Ella Fitzgerald and the Russ Garcia Orchestra. 1957.

Louis Armstrong Meets Oscar Peterson (Compact disc: Verve 825 713-2). With the Oscar Peterson Quartet. 1957.

And the Dukes of Dixieland (Audio-fidelity AFDS-5924). 1958–60.

Great Alternatives (Chiaroscuro 2003). With the Dukes of Dixieland. 1958–60.

Sweetheart (Chiaroscuro 2006). With the Dukes of Dixieland. 1959.

Bing and Satchmo (MGM E-3882). With Bing Crosby. 1960.

The Real Ambassadors (Columbia OS 2250). With the All Stars, Carmen McRae, Lambert, Hendricks & Ross, Dave Brubeck. 1961.

Together for the First Time/The Great Reunion (Mobile Fidelity 2-807). With Duke Ellington. 1961.

THE ALL STARS PLUS
1946–1971

Armstrong's future was sewn up at the 1947 Town Hall concert, when he introduced to great acclaim the small combo that would set the pattern for the various editions of his All Stars. RCA has never issued the entire concert in the U.S., though it was recently issued in France. A compact disc version of *Pops*, subtitled "The 1940s Small-Band Sides" (6378-2-RB) has fifteen of the album's thirty-two selections, plus five numbers from Town Hall (including one, Teagarden's brilliant "St. James Infirmary," on which Armstrong doesn't play), which suggests how inept the custodians of America's classic music can be. Far more egregious are the new Columbia versions of the W. C. Handy and Fats Waller albums; each a montage of original cuts and alternate takes, they masquerade as the much superior original editions—which have now become collector's items. I've noted whether an album presents Armstrong with his All Stars or in another musical setting. Albums identified here and in the preceding category as radio, concert, and TV broadcasts are mostly of doubtful legality but high musical quality.

Pops (Bluebird 5920-1-RB). Big band, All Stars. 1946–47.

With Edmond Hall's All-Stars (Alamac QSR 2411). The Edmond Hall Sextet. Concert broadcast. 1947.

The Complete Town Hall Concert, 1947 (France, RCA NL89746-2). All Stars.

Satchmo at Symphony Hall (MCA2 4057). All Stars. 1947.

Basin Street Blues (France, Jazz Club 2MO56-78139). All Stars, guests. Radio and TV broadcasts. 1947–58.

Reminiscin' with Louis (Italy, Queen Disc 004). Concert, radio broadcasts. All Stars. 1947–50.

At the Eddie Condon Floorshow 1949 (Italy, Queen Disc 010). Concert broadcasts. All Stars and guests.

The All Stars in Philadelphia 1948–1949 (Jazz Archives JA-20). Concert. All Stars.

Satchmo's Golden Favorites (Decca DL 74137). All Stars, choir. 1949–58.

Satchmo Serenades (Decca DL 8211). Sy Oliver Orchestra. 1949–53.

Satchmo Serenades (MCA 1316). Sy Oliver, Toots Camarata, Gordon Jenkins Orchestras. 1949–54.

Old Favorites 1950–1957 (MCA 1335). All Stars.

In Concert at the Pasadena Civic Auditorium (GNP Crescendo 9050). All Stars. 1951.

Plays W. C. Handy (Original: Columbia CSP JCL 591). All Stars. 1954.

Plays W. C. Handy (Columbia CJ 40242). All Stars. 1954.

Rare Performances of the 50's and the 60's (France, CBS 88669). All Stars, Lotte Lenya, Dave Brubeck, Newport International Jazz Band. 1954–66.

At the Crescendo (MCA2 4013). All Stars. 1955.

Satch Plays Fats (Original: Columbia CSP JCL 708). All Stars. 1955.

Satch Plays Fats (Columbia CJ 40378). All Stars. 1955.

Ambassador Satch (Columbia CSP JCL 840). All Stars. 1955.

Chicago Concert (Columbia C2-36426). All Stars. 1956.

Satchmo the Great (Columbia CSP JCL 1077). All Stars, New York Philharmonic directed by Leonard Bernstein. 1956.

Satchmo: A Musical Autobiography Volume 1 (MCA2 4173). All Stars, guests, big band. 1956–57.

Satchmo: A Musical Autobiography Volume 2 (MCA 4174). All Stars, guests, big band. 1956–57.

Louis and the Angels (Decca DL 8488). Sy Oliver Orchestra and choir. 1957.

Verve Silver Collection (Compact disc: Verve 823 446-2). Russ Garcia Orchestra. 1957.

Louis and the Good Book (MCA 1300). All Stars plus organ and choir. 1958.

Satchmo Plays King Oliver (Audiofidelity AFLP 1930). All Stars. 1959.

Snake Rag (Chiaroscuro CR 2002). All Stars. 1959.

Master of Jazz (Storyville SLP-4101). All Stars. 1962.

Hello Dolly! (MCA 538). All Stars plus banjo. 1963–64.

The Essential Louis Armstrong (Vanguard VSD 91/92). All Stars. 1965.

Louis (Mercury SR 61081). All Stars plus banjo. 1965–66.

What a Wonderful World (MCA 2504). All Stars, big band, and strings. 1967–68.

I Will Wait for You (Brunswick 754136). Studio orchestra and choir. 1968.

Disney Songs the Satchmo Way (Buena Vista 4044). The All Stars plus studio orchestra with strings and choir. 1968.

Greatest Hits Recorded Live (Brunswick 754169). All Stars. 1968.

And His Friends (Flying Dutchman AMS-12009). Big band, strings, choir, Leon Thomas. 1970.

Country and Western (Avco Embassy AVE-33022). The Nashville Rhythm Section. 1970.

"The Night Before Christmas" (Continental 45-CR 1001). A reading of the poem. 1971.

Bibliography

A comprehensive bibliography of Louis Armstrong, one of the most written about performers of the century, will require a book of its own and be a valuable addition to the jazz library. The following highly selective list of books and articles provides a variety of interpretations, musical and biographical, as well as a massive amount of information. I've used the original editions except when they've been revised or expanded. Most of the major works are in catalogue from Da Capo, Greenwood, Limelight, and other reprint presses. Three spoken-word recordings are also included here, rather than in the discography. For reasons of space, I've omitted all liner notes, newspaper stories, concert programs and publicity hand-outs (a useful source in Armstrong's case), and—with a few exceptions—articles in jazz magazines.

Allen, Walter C. *Hendersonia.* New Jersey: Jazz Monographs No. 4, 1973.

Armstrong, Lil Hardin. *Satchmo and Me* (recording). New York: Riverside 12-120.

Armstrong, Louis. *Swing That Music.* London: Longmans, 1936.

Armstrong, Louis. *Satchmo: My Life in New Orleans.* New York: Prentice-Hall, 1954.

Armstrong, Louis. "Storyville—Where the Blues Were Born," *True*, November 1947.

Armstrong, Louis. "Europe—With Kicks," *Holiday*, June 1950.

Armstrong, Louis. "Jazz on a High Note," *Esquire*, December 1951.

Armstrong, Louis. "Why I Like Dark Women," *Ebony*, August 1954.

Armstrong, Louis. "It's Tough to Top a Million," *Our World*, August 1956.

Armstrong, Louis. "Good-bye To All Of You From . . . ," *Esquire*, December 1969.

Armstrong, Louis. "Scanning the History of Jazz," *Esquire*, December 1971.

Armstrong, Louis. *Satchmo* (recording). Glendale: Varese 8106.

Armstrong, Louis. *Talks about Louis Armstrong* (recording). Anaheim: Mark-56 690.

Armstrong, Lucille, with Pat Cunningham. "Life with Louie!" *Color*, December 1952.

Avakian, George. "Louis Armstrong." Shapiro, Nat, and Nat Hentoff. *The Jazz Makers.* New York: Rinehart, 1957.

Bankhead, Tallulah. "The World's Greatest Musician," *Ebony*, December 1952.

Barker, Danny. *A Life in Jazz.* New York: Oxford, 1986.

Basie, Count, and Albert Murray. *Good Morning Blues: The Autobiography of Count Basie.* New York: Random House, 1985.

Bechet, Sidney. *Treat It Gentle.* London: Cassell, 1960.

Bigard, Barney, with Barry Martyn. *With Louis and the Duke.* New York: Oxford, 1986.

Black, Charles L., Jr. *The Humane Imagination.* Woodbridge: Ox Bow Press, 1986.

Blesh, Rudi. *Shining Trumpets.* New York: Knopf, 1946.

Borneman, Ernest. " 'Bop Will Kill Business Unless It Kills Itself First'— Louis Armstrong," *Down Beat*, April 7, 1948.

Brooks, Edward. *The Bessie Smith Companion.* New York: Da Capo, 1982.

Caffey, H. David. "The Musical Style of Louis Armstrong," *Journal of Jazz Studies*, Fall 1975.

Callender, Red, with Elaine Cohen. *Unfinished Dream: The Musical World of Red Callender.* London: Quartet, 1985.

Chilton, John. *Sidney Bechet: The Wizard of Jazz.* New York: Oxford, 1987.

Clayton, Buck, with Nancy Miller Elliott. *Buck Clayton's Jazz World.* New York: Oxford, 1987.

Collier, James Lincoln. *Louis Armstrong: An American Genius.* New York: Oxford, 1983.

Condon, Eddie, with Thomas Sugrue. *We Called It Music.* rev. ed. New York: Da Capo, 1988.

Crouch, Stanley. "Laughin' Louis," *The Village Voice,* August 14, 1978.

Crowther, Bruce, and Mike Pinfold. *The Jazz Singers.* Poole: Blandford Press, 1986.

Dance, Stanley. *The World of Swing.* New York: Scribners, 1974.

Dance, Stanley. *The World of Earl Hines.* New York: Scribners, 1977.

Ellington, Duke. *Music Is My Mistress.* Garden City, N.Y.: Doubleday, 1973.

Feather, Leonard. *From Satchmo to Miles.* New York: Stein and Day, 1972.

Feather, Leonard. *The Jazz Years: Earwitness to an Era.* London: Quartet, 1986.

Feather, Leonard. "Pops Pops Top on Sloppy Bop," *Metronome,* October, 1949.

Ferguson, Otis. *The Otis Ferguson Reader.* Highland Park: December Press, 1982.

Finkelstein, Sidney. *Jazz: A People's Music.* New York: Citadel, 1948.

Freeman, Bud. *You Don't Look Like a Musician.* Detroit: Belamp, 1974.

Giddins, Gary, Dan Morgenstern, and Stanley Crouch. "Armstrong at 85," *The Village Voice,* August 27, 1985.

Gillespie, Dizzy, with Al Fraser. *To Be or Not to Bop.* Garden City, N.Y.: Doubleday, 1979.

Gioia, Ted. *The Imperfect Art.* New York: Oxford, 1988.

Gitler, Ira. *Swing to Bop.* New York: Oxford, 1985.

Glenn, Tyree. "Unforgettable Satchmo," *Reader's Digest,* December 1971.

Goddard, Chris. *Jazz Away from Home.* London: Paddington Press, 1979.

Goffin, Robert. *Horn of Plenty: The Story of Louis Armstrong.* New York: Allen, Towne & Heath, 1947.

Hadlock, Richard. *Jazz Masters of the 20's.* New York: Macmillan, 1965.

Hammond, John, with Irving Townsend. *John Hammond on Record.* New York: Summit, 1977.

Harrison, Max, Charles Fox, and Eric Thacker. *The Essential Jazz Records.* Westport: Greenwood Press, 1984.

Hentoff, Nat, and Albert J. McCarthy. *Jazz.* New York: Rinehart, 1959.

Hentoff, Nat. *Jazz Is.* New York: Random House, 1975.

Hodes, Art, and Chadwick Hansen. *Selections from the Gutter.* Berkeley: University of California, 1977.

Hodier, Andre. *Jazz: Its Evolution and Essence.* New York: Grove Press, 1956.

Jones, LeRoi. *Blues People.* New York: Morrow, 1963.

Jones, Max. *Talking Jazz.* New York: W. W. Norton, 1988.

Jones, Max, and John Chilton. *Louis: The Louis Armstrong Story 1900–1971.* rev. ed. New York: Da Capo, 1988.

Kaminsky, Max, with V. E. Hughes. *My Life in Jazz.* New York: Harper and Row, 1963.

King, Larry. "Everybody's Louis Armstrong," *Harper's,* November 1967.

Kolodin, Irving. "All God's Chillun Got Fun," *Americana,* February 1933.

Lyttelton, Humphrey. *The Best of Jazz.* New York: Taplinger, 1979.

Lyttelton, Humphrey. *The Best of Jazz II.* New York: Taplinger, 1982.

Marquis, Donald M. *In Search of Buddy Bolden.* Baton Rouge: Louisiana State University Press, 1978.

Matthews, Jim. *Satchmo.* Hollywood: Collector's Copy, 1971.

McCarthy, Albert. *Louis Armstrong.* London: Cassell, 1959.

Merryman, Richard. *Louis Armstrong –a Self-Portrait.* New York: Eakins Press, 1971.

Mezzrow, Mezz, and Bernard Wolfe. *Really the Blues.* New York: Random House, 1946.

Millstein, Gilbert. "Africa Harks to Satch's Horn," The New York *Times Magazine,* November 20, 1960.

Morgenstern, Dan. "Book Review. Louis Armstrong: An American Genius," *Annual Review of Jazz Studies 3,* 1985.

Morgenstern, Dan, and Ole Brask. *Jazz People.* New York: Abrams, 1976.

Murray, Albert. *Stomping the Blues.* New York: McGraw-Hill, 1976.

Ostransky, Leon. *Jazz City.* Englewood Cliffs, N.J.: Prentice-Hall, 1978.

Panassie, Hughes. *Louis Armstrong.* New York: Scribners, 1971.

Pinfold, Mike. *Louis Armstrong.* New York: Universe Books, 1987.

Rose, Al. *Storyville, New Orleans.* University, Alabama: University of Alabama Press, 1974.

Rose, Al, and Edmond Souchon. *New Orleans Jazz: A Family Album.* rev. ed. Baton Rouge: Louisiana State University Press, 1984.

Russell, William. "Louis Armstrong." Ramsey, Frederick, Jr., and Charles Edward Smith. *Jazzmen.* New York: Harcourt, Brace, 1939.

Sales, Grover. *Jazz: America's Classical Music.* Englewood Cliffs, N.J.: Prentice-Hall, 1984.

Schuller, Gunther. *Early Jazz: Its Roots and Musical Development.* New York: Oxford, 1968.

Shapiro, Nat, and Nat Hentoff. *Hear Me Talkin' to Ya.* New York: Rinehart, 1955.

Smith, Charles Edward, with Frederick Ramsey, Jr., Charles Payne Rogers, and William Russell. *The Jazz Record Book.* New York: Smith & Durrell, 1942.

Smith, Jay D., and Len Guttridge. *Jack Teagarden: The Story of a Jazz Maverick.* London: Cassell, 1960.

Stearns, Marshall. *The Story of Jazz.* rev. ed. New York: Oxford, 1970.

Stewart, Rex. *Jazz Masters of the 30's.* New York: Macmillan, 1972.

Teagarden, Jack. "The World's Greatest Horn Player," *Varsity,* December 1948.

Westerberg, Hans. *Boy From New Orleans: A Discography of Louis "Satchmo" Armstrong.* Copenhagen: Jazzmedia, 1981.

Williams, Martin. *Jazz Masters of New Orleans.* New York: Macmillan, 1967.

Williams, Martin. *The Jazz Tradition.* rev. ed. New York: Oxford, 1983.

Wright, Laurie, Walter C. Allen, and Brian A. L. Rust. *King Oliver.* Essex: Storyville, 1987.

Acknowledgments

So many hands contributed to this book. In 1974 Phoebe Jacobs, the publicist and a close friend of Lucille Armstrong's, arranged for me to interview Mrs. Armstrong. The article I wrote ended up in storage when the magazine that commissioned it went out of business. Mrs. Armstrong died of cardiac arrest on October 3, 1983; a tireless promoter of her husband's art, she was in a Boston Hotel that day, about to receive a citation from Governor Michael Dukakis. Three years later, Phoebe asked me out to the Armstrong house in Corona, Queens. It was like walking through a shrine. After examining photo albums, tapes, and papers, I asked Toby Byron to visit the house with us. Toby and I later met with executives of the Louis Armstrong estate—Oscar Cohen, Dave Gold, and Phoebe—and made plans to produce this book and a documentary film on Armstrong. In 1987, the house was taken over by Queens College, partly the result of a campaign by the estate to have it preserved as a state landmark (for years, tourists from Japan and Europe searched it out thinking it was a landmark). During that transition, my access to the archive was curtailed. Fortunately, Phoebe had had the foresight to preserve copies of the manuscripts identified here as *Archive*, entrusted to her as part of the Lucille Armstrong Collection.

In searching out documents relating to Armstrong's birth, we employed the services of attorney William T. Abbott, Jr., and writer Tad Jones, an authority on New Orleans music and a coauthor of *Up From the Cradle of Jazz*. Tad, in true Lew Archer fashion, sussed out census reports and followed leads that led to the baptismal registry of the Sacred Heart of Jesus Church and certification of Louis Armstrong's true birthdate (August 4, 1901). Bill Abbott helped us acquire Armstrong's FBI files through the Freedom of Information Act, as well as information regarding the Milne Municipal Boys' Home. Harold S. Kaye sent me Armstrong's passport application and Mama Lucy's marriage certificate.

Al Rose and his wife, Diana Rose, who know the jazz-related significance of every house and street in New Orleans, provided guided tours of the city. Eddie Edwards, of the Louis Armstrong Foundation, guided us to and through Boutte. The near-legendary archivist and writer Bill Russell was most generous with his comprehensive files, which include articles not found in institutional archives. Danny Barker and his wife, Blue Lu Barker, were most hospitable.

Don Marquis, of the Louisiana Historical Center and the Louisiana State Museum, made available many documents collected for an ambitious exhibit he is preparing for the museum in 1989. I drew heavily on the comprehensive jazz archives at Tulane and Rutgers universities. Curtis Jerde, who administers the William Ransom Hogan Jazz Archive at Tulane, and members of his staff, particularly Richard B. Allen, Alma Williams, and Bruce Raeburn, were most helpful. I am expecially grateful to Dan Morgenstern at Rutgers, who allowed me limitless access to the files, including numerous letters, the original typescript to *Satchmo: My Life in New Orleans*, and the Armstrong manuscripts identified here as *Goffin*. He also helped with photo captions. But my debt to Dan goes far beyond that; his writings on Armstrong—a diaspora of liner notes and fugitive articles waiting to be bound in a book—are among the most sensitive and perceptive we have. I am also indebted to Jack Bradley, whose deep love of Armstrong comes through in his many photographs. His collection of Armstrongiana is an inexhaustible treasure.

The generous research assistance of a few friends greatly eased the writing of this book. Mary Cleere Haran, a wonderful singer and actress, is also an experienced and indefatigable researcher who finds documents that elude everyone else; though she performed nightly at the Ballroom, she journeyed to libraries by day and waded through my taped interviews and other materials. Loren Schoenberg, gifted saxophonist and disc jockey, and a key figure in the American Jazz Orchestra, helped me with interviews and accumulated many hours of material on tape. Will Friedwald helped me assemble the discography. I would have been hard pressed without the copying and collating facilities provided me by Norman Halper and his staff at Aaron Halper and Company.

Toby Byron juggled all the components of the enterprise and shared my obsession with digging up new material and certifying facts. He and I were greatly assisted by Rick Saylor, whose good humor was most appreciated, though not necessarily in Cessna aircraft. Kendrick Simmons helped gather information in New Orleans. Veronica Windholz's copyediting was a valued safety net. Kathleen and Linda Gates, of Gates Studio, designed the book with impressive attention to detail. I thank my agent, Emilie Jacobson. I am delighted to have had the chance to work with Paul Bresnick of Doubleday, who understood what I was trying to do from the beginning, suggested the title (which didn't seem so obvious to me), and steered the book past several obstacles.

I am indebted to those who gave me interviews; to those who responded to a printed query with anecdotes, letters, and pictures; to those who provided other kinds of assistance. They include Milt Gabler, Danny Barker, Jack Bradley, Doc Cheatham, Sallie (Mrs. Trummy)

Young, Lassie Joseph, Andrea Young, Milt Hinton, Sy Oliver, Bob Haggart, Joe Wilder, George Chisolm, Richard Gibson, Herb Ellis, Arvell Shaw, Benny Carter, Bud Freeman, Ruby Braff, Kenny Davern, Marty Napoleon, Jean Bach, Barbara Carroll, Barbara Lea, William E. Hassan, Harold S. Kaye, Charles Graham, Johnny Simmen, Francis J. Walsh, Julius Rosen, Stan Wheeler, Ella Merkel DiCarlo, Norma M. Murchio, Archie Smith, Ed Berger, Martin Williams, Lou Jacobs, Bessie Williams, Gail Hightower, George T. Simon, Sam Perlman, Don Hunstein, Jay Emery, Jaynie Botsford, Dodie Simmons, Jesse Bryant, Arlene Kerstetter, Harry Parsons, Fred Danzig, Roman Zaharchuk, Jerry Czajkowski, Alan Angele, Peter Kirchoff, Anna Beverwijk, Robert Barger, and, of course, Lucille Armstrong.

The contribution of my wife, Deborah Eve Halper, to this book and everything else I do transcends a page of acknowledgments. But I point out her help in collating thousands of documents; her forbearance when I disappeared into my office for several weeks to write the text; her editorial advice; her enthusiasm; her inspiration.

G. G.

My hat goes off, particularly to Bill Abbott, Tad Jones, Jack Bradley, and Phoebe Jacobs.

Kathleen Gates has been absolutely superb through it all, as has her ever attentive associate, Linda Gates. Rick Saylor tied much of it together and is indispensable. In addition to and including those acknowledged by Gary, I'd like to thank Jeff Atterton, John Berg, Donald Blackman, Janie Botsford, Mark Cantor, John Chominsky and Pro Lab, Mary Cleere Haran, Oscar Cohen, Fritz Diekmann, Jerry Durkin, David Gold, Elliot Groffman, Klaus Hallig, Don Hunstein, Karl Knudsen, Richard Merkin, Dan Morgenstern, Al Rose, Bill Russell, Kendrick Simmons, George Simor, JoDee Stringham, Rupert Surcouf, Martin Williams, Veronica Windholz, and Allyson.

At Doubleday and Dolphin, my hearty thanks and gratitude to Jim Fitzgerald, Peter Kruzan, Alex Gotfryd, Keith Dawson, Mark Garofalo, Nancy Stauffer—and I cannot stress enough—Michele Martin and Paul Bresnick.

And to Gary: I haven't words for the depth with which your insights, enthusiasms, and love for this music constantly enrich my life. Thank you!

T.R.B.

Photography Credits

Almost half of the photographs in *Satchmo* have been made available exclusively for use in this book through the estate of Louis Armstrong and Queens College. Many are previously unpublished. We are indebted to President Shirley Strum Kenny and her staff at Queens College for allowing us use of them. We have made every effort to locate the copyright owner for each photograph in the book. Of the photographs culled from Armstrong's personal collection, many have no documentation. All photographs credited to Louis Armstrong Estate and Queens College are listed here as "LAE/QC." All photographs credited to Louis Armstrong Estate are listed as "LAE."

Page 1: Photograph by Don Hunstein, courtesy of Jack Bradley Collection.
Pages 2–3: David Redfern.
Page 4: Jean-Pierre Leloir.
Page 5: David Redfern.
Pages 6–7: Photograph by Don Hunstein, courtesy of Jack Bradley Collection.
Page 8: Jean-Pierre Leloir.
Page 9: Jean-Pierre Leloir.
Page 11: (Top) Courtesy of LAE/QC.
Page 11: (Bottom) Nancy Nugent.
Page 12: Jean-Pierre Leloir.
Page 13: Jean-Pierre Leloir.
Page 14: (Top) Courtesy of LAE.
Page 14 (Bottom) Courtesy of LAE.
Page 15: Courtesy of LAE/QC.
Page 16: Courtesy of LAE/QC.
Page 17: Courtesy of LAE/QC.
Pages 18–19: Courtesy of LAE/QC.
Page 21: Courtesy of LAE/QC.
Page 22: John Loengard, Life Magazine © Time Inc.
Page 23: Courtesy of Jack Bradley Collection.
Page 25: Photograph by Jean-Pierre Leloir.
Page 26: Courtesy of LAE/QC.

Page 27: David Redfern.
Pages 28–29: Courtesy of Institute of Jazz Studies, Rutgers University.
Pages 30–31: William Gottlieb.
Page 32: Courtesy of Jack Bradley Collection.
Page 33: Courtesy of Gary Giddins Collection.
Page 34: Courtesy of LAE/QC.
Page 35: Courtesy of LAE/QC.
Page 36: Courtesy of William Hogan Jazz Archive, Rose and Souchon Collection, Tulane University.
Page 37: Courtesy of LAE/QC.
Page 39: Photograph by Ava Studio, courtesy of LAE.
Page 40: Courtesy of LAE.
Page 42: Courtesy of LAE/QC.
Page 43: (Top) Courtesy of William Hogan Jazz Archive, Rose Collection, Tulane University.
Page 43: (Bottom) Courtesy of Jack Bradley Collection.
Page 44: Courtesy of LAE/QC.
Page 45: Courtesy of Jack Bradley Collection.
Page 46: Jean-Pierre Leloir.
Page 48: Courtesy of Toby Byron/ Multiprises.
Page 49: (Top) Courtesy of Toby Byron/ Multiprises.
Page 49: (Middle) Courtesy of Toby Byron/Multiprises.
Page 49: (Bottom) Courtesy of Toby Byron/Multiprises.
Page 50: Courtesy of LAE.
Page 54: Courtesy of LAE.
Page 55: Courtesy of LAE/QC.
Page 56: Courtesy of LAE.
Page 57: Charles Peterson.
Page 58: Photograph by William Russell, courtesy of William Hogan Jazz Archive, Tulane University.
Page 59: Photograph by William Russell, courtesy of William Hogan Jazz Archive, Tulane University.
Page 60: David Redfern.
Page 61: William Gottlieb.

Page 63: Courtesy of LAE.
Page 64: Courtesy of LAE/QC.
Page 65: Courtesy of LAE.
Page 66: Courtesy of LAE/QC.
Pages 68–69: Courtesy of William Hogan Jazz Archive, Rose Collection, Tulane University.
Page 70: Courtesy of William Hogan Jazz Archive, Rose Collection, Tulane University.
Page 71: (Top) Courtesy of William Hogan Jazz Archive, Rose and Souchon Collection, Tulane University.
Page 71: (Bottom) Courtesy of William Hogan Jazz Archive, Tulane University.
Page 72: Courtesy of LAE/QC.
Page 73: Courtesy of LAE/QC.
Page 75: (Top) Courtesy of LAE/QC.
Page 75: (Bottom) Courtesy of LAE/QC.
Page 76: Courtesy of Institute of Jazz Studies, Rutgers University.
Page 77: Courtesy of Institute of Jazz Studies, Rutgers University.
Page 78: Courtesy of LAE/QC.
Page 80: Courtesy of William Hogan Jazz Archive, Rose and Souchon Collection, Tulane University.
Page 83: Courtesy of LAE/QC.
Page 85: Courtesy of LAE/QC.
Page 86: (Top) Photograph by Don Hunstein, courtesy of Jack Bradley Collection.
Page 86: (Bottom) Photograph by Don Hunstein, courtesy of Jack Bradley Collection.
Page 87: Photograph by Don Hunstein, courtesy of Jack Bradley Collection.
Pages 88–89: Courtesy of LAE/QC.
Page 91: Courtesy of LAE/QC.
Page 93: Courtesy of William Hogan Jazz Archive, Rose and Souchon Collection, Tulane University.
Page 95: Courtesy of LAE/QC.
Page 96: Courtesy of LAE/QC.
Page 97: Courtesy of LAE.

Page 98: Courtesy of LAE/QC.
Page 101: Courtesy of LAE/QC.
Page 102: (Top) William Gottlieb.
Page 102: (Bottom) David Redfern.
Page 103: Charles Peterson.
Page 104: Courtesy of LAE/QC.
Page 105: Courtesy of LAE/QC.
Page 108: (Top) Courtesy of LAE/QC.
Page 108: (Bottom) Courtesy of LAE/QC.
Page 109: (Top) Courtesy of LAE/QC.
Page 109: (Bottom) Courtesy of Harold S. Kaye Collection.
Page 110: Courtesy of LAE.
Page 111: Courtesy of LAE.
Page 112: Photograph by Rockwell O'Keefe, courtesy of Institute of Jazz Studies, Rutgers University.
Page 113: Courtesy of LAE/QC.
Pages 114–115: Courtesy of LAE.
Page 116: Courtesy of Ken Whitten.
Page 117: Courtesy of Floyd Levin Collection.
Page 119: (Top left) Courtesy of LAE/QC.
Page 119: (Top right) Courtesy of LAE/QC.
Page 119: (Bottom left) Courtesy of LAE/QC.
Page 119: (Bottom right) Courtesy of LAE/QC.
Page 120: Courtesy of LAE/QC.
Page 121: Courtesy of LAE.
Pages 122–123: Courtesy of LAE/QC.
Page 124: Courtesy of LAE.
Page 125: Photograph by Jan White, courtesy of William Hogan Jazz Archive, Tulane University.
Page 126: Courtesy of LAE/QC.
Page 127: Courtesy of LAE.
Page 128: Courtesy of LAE/QC.
Page 129: Courtesy of LAE/QC.
Page 130: Courtesy of LAE/QC.
Page 131: Courtesy of LAE/QC.
Pages 132–133: Courtesy of LAE/QC.
Page 134–135: Courtesy of Institute of Jazz Studies, Rutgers University.
Page 136: Courtesy of LAE/QC.

Page 137: (Top) Courtesy of Institute of Jazz Studies, Rutgers University.

Page 137: (Bottom) Courtesy of LAE/QC.

Page 138: (Top) Courtesy of Jack Bradley Collection.

Page 138: (Bottom) Courtesy of Jack Bradley Collection.

Page 139: (Top) Courtesy of Gary Giddins Collection.

Page 139: (Bottom) Courtesy of LAE/QC.

Page 140: Courtesy of LAE/QC.

Page 142: Courtesy of LAE/QC.

Page 143: Courtesy of LAE.

Pages 144–145: Courtesy of LAE.

Page 146: Courtesy of LAE.

Page 147: Courtesy of LAE.

Page 148: (Top) Courtesy of LAE/QC.

Page 148: (Bottom) Courtesy of LAE/QC.

Page 149: (Top) Courtesy of LAE/QC.

Page 149: (Bottom) Courtesy of LAE/QC.

Page 150: Courtesy of LAE/QC.

Page 151: Courtesy of LAE.

Page 152: (Top) Courtesy of LAE/QC.

Page 152: (Bottom) Courtesy of Richard Merkin.

Page 153: Photograph by Bill Mark, courtesy of LAE/QC.

Page 154: Courtesy of Jack Bradley Collection.

Page 155: Courtesy of LAE.

Page 157: (Top) Courtesy of LAE/QC.

Page 157: (Bottom) William Gottlieb.

Page 158: Courtesy of LAE.

Page 159: Courtesy of LAE/QC.

Page 160: (Top) Courtesy of LAE/QC.

Page 160: (Bottom) Courtesy of LAE/QC.

Page 161: (Top) Courtesy of LAE.

Page 161: (Bottom) Courtesy of LAE.

Page 162: Weegee.

Page 163: Courtesy of LAE/QC.

Page 164: Jean-Pierre Leloir.

Page 165: Courtesy of Sally Young Collection.

Page 166: (Top) Photograph by Jan Greve, courtesy of LAE/QC.

Page 166: (Bottom) Courtesy of LAE.

Page 167: (Top) Courtesy of LAE/QC.

Page 167: (Bottom) Courtesy of LAE/QC.

Page 169: Courtesy of Time Inc.

Pages 170–171: Movie posters, stamps, decanters, awards, lip salve, and magazine, photographs by Don Hunstein, courtesy of Jack Bradley Collection; horns, record jackets, and 78 rpm records, photographs by Jan White, courtesy of Louisiana State Museum, Jazz Collection.

Pages 172–173: Dan Wynn.

Pages 174–175: Jean-Pierre Leloir.

Page 176: Courtesy of Life Magazine © Time Inc.

Page 178: Jean-Pierre Leloir.

Page 179: (Top) Courtesy of LAE.

Page 179: (Bottom) Courtesy of LAE.

Page 180: Courtesy of LAE.

Page 181: Courtesy of LAE/QC.

Page 182: (Top) Courtesy of LAE/QC.

Page 182: (Bottom) Courtesy of LAE/QC.

Page 183: (Top) Courtesy of Institute of Jazz Studies, Rutgers University.

Page 183: (Bottom) William Hassan.

Page 184: Jack Bradley.

Page 185: (Top) Courtesy of Sally Young Collection.

Page 185: (Bottom) Courtesy of LAE/QC.

Page 186: (Top) Charles Peterson.

Page 186: (Bottom) Courtesy of LAE/QC.

Page 187: (Top) Weegee.

Page 187: (Bottom) Weegee.

Page 188: Courtesy of LAE.

Page 189: (Top) Courtesy of LAE/QC.

Page 189: (Bottom) Courtesy of LAE/QC.

Page 190: Jean-Pierre Leloir.

Page 191: Jean-Pierre Leloir.

Pages 192–193: Courtesy of Jack Bradley Collection.

Pages 194–195: Courtesy of LAE.

Page 196: Courtesy of Ken Whitten.

Page 197: Courtesy of LAE.

Page 198: (Top left) Courtesy of LAE/QC.

Page 198: (Top right) Courtesy of Jack Bradley Collection.

Page 198: (Bottom left) Courtesy of LAE/QC.

Page 198: (Bottom right) Courtesy of LAE/QC.

Page 199: (Top left) Courtesy of LAE/QC.

Page 199: (Top right) Courtesy of Jack Bradley Collection.

Page 199: (Bottom left) Courtesy of LAE/QC.

Page 199: (Bottom right) Courtesy of Jack Bradley Collection.

Pages 200–201: Courtesy of LAE/QC.

Page 202: Courtesy of LAE.

Page 203: Courtesy of LAE/QC.

Page 204: Courtesy of LAE/QC.

Pages 204–205: Ed Berger.

Page 206: Courtesy of LAE/QC.

Page 207: Courtesy of LAE/QC.

Pages 208–209: Peter Anderson, Life Magazine © Time Inc.

Page 210: Courtesy of LAE/QC.

Page 211: Courtesy of LAE.

Page 212: (Top) William Gottlieb.

Page 212: (Bottom) Don Hunstein, courtesy of Jack Bradley Collection.

Page 213: Courtesy of William Hogan Jazz Archive, Rose Collection, Tulane University.

Page 214: Courtesy of William Hogan Jazz Archive, Tulane University.

Page 217: (Top) Courtesy of LAE.

Page 217: (Bottom) Courtesy of LAE/QC.

Page 218: (Top) Courtesy of LAE/QC.

Page 218: (Bottom) Courtesy of LAE/QC.

Page 219: (Top) Courtesy of LAE/QC.

Page 219: (Bottom) Courtesy of LAE/QC.

Page 220: (Top) Photograph by William Russell, courtesy of William Hogan Jazz Archive, Tulane University.

Page 220: (Bottom) Photograph by William Russell, courtesy of William Hogan Jazz Archive, Tulane University.

Page 221: Photograph by William Russell, courtesy of William Hogan Jazz Archive, Tulane University.

Page 222: Photograph by Jan Greve, courtesy of LAE/QC.

Page 223: David Redfern.

Page 224: (Top) Photograph by Don Hunstein, courtesy of Jack Bradley Collection.

Page 224: (Bottom) Photograph by Don Hunstein, courtesy of Jack Bradley Collection.

Page 225: (Top) Photograph by Don Hunstein, courtesy of Jack Bradley Collection.

Page 225: (Bottom) Photograph by Don Hunstein, courtesy of Jack Bradley Collection.

Page 226: Photograph by Don Hunstein, courtesy of Jack Bradley Collection.

Page 227: Photograph by Don Hunstein, courtesy of Jack Bradley Collection.

Page 228: (Top) Photograph by Don Hunstein, courtesy of Jack Bradley Collection.

Page 228: (Middle) Photograph by Don Hunstein, courtesy of Jack Bradley Collection.

Page 228: (Bottom) Photograph by Don Hunstein, courtesy of Jack Bradley Collection.

Page 229: Photograph by Don Hunstein, courtesy of Jack Bradley Collection.

Page 230: Photograph by Pro Lab, courtesy of William Russell Collection.

Page 231: Photograph by Pro Lab, courtesy of William Russell Collection.

Page 232: Nancy Nugent.

Page 240: Larry Burrows, Life Magazine © Time Inc.